Women and Global Documentary

WORLD CINEMA SERIES

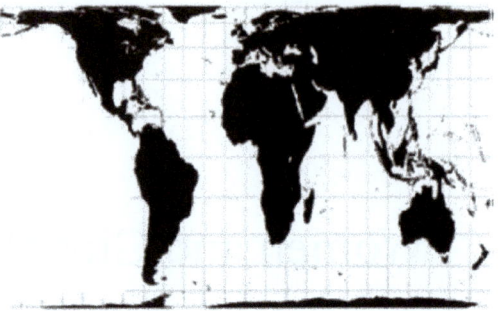

Series Editors:

Lúcia Nagib, Professor of Film at the University of Reading
Julian Ross, Research Fellow at the Leiden University
Advisory Board: Laura Mulvey (UK), Robert Stam (USA), Ismail Xavier (Brazil), Dudley Andrew (USA)

The *World Cinema* series aims to reveal and celebrate the richness and complexity of film art across the globe, exploring a wide variety of cinemas set within their own cultures and as they interconnect in a global context. The books in the series will represent innovative scholarship, in tune with the multicultural character of contemporary audiences. Drawing upon an international authorship, they will challenge outdated conceptions of world cinema and provide new ways of understanding a field at the centre of film studies in an era of transnational networks.

Published and forthcoming in the World Cinema series:

Allegory in Iranian Cinema: The Aesthetics of Poetry and Resistance, Michelle Langford

Animation in the Middle East: Practice and Aesthetics from Baghdad to Casablanca, Stefanie Van de Peer

Basque Cinema: A Cultural and Political History, Rob Stone and Maria Pilar Rodriguez

Brazil on Screen: Cinema Novo, New Cinema, Utopia, Lúcia Nagib

Brazilian Cinema and the Aesthetic of Ruins, Guilherme Carréra

Cinema in the Arab World: New Histories, New Approaches, Edited By Philippe Meers, Daniel Biltereyst and Ifdal Elsaket

Contemporary New Zealand Cinema,
Edited by Ian Conrich and Stuart Murray

Cosmopolitan Cinema: Cross-cultural Encounters in East Asian Film,
Felicia Chan

Documentary Cinema of Chile: Confronting History, Memory, Trauma,
Antonio Traverso

East Asian Cinemas: Exploring Transnational Connections on Film,
Edited by Leon Hunt and Leung Wing-Fai

East Asian Film Noir: Transnational Encounters and Intercultural Dialogue,
Edited by Chi-Yun Shin and Mark Gallagher

Eastern Approaches to Western Film: Asian Reception and Aesthetics in Cinema,
Stephen Teo

Impure Cinema: Intermedial and Intercultural Approaches to Film,
Edited by Lúcia Nagib and Anne Jerslev

Latin American Women Filmmakers: Production, Politics, Poetics,
Edited by Deborah Martin and Deborah Shaw

Lebanese Cinema: Imagining the Civil War and Beyond,
Lina Khatib

New Argentine Cinema,
Jens Andermann

New Directions in German Cinema,
Edited by Paul Cooke and Chris Homewood

New Turkish Cinema: Belonging, Identity and Memory,
Asuman Sune

On Cinema,
Glauber Rocha, edited by Ismail Xavier

Pablo Trapero and the Politics of Violence,
Douglas Mulliken

Palestinian Filmmaking in Israel: Narratives of Place and Identity,
Yael Friedman

Performing Authorship: Self-inscription and Corporeality in the Cinema,
Cecilia Sayad

Popular Ethiopian Cinema: Love and Other Genre,
Michael W. Thomas

Portugal's Global Cinema: Industry, History and Culture,
Edited by Mariana Liz

Queer Masculinities in Latin American Cinema: Male Bodies and Narrative Representations,
Gustavo Subero

Realism in Greek Cinema: From the Post-War Period to the Present,
Vrasidas Karalis

Realism of the Senses in World Cinema: The Experience of Physical Reality,
Tiago de Luca

Stars in World Cinema: Screen Icons and Star Systems Across Cultures,
Edited by Andrea Bandhauer and Michelle Royer

The Cinema of Jia Zhangke: Realism and Memory in Chinese Film,
Cecília Mello
The Cinema of Sri Lanka: South Asian Film in Texts and Contexts,
Ian Conrich
The New Generation in Chinese Animation,
Shaopeng Chen

The Spanish Fantastic: Contemporary Filmmaking in Horror, Fantasy and Sci-fi,
Shelagh-Rowan Legg
Theorizing World Cinema,
Edited by Lúcia Nagib, Chris Perriam and Rajinder Dudrah

Queries, ideas and submissions to
Series Editor: Professor Lúcia Nagib—
l.nagib@reading.ac.uk
Series Editor: Dr. Julian Ross—
j.a.ross@hum.leidenuniv.nl
Commissioning Editor at Bloomsbury: Veidehi Hans –
Veidehi.Hans@bloomsbury.com

Women and Global Documentary

Practices and Perspectives in the 21st Century

Edited by Najmeh Moradiyan-Rizi
and Shilyh Warren

BLOOMSBURY ACADEMIC
LONDON · NEW YORK · OXFORD · NEW DELHI · SYDNEY

BLOOMSBURY ACADEMIC
Bloomsbury Publishing Plc
50 Bedford Square, London, WC1B 3DP, UK
1385 Broadway, New York, NY 10018, USA
29 Earlsfort Terrace, Dublin 2, Ireland

BLOOMSBURY, BLOOMSBURY ACADEMIC and the Diana logo are trademarks of
Bloomsbury Publishing Plc

First published in Great Britain 2025

Copyright © Najmeh Moradiyan-Rizi and Shilyh Warren, 2025

Najmeh Moradiyan-Rizi and Shilyh Warren have asserted their right under the Copyright,
Designs and Patents Act, 1988, to be identified as Editor of this work.

Cover design: Ben Anslow
Cover image © Hannah Murrell / Unsplash

All rights reserved. No part of this publication may be reproduced or transmitted in any
form or by any means, electronic or mechanical, including photocopying, recording, or
any information storage or retrieval system, without prior permission in writing from
the publishers.

Bloomsbury Publishing Plc does not have any control over, or responsibility for, any third-
party websites referred to or in this book. All internet addresses given in this book were
correct at the time of going to press. The author and publisher regret any inconvenience
caused if addresses have changed or sites have ceased to exist, but can accept no
responsibility for any such changes.

A catalogue record for this book is available from the British Library.

ISBN: HB: 978-1-3504-2290-2
PB: 978-1-3504-2289-6
ePDF: 978-1-3504-2292-6
eBook: 978-1-3504-2291-9

Series: World Cinema

Typeset by Deanta Global Publishing Services, Chennai, India
Printed and bound in Great Britain

To find out more about our authors and books visit www.bloomsbury.com and
sign up for our newsletters.

Contents

Notes on Contributors ix

Introduction *Najmeh Moradiyan-Rizi and Shilyh Warren* 1

Part I   Documentary Initiatives as Feminist Worldbuilding

1   Women Make Movies Globally *Patricia White* 11
2   Transforming Documentary Film Cultures in East Africa: Judy Kibinge and Docubox *Lindiwe Dovey* 27
3   Caravan: Rerouting Transnational Feminist Collaboration Networks *Amal Shafek* 51

Part II   Rereading Public and Private Connections through Documentary

4   Feminist Animated Documentary: Ways of Confronting Violence against Women *Shilyh Warren and Christine Veras* 73
5   Affective Relations and First-Person Enunciation: Daughters/Filmmakers Reformulate the Latin American Documentary *Lorena Cervera* 97
6   Politicizing Familial Space: Women's Post-Fukushima Documentaries as the Creation of Counterpublics *Wakae Nakane* 113

Part III   Reimagining Documentary Activism

7   Iranian Women's Biographical Documentaries as Sites of Recognition and Advocacy: An Ecofeminist Reading *Najmeh Moradiyan-Rizi* 133
8   *Que se vayan ellos*: Beyond Resilience in Puerto Rican Social Justice Documentary *Zaira Zarza* 151
9   *The Art of Work Is a Work of Art*: Feminist Theater and Live Documentary *Kim Munro* 169

Part IV Documentary Voice and Feminist Perspectives

10 "Are We on the Same Page Here?": Moving Beyond "Us" and "Them" in *nîpawistamâsowin: We Will Stand Up* and *Kímmapiiyipitssini: The Meaning of Empathy* Gail Vanstone ... 187

11 Making Documentary Media: Approaches to the Deep Image *Aparna Sharma and Priya Sen* ... 211

12 Feminism as Documentary Method: A Conversation *Irene Lusztig, Hannah Jayanti, Noorafshan Mirza, Rosa-Johan Uddoh, and Andrea Luka Zimmerman* ... 233

References ... 255
Index ... 278

Contributors

Lorena Cervera works as Senior Lecturer in Film Production at Arts University Bournemouth and holds a PhD in Film Studies from University College London. She has published several articles and book chapters on Latin American documentary, women's cinema, feminist filmmaking, film collectives, and practice as research, including in *Feminist Media Studies* and *Jump Cut: A Review of Contemporary Media*. Her first monograph, *A Feminist Counter-History of Latin American Documentary*, will be published by Routledge in 2025. As a filmmaker, she has directed *Pilas* (2019) and *Processing Images from Caracas* (2022) and has co-directed *#PrecarityStory* (2020).

Lindiwe Dovey is a researcher, teacher, film curator, and filmmaker. She is Professor of Film and Screen Studies at SOAS University of London and the Principal Investigator of the ERC-funded project "African Screen Worlds: Decolonising Film and Screen Studies" (www.screenworlds.org), which has brought together an international team to try to make Screen Studies and the film industry more globally representative in creative, critical, and activist ways. Through this project, Lindiwe has directed the films *Out of the Box: The Screen Worlds of Judy Kibinge* (2023) and *From One Woman to Another: The Screen Worlds of Bongiwe Selane* (2023).

Hannah Jayanti is a documentary filmmaker whose work centers on process-driven and formally expansive non-fiction as ethical and political practices. Through this lens, she circles around questions of place, listening, memory, and time. As of 2024, she is exhibiting and working on *Topography*, a multimedia documentary project exploring land use that includes live-edited performances, installations, community collaborations, and films. Previous work includes the speculative documentary *Truth or Consequences* (2020) and the VR documentary *Blackout* (2017). Her work has screened at IFFR,

Sheffield, Dok Leipzig, Tribeca, Transmediale, Smithsonian, and the Museum of the Moving Image, among many others.

Irene Lusztig is a feminist filmmaker, archival researcher, educator, and amateur seamstress. She works in a space of delicate mediation between people, their pasts, and the present-tense spaces and landscapes where unresolved histories bloom and erupt. She is the director, producer, and editor of four acclaimed feature-length documentaries that have screened widely in festivals: *Reconstruction* (2001), *The Motherhood Archives* (2013), *Yours in Sisterhood* (2018), and *Richland* (2023). Her work has been screened around the world, including at the Berlinale, Tribeca, MoMA, and IDFA. She teaches filmmaking at UC Santa Cruz, where she is Professor of Film and Digital Media.

Noorafshan Mirza's work engages with contradictions of inequality, power, privilege, and (non)participation. Her collaborative practice spans moving image, installation, workshops, sound, text, and performed actions. Recent exhibitions include *The Scar* at the Delfina Foundation (September–December 2018) and *The Scar* at HOME (February–April 2018), *The Embassy of Non Participation* at the Sydney Biennale (April–June 2016), *MIRRORCITY* at the Hayward Gallery (October–January 2015), *The Unreliable Narrator* at the Whitechapel Gallery (January–March 2015), *The New Deal* at the Walker Art Centre (April–July 2013), and *Guest of Citation* at Performa 13 (2013).

Najmeh Moradiyan-Rizi is Assistant Professor of Film Studies at the Old Dominion University. She holds a PhD in Film and Media Studies and a Graduate Certificate in Women, Gender, and Sexuality Studies from the University of Kansas. She is the author of "Iranian Women, Iranian Cinema: Negotiating with Ideology and Tradition" (*Journal of Religion and Film*, 2015) and "The Acoustic Screen: The Dynamics of the Female Look and Voice in Abbas Kiarostami's *Shirin*" (*Synoptique*, 2016) as well as several book chapters and book reviews.

Kim Munro is a documentary researcher and practitioner whose work across installation, film, audio, and performance explores entangled histories of place, people, and archives. Kim has written on a range of documentary styles, genres, and forms and is the co-editor of *Constructions of the Real: Intersections* of *Documentary-Based Film Practice and Theory* (2023, Intellect). Kim was the conference programmer for the Australian International Documentary Conferences (AIDC), and in 2023 founded the Adelaide-based Documentary Film Society. Currently, she is based at the University of South Australia in Adelaide as a lecturer in Film and Television.

Wakae Nakane is a PhD candidate in the Division of Cinema and Media Studies at the USC School of Cinematic Arts. Her research interests include essay film, Japanese documentary and experimental film, and feminist film theory and historiography. Her publications include "Constructing an Intimate Sphere Through Her Own Female Body: Naomi Kawase's Documentary Films" in *Female Authorship and the Documentary Image* (2018) and "Female Performers as Authors: Documentary Film *Extreme Private Eros: Love Song 1974* and the Women's Liberation Movement" in *Eizogaku* (2016, Japanese). She curated film screening events featuring experimental films by female filmmakers in Japan for the Pacific Film Archive in Berkeley, California, and online platforms.

Priya Sen is an independent filmmaker and artist whose work explores forms of tenuousness and ambiguity within realist documentary and simultaneously plays with narrative modes and cinematic gestures. She is interested in eclectic, itinerant, and egalitarian film forms and the manners of presence that accompany each work. Sen's work has screened at festivals and venues in India and globally. She received an MA from Jamia Millia Islamia, Delhi, and an MFA in film and media arts from Temple University, Philadelphia, and is currently a Radcliffe Fellow at the Harvard Radcliffe Institute, 2023–4.

Amal Shafek has a doctorate in Humanities from the University of Texas at Dallas. She is a lecturer of Transnational Cinema and World Cinema at UT Dallas. Her research focuses on women's documentary filmmaking in the Middle East, transnational feminist film theory and practice, postcolonial trauma studies, trauma representations, and first-person cinema. She is also an aspiring documentary filmmaker.

Aparna Sharma is a documentary filmmaker and scholar. Her films focus on cultural heritage and material culture practices in the South Asian and adjoining regions. Her recent films include *Mihin Sutta, Mihin Jibon* (*The Women Weavers of Assam*, 2019, Royal Anthropological Institute) and *Playing the Flute in Shanghai* (co-directed with Helen Rees, 2021, PAN Records). She is committed to writing about non-mainstream film practices with an emphasis on documentary. Her book *Documentary Films in India: Critical Aesthetics at Work* examines non-canonical documentary practices (2015). She is presently developing an open-access digital media archive of visual anthropological materials from Northeast India.

Rosa-Johan Uddoh is an interdisciplinary artist working toward radical self-love, inspired by Black feminist practice. Through performance, writing, film, and multi-media installation, she explores the effects of popular culture on self-formation. Rosa is a lecturer in Performance at Central Saint Martins, London. She was shortlisted for the Jarman Award in 2022. She has had critically acclaimed shows in the UK and internationally, including at Focal Point Gallery, Bluecoat, Pioneer Works, and Bergen Kunsthall. Rosa's work has been profiled in *Art Monthly*, *The New York Times*, and *Nordic Art Review*, and her first book, *Practice Makes Perfect*, was published in 2022.

Gail Vanstone is Associate Professor in the Department of Humanities at York University, Toronto. She works at the intersection of feminist theory and women's documentary film production. She is the author of *D Is for Daring* (2007), a history of Studio D, a feminist film unit at Canada's National Film Board, and, with Brian Winston and Wang Chi, *The Act of Documenting* (2017). She has published essays, such as "'*Scriptrix narrans*': Digital Documentary Storytelling's Radical Potential" (2018) and, with Winston, "'This Would Be Scary to Any Other Culture . . . But to Us It's So Cute?': Radicalism of Fourth Cinema from *Tangata Whenua* to *Angry Inuk*" (2019).

Christine Veras researches the integration of physical and digital technologies to explore the multimedia possibilities of animation. Her background in animation studies combines history, theory, and practice, positioning her as a scholar and practitioner. As the director of experimenta.l., the experimental animation lab, she fosters collaboration and encourages the exploration of animation through a variety of hands-on techniques. She earned her PhD from Nanyang Technological University Singapore. Veras invented the Silhouette

Zoetrope (aka Silhotrope), a patented animated optical illusion device. She is Assistant Professor teaching and researching at UT Dallas's Bass School of Arts, Humanities, and Technology.

Shilyh Warren is the author of *Subject to Reality: Women and Documentary* (University of Illinois Press, 2019) and numerous essays and book chapters on the history and impact of women's documentary filmmaking. She earned a PhD in Literature from Duke University and an MA in Comparative Literature from Dartmouth College. Currently, her work explores the entangled histories of psychoanalysis, feminism, and cinema. She is Associate Professor of Film Studies and Associate Dean of Graduate Studies in the Bass School at the University of Texas at Dallas.

Patricia White, Centennial Professor of Film and Media Studies, is currently Coordinator of Gender and Sexuality Studies and Director of the Aydelotte Foundation at Swarthmore College. Her books include *Rebecca*, *Women's Cinema/World Cinema: Projecting Contemporary Feminisms*, and *Uninvited: Classical Hollywood Cinema and Lesbian Representability*, and, with Timothy Corrigan, *The Film Experience*. She is a member of the *Camera Obscura* editorial collective and serves on the board of Women Make Movies.

Zaira Zarza is Assistant Professor in the Department of Art History and Film Studies at Université de Montréal. As a programmer, she worked at the Toronto (TIFF) and Cartagena (FICCI) international film festivals. She also directed the Latin American Studies Association (LASA) Film Festival, Boston, 2019. Zarza published *Caminos del cine brasileño contemporáneo* (Ediciones ICAIC) in 2010 and founded *Roots and Routes*, a project that promotes Cuban diasporic film and media. She co-curated the exhibition *L'espace de plateformes* (Carrefour des arts et de sciences, UdeM, 2023–4). Her current research focuses on Latin American and Caribbean documentary activism and Latinx-Canadian cinemas.

Andrea Luka Zimmerman is a Jarman award-winning artist and filmmaker whose multi-layered practice explores fragile refusals and counter memories, itinerant lives, human and otherwise, in relation to structural and political injustice. Andrea has made five acclaimed feature-length films: *Taskafa*,

Stories of the Street (2013), *Estate, a Reverie* (2015), *Erase and Forget* (2017), *Here for Life* (2019), and *Wayfaring Stranger* (2024). Her work has screened widely around the world, including at Berlinale, Locarno, BAFICI, and IFFR festivals, in cinemas and galleries, in community and activist spaces, and is held in collections and archives. Her collected films are released on Blu-ray by Second Run.

Introduction

Najmeh Moradiyan-Rizi and Shilyh Warren

In recent years, we have witnessed extraordinary momentum, visibility, and support for women filmmakers around the globe. Headlines in 2021 and 2022 celebrated Oscar wins for Best Director for women two years in a row: Chloé Zhao for *Nomadland* and Jane Campion for *The Power of the Dog*. Under increasing pressure from critics, the Cannes Film Festival has also increased the presence of women directors in competition, although in 2022, that meant only a quarter of the films under consideration for the most prestigious awards. Noticeably, Cannes' Palme d'Or in 2021 and 2023 went to French women filmmakers, Julia Ducournau for *Titane* and Justine Triet for *Anatomy of a Fall*, respectively.

More significant perhaps are the steady gains made by women documentary filmmakers across the globe. Historically, documentary filmmaking has always welcomed women with greater enthusiasm than the narrative filmmaking industry, and the momentum created by decades of women documentary filmmakers continues to accelerate in the twenty-first century. From production grants to festival presentations and programming, from streaming platforms to award ceremonies, and from academic publications and conferences to professional training opportunities, women and documentary have received increasing consideration. In 2022, Laura Poitras was awarded the Golden Lion for best film at the 79th Venice International Film Festival for her documentary *All the Beauty and the Bloodshed* (2022), and Danish filmmaker Lea Glob received the International Documentary Film Festival Amsterdam (IDFA) Award for Best Feature-Length Documentary for *Apolonia, Apolonia* (2022). In 2023, Sara Dosa's *Fire of Love* (2022) was nominated for an Oscar for Best Documentary Feature.

In recent years, women documentarians from the Global South have also achieved major success on the global stage. In 2020, Iranian documentarian Firouzeh Khosrovani's *Radiograph of a Family* was awarded the IDFA Award for

Best Feature-Length Documentary. In 2021, Indian filmmaker Payal Kapadia's *A Night of Knowing Nothing* received Cannes Film Festival's Golden Eye Award for best documentary. Tunisian filmmaker Kaouther Ben Hania's documentary *Four Daughters* received an Oscar nomination for Best Documentary Feature Film at the 2024 Academy Awards. The film was also one of two documentaries in 2023 to earn a coveted spot in the main competition at the Cannes Film Festival. As is so often the case, however, the lion's share of global attention remains trained on women filmmakers from Europe and North America. Despite these notable exceptions, films by women documentarians, especially from the Global South, are less often seen, distributed, and studied due to persistent geopolitical, financial, artistic, and academic hierarchies impacting access to and engagement with these works.

Feminist distribution and exhibition networks pressure this North–South discrepancy, however. In August 2021, as the world was watching the Taliban's takeover of Afghanistan, the nonprofit media organization Women Make Movies (WMM) curated a selection of ten documentary films from their collection on Afghan women's lives and experiences. The series, titled "Voices of Afghan Women," was made available to the public for free streaming through September 21, 2021. "As the rights and lives of women in Afghanistan are threatened, it is important for people all over the world to hear the voices of Afghan women," said WMM Executive Director Debra Zimmerman (Women Make Movies 2021). The collection's award-winning documentary films, such as Rokhsareh Ghaemmaghami's *Sonita* (2015)—winner, among others, of the IDFA Audience Award and the Sundance Film Festival Grand Jury Prize-World Documentary—Sahra Mani's *A Thousand Girls Like Me* (2018)—winner, among others, of Full Frame Film Festival's Center for Documentary Studies Filmmaker Award—and Eva Mulvad and Anja Al-Erhayem's *Enemies of Happiness* (2006)—winner, among others, of Human Rights Watch Film Festival's Nestor Almendros Prize—all attested, on the one hand, to the co-production practices and festival circulation of these films within a global context and, on the other hand, to the power of digital technologies facilitating worldwide streaming of these films during a critical historical moment exacerbated by a global pandemic.

This edited collection channels new attention to the changing landscape and increasingly urgent demand for feminist documentary filmmaking from around the globe. We are feminist scholars who bring together a range of diverse authors to investigate the global, institutional, political, and artistic dynamics that have impacted women's documentary practices in the twenty-first century and their implications for women's authorship, political subjectivity, and documentary representation. How do these dynamics and conditions shape women's opportunities as filmmakers as well as contribute to transnational feminist politics, expanded definitions of feminist documentary, and trends in documentary scholarship? Considering the intensified conditions brought forth by neoliberalism, globalization, digital expansion, war, displacement, and the climate crisis, there exists an urgent need to re-evaluate not only the significance of women's documentary practices and their contributions to feminist worldbuilding but also the state of documentary studies as it engages with the political, aesthetic, and industrial questions raised by increasing numbers of women filmmakers. Women's documentaries tend to prioritize and promote global awareness, alternative modes of allyship, and advocacy for those most marginalized by the legacies of colonialism, patriarchy, and capitalism; situating these global concerns at the center of documentary film scholarship promises to shift long-standing debates in documentary studies about the aesthetics and politics of realism and the significance of women's authorship.

Published in 1999, the pioneering collection *Feminism and Documentary* (University of Minnesota Press) examined the interrelation of feminism and documentary as then "one unbounded and mostly uncharted universe" (3). Emphasizing the lack of engagement with films by women in 1970s documentary and feminist film studies, an era that saw the rise of both fields in the United States, the editors, Diane Waldman and Janet Walker, aptly called for the reconsideration of women's contributions and of gender as a useful and integral category of analysis in documentary studies. Since then, anthologies such as *Feminist Worldmaking and the Moving Image*, edited by Erika Balsom and Hila Peleg (MIT Press, 2022); *Female Agency and Documentary Strategies: Subjectivities, Identity and Activism* (Edinburgh University Press, 2018) and *Female Authorship and the Documentary Image: Theory, Practice and Aesthetics* (Edinburgh University Press, 2018), both edited by Boel Ulfsdotter and Anna Backman Rogers; and monographs such as Lisa French's *The Female Gaze in Documentary Film: An International Perspective* (2021), Shilyh Warren's *Subject to Reality: Women and Documentary* (University of Illinois Press, 2019), and Stefanie Van de Peer's *Negotiating Dissidence: The Pioneering Women of Arab*

Documentary (Edinburgh University Press, 2017) have substantially furthered discussions on women's non-fiction filmmaking and gender issues in relation to documentary studies and practice.

These volumes are significant and generative interventions in the expanding field of feminist documentary studies. French, for example, makes a case for the particularity of "the female gaze" as the defining feature of women-directed documentaries. She claims that women's "experiences and perceptions are in part coloured by the life they lead in female bodies, and how their sex and gender are regarded or treated in their culture" (2021: 35). For French, the "female gaze" is marked by a quality she calls "intimacy," which women prioritize in their work (2021: 37). Intimacy might be detected in women's ability to make more sensitive and nuanced films about other women and girls or in the kind of empathy that women, as a result of socialization, bring to stories about the needs of others. Despite decades of disagreement about terms such as "essentialism" and "authorship" at the core of debates about women's cinema writ large, French emphatically makes a case that gender matters in specific, embodied ways in women's documentary filmmaking. Resonant with our project, Ulfsdotter and Rogers also insist on the need for a global frame for feminist documentary scholarship and reinvigorate enduring questions about authorship and agency. Their twin volumes also feature interviews, creative essays, and collaborative works by filmmakers and scholars, diversifying methods, modes of research, as well as the field to which we have all committed our energies. Contributors to this volume also engage with these methodological and conceptual questions in diverse ways that, we hope, continue to press the field in new directions.

Our thinking has also been deeply influenced by questions raised and addressed by Patricia White and Lúcia Nagib about the status and definition of world cinema and women's work within that frame. In *Women's Cinema, World Cinema* (Duke University Press, 2015), White makes the case that "women filmmakers from all over" collectively produce and project "a transnational feminist social vision," thereby contesting the perception that feminist activism is either "relegated to the past or projected onto the developing world" (2015: 4–5). Throughout her landmark book, White consistently writes "women's cinema" back into the category of "world cinema." Focused primarily on narrative features, which are more likely to become festival darlings and thus signal the emergence of global women auteurs, White's project lays the groundwork for our own investigation in the realm of documentary, which her contribution to this edited collection extends. Nagib's most recent book, *Realist Cinema as World Cinema* (Amsterdam University Press, 2020), advances the claim that thinking through realism and realist cinema productively helps us understand what we mean by world cinema, or "what 'world cinema' actually stands for" (2020: 19). For Nagib, however, realism is concretely a mode of production, rather than a vaguely formal or philosophical question constrained to the text itself or even a possible mode of reception. Documentaries figure prominently in Nagib's analysis, although her focus on the site of production and "the crews and casts who choose to produce rather than just reproduce reality" also pressure traditional modes of inquiry in documentary studies (2020: 23). Nagib and White model the stakes of our collective attention to filmmakers (broadly conceived), ethics, politics, and the extremely real ground on which our inquiry delicately rests.

By prioritizing global practices and emphasizing the enduring connections between feminist activism and documentary filmmaking, however, this edited collection makes a new contribution to the field, expanding the range of issues, authors, and networks that shape the work of women filmmakers in terms of both production and reception. The overall promise of the volume is to re-investigate the particularities of global women's documentary practices in tandem with progressive social changes and movements in the twenty-first century, with a special focus on the Global South. This specific focus is important for our collection as there is still a great need to address the persistent geopolitical, financial, artistic, and academic hierarchies impacting access to and engagement with women's work in and from the Global South. As Raewyn Connell observes, "The problem is not a deficit of ideas from the global periphery—it is a deficit of recognition and circulation. This is a structural problem in feminist thought on a world scale" (2015: 52). Our hope is that this volume contributes to the "new and globally inclusive ways" of conceiving feminist scholarship urged by Connell, by highlighting women's documentary practices and scholarship from the Global South as well as alternative and emergent networks of production and reception from around the globe (2015: 53). Therefore, the authors in this collection pay particular attention to the Global South by examining new forms of documentary activism, institutions, audience outreach, and informal networks of collaboration among women filmmakers; investigating new voices, aesthetics, and public and private spaces; and revising national and international narratives about the origins and legacies of political filmmaking. The chapters focus on filmmakers from East Africa, Latin America, South Asia, East Asia, the Middle East, and North Africa, as well as decolonial practices in the Global North based on Indigenous filmmaking and feminist documentary institutions such as WMM.

Increasing scholarship on women and documentary is concomitant with the rise of women's documentaries across the globe that have had a crucial impact on progressive sociocultural and political changes, bringing much-needed visibility and advocacy to gender issues and women's rights discourses, as well as the trend toward global frameworks in documentary studies.

Boel Ulfsdotter and Anna Backman Rogers rightly argue that "women's increasing claims to equal societal rights and vocalisation on a global scale have had a decisive impact on female agency in relation to the documentation of contemporary issues" (2018: 1). Given the considerable role women play in the documentation of and reflection on crucial contemporary issues, this edited collection aims to reconsider the connections between women's and gender studies and documentary film studies through an examination of women's contemporary documentary practices and their transformative impacts within a global context. In doing so, the volume engages with both the textual (representational and thematic) and the contextual (practical and institutional) aspects of women's documentary practices, further connecting them to various progressive political, social, and academic transformations. Taken together, the chapters investigate the conditions and results of women's documentary practices in terms of production, distribution, and exhibition across the world as well as their aesthetic and representational strategies and approaches. Additionally, some chapters examine curatorial/programming, institutional, and collaborative practices that contribute to feminist worldbuilding as well as help bring about visibility and engagement with urgent gender issues, especially those beyond the immediate and familiar academic scope of the Global North.

The volume is divided into four main parts, each containing three chapters. Part I, "Documentary Initiatives as Feminist Worldbuilding," features works by established and emergent scholars discussing women's initiatives and networks involved in feminist documentary. Patricia White lays out the significant role of WMM in supporting women documentarians transnationally and expanding the reach of women's documentaries, particularly those from the Global South, to international audiences. Lindiwe Dovey explores the essential work of Kenyan filmmaker Judy Kibinge, particularly as the executive founder and creative director of the Nairobi-based initiative Docubox, and the ways it has supported women's documentary practices in East Africa. Amal Shafek focuses on the Cairo-based organization Between Women Filmmakers Caravan, which aims to foster Arab women's filmmaking practices and enhance transnational feminist solidarity and exchange across the world, with a special focus on the Global South collaborations between Latin America and the Middle East.

Part II, "Rereading Public and Private Connections through Documentary," engages with the dynamics of private and public spaces as presented in women's documentaries. Shilyh Warren and Christine Veras examine independent, feminist animated documentaries from Turkey, Brazil, India, and Slovenia that take aim at the global problem of enduring violence against women by featuring very personal stories from survivors and activists. Lorena Cervera rereads the history of Latin American documentary and its sociopolitical contexts to focus on recent women's practices that engage with daughter/filmmakers' connection to their fathers, thus presenting a cross-generational and affective discourse in regard to Latin American documentary. Wakae Nakane, on the other hand, works with the politicization of familial space in women's post-Fukushima documentaries with a focus on the aesthetic strategies used by Japanese women filmmakers to disrupt private/public boundaries in order to bring about social, political, and familial connectivity in a post-disaster society.

Part III, "Reimagining Documentary Activism," highlights various forms of documentary activism that have emerged across the world in order to expand the range of issues that shape women's progressive and crucial efforts in the twenty-first century. Najmeh Moradiyan-Rizi employs an ecofeminist lens to examine Iranian women's biographical documentaries as a form of activism that effectively revives the female voice and subjectivity in Iranian society and culture, further offering crucial acts of environmental protection and advocacy. Zaira Zarza explores Puerto Rican women's documentary activism that aims to enhance social justice and grassroots activism against persisting coloniality, hegemonic capitalism, and financial instability. Kim Munro discusses her hybrid theater documentary project, *The Art of Work Is a Work of Art*, in order to examine the intersections of live theater and documentary in relation to histories of feminism and queerness within an Australian context.

Part IV, "Documentary Voice and Feminist Perspectives," highlights practices of filmmakers who expand the forms and possibilities of feminist documentary. Gail Vanstone's focus on Canadian Indigenous filmmakers explores the notion of "braided narratives" as a radical pathway to a new, decolonized worldview. Aparna Sharma and Priya Sen reflect on their documentary practice in a conversation that develops a cinematic mode of inquiry they call "the deep image," as a way to complicate our apprehension of social realities in contemporary India. The final chapter presents a collective conversation between artist-filmmakers—Irene Lusztig, Hannah Jayanti, Andrea Luka Zimmerman, Noorafshan Mirza, and Rosa-Johan Uddoh—that reflexively foregrounds processes and practices, including in the writing of the chapter itself, and prioritizes listening, vulnerability, and power-sharing at the scene of documentary encounters. Collectively, these essays lay the groundwork for a new conversation in feminist documentary studies—one that looks decisively at the *contemporary* and *global* landscape of women's non-fictional work, which is typically produced outside of capital-intensive, exclusionary realms of industry, and instead operates in committed collaboration with activists, communities, and nonprofitable educational and advocacy networks that form the vital vascular system of transnational feminism.

Part I

Documentary Initiatives as Feminist Worldbuilding

1

Women Make Movies Globally

Patricia White

As the contributors to this volume richly demonstrate, feminist documentary occupies many spaces and takes multiple forms globally. Grassroots activist and training films, NGO and television commissions, and observational and personal documentaries are just a few of these practices. Positioning such work in institutional terms, this chapter addresses the role of the US nonprofit feminist media arts organization Women Make Movies (WMM) in the global circulation and definition of feminist documentary from the perspective of a feminist scholar and educator who serves on the WMM board.[1] With its distribution collection comprising nearly 700 films by and about women, many from the Global South, WMM shapes the US educational market for non-fiction feminist films and, through its advocacy efforts and Production Assistance Program, impacts the funding, festival, and streaming prospects for many more documentaries by and about women, inclusively defined. Through networking, acquisitions from around the world, and the subject matter of much of the work, WMM engages in transnational feminist politics of solidarity and decoloniality.

From the grassroots organizing of the early 1970s to the post #MeToo reckoning of recent years, WMM has participated in transnational networks of feminist media activism, advocacy, exhibition, preservation, and scholarship. At the same time, the organization has sustained itself for most of its more than fifty-year history in an unfriendly arts funding environment through its distribution income and fees from workshops and fiscal sponsorship and is deeply ensconced in the documentary film ecosystem. Under executive director Debra Zimmerman since 1983, WMM has become, as B. Ruby Rich notes, an "influential international hub and a tireless promoter of women's filmmaking—a veritable NGO unto itself" (2013: 159). The WMM distribution collection consists primarily of documentaries, with some significant experimental, narrative, and animated works, which circulate to universities, festivals, media arts centers, and community groups, primarily but not exclusively within the United States. WMM also functions as a resource for countless programmers, festival organizers, educators, and grassroots groups that want to bring feminist issues and the work of women filmmakers to audiences worldwide.

Digital culture has vastly expanded the potential of global media flows, including non-fiction filmmaking, outside the domination of the Global North. Yet, constraints on the production and circulation of work about and especially by women from the Global South are still considerable. WMM has maintained a longstanding commitment to seeking out and promoting such work and to facilitating local infrastructures for sustaining it through festivals, consulting, and other initiatives. Documentaries distributed by WMM have achieved significant festival and awards exposure. Examples include *Sonita*, a portrait of an Afghan teenage rapper and marriage resister living in Iran, by Rokhsareh Ghaemmaghami, which won the 2015 World Cinema Documentary Grand Jury Prize at the Sundance Festival, and *Saving Face* (Daniel Junge and Sharmeen Obaid-Chinoy), about misogynist acid attacks in Pakistan, which won the short documentary Oscar in 2012. Shalini Kantayya's successful *Coded Bias* (2020) is exemplary of WMM's current profile. Made in the United States with the support of progressive initiatives in independent documentary, including Ford Foundation's JustFilms and Chicken and Egg, by a second-generation Indian-American filmmaker, the film offers an intersectional feminist critique of the neoliberal surveillance world order.

Just as important as addressing timely topics and participating in the festival and awards circuit, documentaries acquired by WMM remain accessible for years and even decades through its nontheatrical distribution catalog. This repository of transnational feminist filmmaking encompasses diverse modes; reflexive works by Trinh T. Minh-ha and observational documentaries by Kim Longinotto, cornerstones of the WMM collection, take up different epistemologies and ethics of cross-cultural encounter (Nichols 1991). But at the time of writing, such high-profile films as Oscar-nominees *To Kill a Tiger* (Nisha Pahuja, 2022) and *Cameraperson* (Kirsten Johnston, 2016) are associated with WMM through its Production Assistance Program rather than its distribution program. The precarity of educational distribution reflects broader challenges to sustainability in the higher education and documentary landscapes, with shrinking university acquisition budgets and cries of a "doc apocalypse," as streamers and investors pull out of the sector (Kohn 2023). After reflecting on how WMM's feminist commitments have determined its place in the documentary ecosystem over the years, I will conclude by briefly discussing two WMM documentaries that speak to the promises and challenges of contemporary transnational feminist non-fiction filmmaking.

Distribution Matters

Neither a funder nor a production company, and operating outside the industrial entertainment world of "movies," the organization has a somewhat misleading name. WMM evolved its role and reputation as a distributor within the feminist media community. Founded in 1972 by Ariel Dougherty and Sheila Paige (with Dolores Bogowski) to teach production to New York City women and girls, WMM is one of many feminist media groups established in the period, in the United States and beyond. Dougherty and her co-organizers reached out to more than 100 such groups in planning the 1975 New York Conference of Feminist Film and Video Organizations.[2] The event's "Ongoing Manifesto" stated: "as feminists working collectively in film and video we see our media as an ongoing process both in terms of the way it is made and the way it is distributed and shown. We do not accept the existing power structure and we are committed to changing it by the content and structure of our images and by the way we relate to each other in our work and with our audience" (Conference 1975). Ensuring access to women's films through grassroots distribution was integral to this process.

Consistent with this philosophy, WMM both exhibited and distributed its workshop films as well as its own productions. By 1975 the organization had picked up several titles for distribution from women's filmmaking groups in the UK and Australia and created a staff position to meet the demand, particularly for the WMM production *Healthcaring: From Our End of the Speculum* (Denise Bostrom and Jane Warrenbrand, 1976).[3] By the early 1980s, WMM's collection included films by avant-garde feminist filmmakers Lizzie Borden, Su Friedrich, Barbara Hammer, and Marjorie Keller as well as documentary and narrative titles. But internal divisions around race and class politics and organizational mission, and a funding crisis, prompted reorganization and a strategic decision to focus on distribution. Zimmerman, who had come to the organization on the government-funded jobs training program, the Comprehensive Employment and Training Act (CETA), was appointed director in 1983. WMM's next catalog featured a significant number of acquisitions, including works from the Global South in the series "As Women See It" and "Punto de Vista: Latina," discussed in more detail below.

Connecting production and exhibition in media circulation, distribution lacks the glamor of both. But distribution is a means of nurturing publics, from the local to the transnational, around issues, perspectives, and aesthetics. In the 1980s, other mission-driven peer organizations similarly weathered arts funding and political vicissitudes through earned income from educational distribution. New Day, which also started in the 1970s to distribute feminist films made by its founders, functions as a collective for US-based makers (Coffman and Stein 2018), and California Newsreel and Third World Newsreel feature significant work by filmmakers from the Global South alongside US filmmakers of color. Sister organizations like Iris and Serious Business in California (Freude 1979), Circles and COW in the UK (later merged as Cinenova), Video Femmes and GIV in Canada, and Cinemien in the Netherlands shared WMM's mission to distribute work by and about women and carried some of the same titles. Women's film festivals, grassroots groups, and media arts centers provided exhibition outlets and contexts for discourse about and networking around women's media work, including a significant emphasis on global issues. As most of the other feminist distributors went under, the large US educational market sustained WMM, which saw its business shift from 16mm rentals to institutional VHS sales, which could return a significant share of revenue to filmmakers.

The US university library market, which encompasses nearly 3,600 post-secondary institutions, is the primary sector for WMM's distribution service. The customer base also includes public libraries, K–12 education, media art centers, and community groups. Educational distribution is the *how* of WMM's survival—the *what* encompasses hundreds of works by and about women addressing such issues as abortion, women and work, the legacies of writers and musicians, race and ethnicity, peace and conflict in Central America and the Middle East, gender and sexual identity, and more.

While decisions about which films to acquire for distribution are based on multiple factors, including aesthetic criteria and political convictions, viability in the educational market is crucial. While institutional library media selections are governed by policy, budget, and format and license restrictions, the community-building function of distribution carries over to higher education. Feminist faculty and librarians often drive institutional purchasing of WMM titles, and teaching and writing about particular films makes a profound mark on generations of students who will themselves become filmmakers, critics, curators, and scholars as well as on knowledge production across a number of fields.

It is a truism in feminist film studies that the scholarly preference for formally challenging work led to the marginalization of scholarship on documentary in the field (Lesage 1990; Warren and Lesage 2022). And indeed, films from WMM's New Directions collection—including Sally Potter's *Thriller* (1979), Michelle Citron's *Daughter Rite* (1978), and Trinh T. Minh-ha's *Reassemblage* (1982), all of which received significant scholarly attention in the early 1980s—long ranked among the catalog's top sellers. But experimental works were and remain vastly outnumbered in the WMM collection by more straightforward documentaries. There are many more films by and about women in circulation than the few that have been canonized by scholars, and this breadth is crucial to feminist film history. Whether experimental or more conventional in form, all of the works in the WMM collection are distinguished by the filmmakers' positionality. WMM specifies that at least one of the directors of a film considered for distribution identify as a woman. Rather than an essentialist position, this is an epistemological one that insists on access to the means of production. Subjectivity and address are fundamental values of feminist film culture; each of the hundreds of films in the collection contributes to documentary filmmaking as feminist worldbuilding (Balsom and Peleg 2022).

WMM's mission to distribute films by *and about* women also poses ethical questions about speaking on others' behalf. One of Zimmerman's first acquisitions by women filmmakers from the Global South was a collection of five 30-minute films depicting women and girls from developing countries entitled *As Women See It*. German producer Pierre Hoffmann tapped an extraordinary lineup of filmmakers engaged in grassroots and political filmmaking. Safi Faye, heralded as the first sub-Saharan African woman director to direct a feature film, contributed *Selbe: One among Many/Selbe et tantes d'autres* (1983). Deepa Dhanraj and the Yugantar Collective made *Sudesha* (1983), about a woman involved in Chipko forest preservation activism in India. Egyptian activist director Ateyyat El Abnoudy focused on the double standard in *Permissible Dreams* (1983), portraying the farm and domestic labor of Oum Said, and María Barea's *Women of El Planeta* (1983) was produced with a neighborhood indigenous women's group in Peru. In *Pan y Dignidad* (1982), María José Alvarez gave a picture of women in Nicaragua that balanced the many solidarity films on Central America made by North American women. The films in *As Women See It* were marred by Eurocentric framing, however, with the protagonists' voice-overs dubbed into English. While the films position Third World women "under Western eyes," to cite Chandra Mohanty's critique of Western feminist social science, these filmmakers' collaborative visions made these five short documentaries more than a panorama of international development concerns (Mohanty 1984).

WMM expanded its connections with women filmmakers from the Global South through participation in Filmforum/Nairobi, part of the nongovernmental forum accompanying the UN End of Decade for Women in 1985. WMM board member Joanne Sandler worked at the International Women's Tribune Center, which coordinated with Studio D, the women's studio of the National Film Board of Canada, to organize the film forum. Zimmerman participated on the steering committee and met filmmakers and activists from all over the globe in Nairobi, seeding a collection of films that continues to expand.

Inclusivity and antiracism guided WMM's distribution mission as film and video by North American multicultural artists burgeoned in the 1980s. WMM distributed films by Black US women filmmakers and videomakers Ayoka Chenzira, Julie Dash, Linda Gibson, Michelle Parkerson, Kathe Sandler, and Fronza Woods, along with the National Black Women's Health Collective's documentary for girls, *Becoming a Woman*. Asian-American videomakers included Shu Lea Cheang, Rea Tajiri, and Janice Tanaka. In 1988 the Association of Independent Video and Filmmakers, on whose board Zimmerman served, successfully lobbied Congress for dedicated funding for independent programming from underrepresented groups. The establishment of the Independent Television Service supplemented the public television minority programming consortia and other limited US funding resources and outlets for such productions, and WMM linked filmmakers with such opportunities through its Production Assistance Program.

A notable exception to Anglophone hegemony in the circulation of feminist film at this time was the program of 16mm films released by WMM in 1984, Punto de Vista: Latina. Zimmerman worked with Bienvenida Matías and Catherine Benamou to curate and screen films by and about Latinas throughout the New York City boroughs. Looking for work for the series, they soon found they needed to extend the effort beyond US borders, and the curators connected with women's film groups working in Latin America like Cine Mujer in Mexico and Grupo Chaski in Peru (Zimmerman 2017; Benamou and Matías 2013). Accompanied by a study guide, Punto de Vista: Latina included Susana Blaustein Muñoz's autobiographical lesbian short *Susana* (1980) and Lourdes Portillo's drama *After the Earthquake/Despues del Terremoto* (1979) as well as an early short by acclaimed Mexican director María Novaro (*An Island Surrounded by Water/Una isla rodeado de agua*, 1985). Exiled Chilean filmmaker Valeria Sarmiento contributed an hour-long documentary on machismo shot in Costa Rica, *Un hombre, cuando hombre es* (1982).

Reflecting on the experience, Benamou comments:

> Women Make Movies has been much more than a distributor over the years, providing support (logistical, technical, and pedagogical) for women directors and filmmakers-in-the-making across the globe. Occupying an interstitial space with respect to initiatives by filmmakers of diverse national and ethnic backgrounds, the organization has maintained a steady presence in global feminist forums as well as minority-oriented production and networking initiatives within the US. (Benamou and Matías 2013: 135)

Several of the included works are the subject of recent scholarship recovering the robust early feminist film movement in Latin America (Soto 2022; Seguí 2022).

Punto de Vista: Latina opened unto a wider feminist film culture intersecting with hemispheric social justice and cultural activism. "[D]uring a decade marked by the beginning of neoliberal cultural politics at home and US-sponsored armed conflict in Central America . . . . We took these women's images as a sign of peace and the promise of restitution" (Benamou and Matías 2013: 140–1), Benamou recalls. Shortly afterward, Blaustein and Portillo's

Las Madres: The Mothers of Plaza del Mayo (1985) marked a breakthrough for Latin American women's issues and Latina filmmaking with its Academy Award nomination for best documentary. WMM distributed that film and subsequently acquired such key Latin American works as Marta Rodriguez and Jorge Silva's documentary about women in Colombia's flower industry, *Love, Women and Flowers* (1988); Marilu Mallet's moving meditation on life in exile from Chile, *Unfinished Diary* (1989); and, more recently, Albertina Carri's *The Blonds* (2003), Natalia Almada's *El General* (2009), and Celina Escher's *Fly So Far* (2021) (Figure 1.1).

Consistent with the border-crossing exemplified in Punto de Vista: Latina, many works in WMM's collection could be characterized, following Hamid Naficy (2001), as "accented" cinema—films by exilic, diasporan, or ethnic/hyphenate filmmakers working in the Global North. On staff at WMM, I helped release Trinh T. Minh-ha's *Surname Viet Given Name Nam* (1988). The feature film anchored a curated program of new works on cultural identity, exile, and diaspora at Anthology Film Archives. Changing the Subject included 16mm shorts and videos by Ngozi Onwurah, Maureen Blackwood, Mona Hatoum, Pratibha Parmar, and Tracey Moffatt, among others. The notable diversity of filmmakers and their challenges to "straight" documentary forms inaugurated new conversations in feminist filmmaking and scholarship, including writing by Trinh and Parmar. Ella Shohat foregrounded many of these WMM works in her landmark essay,

Figure 1.1 Teodora Vásquez in *Fly So Far*. Directed by Celina Escher, 2021. Image courtesy of Women Make Movies.

"Post-Third-Worldist Culture: Gender, Nation, and the Cinema" (1996), arguing that the whiteness of the feminist film canon and the masculinism of third-worldist militant filmmaking have overshadowed the significant work of women of color and women from the Global South at the overlap of both movements. From portraits to essay films, such works put the epistemologies of intersectional, transnational feminism into the public sphere.

Given inadequate public funding for educational and independent media in the United States, WMM has long showcased work from outside the country. Films from Canada's Studio D, founded in 1974, and the UK Black British workshops, which in the 1980s provided access to the means of production for people of color and encouraged experimental work, have made a significant impact in the United States through WMM. Indeed, partnerships with filmmakers from the UK like Parmar (who also produced work for Channel 4's queer program *Out on Tuesday*, 1989–94) and documentarian Kim Longinotto have helped define the WMM collection over the years. Longinotto is the single best-represented filmmaker, with seventeen films currently in distribution. BBC and other commissions have supported a career that would be impossible to sustain in the US context without independent wealth. Longinotto's works, including *Dream Girls* (1993), *Divorce Iranian Style* (1998), *Sisters in Law* (2005), and *Pink Saris* (2010), identify WMM with transnational feminism as both subject matter and institutional practice. Longinotto's work is characterized by a politics of solidarity and by an effort to particularize her perspective as a white woman, even as it depicts women from other cultures and classes for an audience in the Global North (White 2006). However, work by and about women from the Global South is an acquisition priority for WMM, consistent with a transnational feminist political scrutiny of extractive documentary practice.

With a critical mass of WMM acquisitions on global issues in the 1990s and into the twenty-first century, it becomes possible to address relations of power in representation by comparing films made from different standpoints in various modes with diverse funding arrangements. For example, how does the rhetorical framing of the 1999 series Girls Around the World contrast with that of As Women See It? Both were commissioned by European television from women filmmakers about girls and women in the Global South; how do Maria Barea's contributions to both inscribe her positionality as a filmmaker? How does Pakistani director Sabiha Sumar's short made for Girls Around the

World inflect the filmmaker's ongoing inquiry into South Asian female lives in her other documentaries distributed by WMM or her feature film *Silent Waters/Khamosh Pani* (2003)? How effective is the strategy of "giving voice" in *Afghanistan Unveiled* (2004), which highlights the work of young Afghan women in the Aina Women Filming Group collaborating with French television journalist Brigitte Brault? The multiplicity of the collection complements a long-standing commitment to self-reflexivity. Among the most trenchant critics of the ethnographic gaze at non-Western women, Trinh Minh-ha continues her deconstruction of the documentary eye's neutrality in her latest WMM release, *What About China?* (2021).

Boel Ulfsdotter and Anna Backman Rogers use the concepts of authorship and agency to frame two valuable recent essay collections on international feminist documentary practice: *Female Agency and Documentary Strategies: Subjectivities, Identity and Activism* (2019) and *Female Authorship and the Documentary Image: Theory, Practice and Aesthetics* (2022). These concepts inform the enunciative strategies of WMM releases on such topics as women's human rights, sexual violence in conflict zones, feminicide, early marriage, and girls' education. In the area of international women's human rights, the Bosnian documentary *Calling the Ghosts* (Mandy Jacobsen and Karmen Jelincic, 1996) and Lisa F. Jackson's *The Greatest Silence: Rape in the Congo* (2007) used authorial experience to depict their subjects' agency in changing international law around rape as a war crime. Thus, the collection *as* collection invites scholarly, activist, curatorial, and archival attention. Some curatorial work is undertaken by the organization itself. For example, in the immediate aftermath of 9/11, amid rising Islamophobia, WMM made a collection of nine films by and about Muslim women available to customers for free to screen and discuss. The initiative, Response to Hate, had considerable impact and WMM used the model at other times of crises, such as the US withdrawal of troops from Afghanistan and the overturning of *Roe v. Wade*.

However, financial, political, and technological threats to the sustainability of WMM's distribution model have intensified in the twenty-first century. The educational market has been eroded by media privatization, online aggregators and streamers, as well as waning public faith in higher education. While platforms like Netflix put many important independent documentaries before the public eye, their exclusive terms make many excellent films unavailable through educational distribution and thus university collections.

#MeToo raised consciousness about the social and economic struggles faced by women behind the camera, and the film world has become more nominally feminist. But big-budget documentaries with high-profile and celebrity producers promulgating popular feminism and popular feminist causes crowd out more grassroots efforts. Finally, the documentary boom, fed by new platforms and equity investors, has gone bust, leaving nonprofits and independents fighting to maintain a hard-won counterpublic sphere.

In particular, the work of fiction and avant-garde filmmakers, video artists, and animators has become harder for a nonprofit like WMM to distribute successfully as the market contracts. Accordingly, the preponderance of WMM acquisitions are straightforward social-issue documentaries that deploy, to use Bill Nichols's term, "discourses of sobriety," to address vital issues and promote marginalized voices (1991: 3–4). In the midst of existential threats, the organization has adapted and maintained an earned-income base, remarkable for a nonprofit arts organization with explicit political commitments.

Advocacy on the Global Stage

In my discussion of WMM's distribution services, which are limited to the United States, I've invoked a variety of work with transnational subject matter, produced by filmmakers positioned both inside and outside the United States. How does the organization itself function outside the national context? In transnational feminist spaces, WMM represents the film world. In spaces oriented toward film, WMM represents feminist concerns. It is in sites that arise from the intersection of feminism and film that WMM's history is most impactful and its mission most legible, and these have shifted ground over its fifty-year history.

From its beginning in the 1960s and 1970s, the feminist filmmaking movement was transnational. Grassroots groups were active in Europe, North America, Australia, and Latin America, and many women were involved in local and Third World film movements as well. Helping to link these movements, WMM organized two women's film festivals in New York and sent delegations and films to some of the earliest events in Toronto and Berlin, as well as Film Forum Nairobi in 1985 and the hemispheric gathering *Cocina de imágenes* in 1987.

Increasingly, curators, archivists, and scholars are turning their attention to the compelling histories of feminist film organizing and especially to decolonial perspectives that have been marginalized. Under the direction of Daniella Shreir, the journal *Another Gaze* and the online site Another Screen have presented invaluable programming and scholarship, both topical and historical, such as a timely series of films by women in Iran supporting the Women, Life, Freedom movement, and a forum on Sarah Maldoror featuring the filmmaker's daughter. The 1976 Sojourner Truth Festival of the Arts celebrating African American women filmmakers was reprised at the University of Chicago in 2023. Karola Gramann and Heidi Schlüpmann, former editors of *Frauen und Film*, have hosted Remake in Frankfurt since 2018 to highlight feminist film history. Also in Germany, 2023's Feminist Elsewheres program at Arsenal Kino brought together, with minimal resources, films from the international festival and gathering in Berlin in 1973, others from a reprise in 1997, and works from an open call. From these gatherings and programs, more robust networks, archives, and histories of the global dimensions of feminist film history are emerging.

WMM is a touchstone for these conversations around archiving and curation, even as it is a hub for transnational networks with connections to media professionals through organizations like Women and Film and other groups fighting for gender equity in production, programming, criticism, and more, such as Pro Quote in Germany. And it plays a key role within the women's film festival ecosystem. With Films de femmes in Creteil in its forty-sixth year, and the Internationales Frauenfilm Festival in Dortmund/Köln carrying on work started in the 1980s, there remain sites with longstanding commitments to global women's film programming. As North American events waned, others emerged elsewhere: the Seoul International Women's Film Festival, founded in 1997, is sustained by Korean feminist film scholarship and activism and state support of film culture. WMM has long histories with all of these events and has offered films and curated programs to launch other festivals on several continents. The women's film festival in Taiwan pays homage in its very name: Women Make Waves; Filmmor in Turkey credits Zimmerman as a founding influence, and she has been instrumental to events in Latin America, Eastern Europe, and Africa.

WMM long functioned as one of the few explicitly feminist organizations in the international documentary ecosystem, which has seen enormous growth in recent decades. International documentary markets have always been an important site for WMM's acquisition and sales, and the organization's status in this sector has only grown with initiatives toward gender equity. WMM's success as a distributor in the US nontheatrical market represents a significant sales opportunity and an important symbolic force for emerging women artists around the world.

Zimmerman and other staff and board members serve on panels, juries, and pitch sessions at international documentary showcases like IDFA (International Documentary Film Festival), CPH:DOX in Copenhagen, Sheffield in the UK, and Hot Docs in Toronto. WMM's consistent feminist presence at such events has held broadcasters and funders accountable to gender equity in their policies at the same time as it makes the feminist commitments of filmmakers and potential audiences visible. Its name alone gives it a seat at the table.

WMM continues to work at the epicenter of innovative, high-profile feminist filmmaking internationally through its Production Assistance Program, which has become ever more vital even as the outlook for nonprofit distribution grows more uncertain. Through fiscal sponsorship (using its nonprofit status as a conduit for funds from donors and foundations), workshops, and consultations, WMM supports work by many of today's most celebrated women documentary filmmakers. Feature documentaries by Laura Poitras (*Citizen 4*, 2014), Dawn Porter (*Trapped*, 2016), Sandi Tan (*Shirkers*, 2018), and Nanfu Wang (*Hooligan Sparrow*, 2016), among others, have won accolades at Sundance, received Oscar nominations, and secured Netflix deals. Not only do these films receive transnational exposure, but they are also often transnational in production and subject matter. Tan and Wang are representative of a growing group of diasporan directors, many of whom have attended film school in the United States, whose perspectives have energized US documentary culture. The Production Assistance Program even supports women directors based outside the United States, like South African poet Milisuthando Bongela.

Bongela's debut film, the personal documentary *Milisuthando*, a South African–Colombian co-production made in association with Multitude Films, premiered at Sundance in 2023 and went on to screen at IDFA, Hot Docs, and many other festivals. In it, Bongela uses voice-over, historical footage, vignettes, and intimate interviews to explore the legacy of growing up in a country that no longer exists: the Transkei, a Black state lasting between 1976 and 1994 under the South African apartheid regime. The film is structured in five parts, around memories, dreams, and encounters exploring the contradictions of race and national identity, family and friendship, art and politics. As the voice-over asks, underscored by the text onscreen: "Who will you become because of where you come from?" Starting with footage of an anonymous Black woman who stripped at the foot of the Mandela statue, *Milisuthando* considers the female body in relation to the body politic. Bongela's voice, figuratively and literally, distinguishes a film that will become a touchstone in decolonial feminist theory and cultural practice.

Another extraordinary documentary, *Bye Bye Tiberias*, was acquired for distribution by WMM after festival exposure in 2023 and given a limited theatrical release. Lina Soualem's film is also a feature-length first-person documentary about generations of women and the unresolved legacy of a country of origin under erasure. In it, Soualem journeys with her mother, acclaimed Palestinian actor Hiam Abbass, to her childhood home and back to the village by Lake Tiberias from which Abbass's grandparents and their children were displaced by the Israeli occupation in 1948 (Figure 1.2).

Bye Bye Tiberias relies on photos and video footage to establish the filmmaker's lineage within four generations of women. Her mother and aunts feature in footage from before and after her grandmother's death; home movies capture Lina's childhood visits to her grandmother's home. Her

Figure 1.2 Hiam Abbass and Lina Soualem in *Bye Bye Tiberias*. Directed by Lina Soualem, 2023. Credit: Frida Marzouk, Beall Productions. Image courtesy of Women Make Movies.

great-grandmother is remembered by Abbass, who singles out a photo from before she was born to which she bears a striking resemblance. Soualem's own present-tense on-camera appearances are sparing; scenes in which she and her mother pin family photographs on the wall capture tender but terse mother-daughter dynamics. While the overriding narrative is one of dispossession, including haunting newsreel footage of the Nakba, in her mother's story, leaving home was a declaration of independence. Abbass's desire to be an actor and conflicts with her father around her sexual expression propelled her to France, where Lina was later born. The daughter's gentle prodding to memory is greeted with a notable lack of sentimentality by Abbass, who also shows great tenderness with her own mother and affection with her sisters. It is fascinating to see this striking actor, best known to US audiences for her role in the TV drama *Succession* (2018), among the women of her family of origin. But the distance she chose for herself and bequeathed to her daughter remains in the frame, echoing the family's displacement from the shores of Lake Tiberias. The marks of history are lived in deeply gendered ways—when the family was dispossessed of their home, her grandmother was separated from her married sister, who was resettled in Syria. When they finally reunited decades later, the grandmother recounts how they buried their faces in each other's clothing to take in their loved one's scents. Like *Milisuthando*'s imagery of cooking and incense-burning, this anecdote has a synesthetic effect. Both films include physical travel to the filmmakers' grandmothers' houses, but the journey doesn't promise recovery. Instead, the memories tethered to photos, smells, garments, and locks of hair trigger more questions. The place of origin is held in ambivalence, the path to belonging unsettled, as the young women at their center interrogate generational and geopolitical fault lines.

Milisuthando and *Bye Bye Tiberias* carry forward many of the stylistic features Naficy attributes to accented filmmaking and the priorities Shohat relates to post–Third Worldist frameworks, while their transnational itineraries are indicative of the current fraught geopolitical moment. In fact, when asked in 2023 what she found notable in the space of global women's documentary production, Zimmerman singled out the increasing use of personal documentary in films made outside the United States. She has long held the personal documentary to be a foundationally feminist approach to filmmaking (even as male practitioners of the form have grabbed the spotlight) but previously found European programmers dismissive of the approach. If this has changed, it is because women documentarians are using these formats in conjunction with decolonial strategies. *Milisuthando*'s exploration of the entanglement of race, gender, and national politics through memory offers a powerful perspective on South Africa and beyond. And the release of *Bye Bye Tiberias* during the Israel–Hamas War throws into relief gendered histories of displacement and cultural resistance. The films' resonance with formal features of earlier WMM films, from *Surname Viet Given Name Nam* to Rea Tajiri's *History and Memory: For Akiko and Takashige* (1991), maintains the link between WMM's collection and transnational feminist activism, curation, teaching, and scholarship.

WMM's distribution collection is concrete evidence that there is no lack of talent, diversity, precedent, or pipeline when it comes to global feminist media by and about women. In the era in which streaming platforms and neoliberal feminism are reshaping borders and interfaces between public and private, WMM holds a space for independent and critical women's media production, a space that is both precarious and vital. The organization's history shows that women's labor has been key not only to independent filmmaking but also to building the institutions that sustain it. As WMM faces the very real challenges currently confronting feminist documentary globally, "make" may be the most important word in its name.

Notes

1 This essay is dedicated to Michelle Materre, Bérénice Reynaud, and Patricia Zimmermann, wonderful women whose dedication to feminist film advocacy included serving as WMM board members.

2 The Conference of Feminist Film and Video Organizations took place on February 1 and 2, 1975. A companion event in LA the same year, the Feminist Eye, was organized by Frances Reid and Cathy Zheutlin, who formed the production company and distributor Iris Films after meeting photographer Joan E. Biren (JEB) at the New York event. See Samer (2022) for an account of their exhibition venture, Moonforce Media.

3 The films included Gillian Armstrong's short *The Roof Needs Mowing* (1971) and *The Amazing Equal Pay Show* (1974) from the London Women's Film Group. On *The Amazing Equal Pay Show,* see Evans (2016) and Fabian (2018).

2

Transforming Documentary Film Cultures in East Africa

Judy Kibinge and Docubox

Lindiwe Dovey

Introduction: Female Friendship and Feminist Curation in Film

> Women working together in the film industries can bring out the best in one another and stimulate each other in their cinematic endeavours. This is the nature of affinity and affiliations, leading to trusting relationships and friendships, resulting in increasingly successful films. This power of female friendships is increasingly revealing its power in the African film industries. (Bisschoff and Van de Peer 2020: 94)

> [W]e hereby call on you, feminist readers, to take up the mantle of curators and join us in a rising movement to transform and reimagine film history through the liberation of unseen, obscure, badly preserved, long-lost, mutilated, marginalized, and even mischievously counterfactual moving image archives. To curate from the archive is to decide whose history matters in the present. (Hennefeld and Horak 2024: 8)

At the 2009 FESPACO film festival in Ouagadougou, Burkina Faso, I first met the Kenyan filmmaker Judy Kibinge. I was thrilled about this, since—as a researcher, curator, and teacher of African filmmaking—I knew about the revolution she had created in contemporary Kenyan filmmaking through her popular Nairobi-set romantic comedies, *Dangerous Affair* (2002) and *Project Daddy* (2004). Prior to this, very few films had been made in Kenya by Kenyans, despite some notable exceptions, such as Anne Mungai's pioneering

Saikati (1992) and Wanjiru Kinyanjui's *Battle of the Sacred Tree* (1994).[1] At the time I met her, Kibinge had recently made the short film *Coming of Age* (2008) in which—as a "child of independence" born in 1967[2]—she explores both her own and Kenya's "coming of age" through archival footage and a playful, poignant voice-over. In 2009, Kibinge went on to make the stylish mid-length fiction film *Killer Necklace*, adapted from a graphic novel, as part of the Africa-wide M-Net New Directions filmmaking initiative under the leadership of South African film producer Bongiwe Selane.[3] In 2010, I crossed paths with Kibinge again when I was doing research in Kenya and was on the jury of the Kenya International Film Festival, but it was sharing a flat together at the 2011 FESPACO film festival that led to the emergence of a friendship that has ended up greatly enriching both my personal and professional life over the years. Even though I am a white South African woman and Kibinge is a Black Kenyan woman, we have found affinity across our differences in positionality and lived experiences through shared values and through that sense of connection, trust, and curiosity that is the basis of all good friendships.

I preface my discussions of Kibinge's work with our personal story since I do not believe it is possible for any academic to approach their analytical work wholly objectively.[4] Furthermore, my close relationship with Kibinge, and my collaborations and friendships with some of the women filmmakers discussed here, necessitates that I reveal how we have put our affinities into practice. Indeed, I knew about Kibinge's work for many years before formally researching it (in fact, my friendship with her made this idea feel rather bizarre at first); this research has thus organically grown out of ongoing, informal conversations (rather than formal interviews) over many years.[5]

My deep respect for Kibinge and her work has led me not only to teach, curate, and research her films but also, most recently, to make a feature-length documentary film titled *Out of the Box: The Screen Worlds of Judy Kibinge* (Dovey 2023b) as part of the ERC-funded "African Screen Worlds: Decolonising Film and Screen Studies" project for which I have been principal investigator (2019–25). Alongside this film about Kibinge, I have made a companion film, titled *From One Woman to Another: The Screen Worlds of Bongiwe Selane* (Dovey 2023c), about a South African female film producer who led the first iteration of a program called "Female Only Filmmakers" (2013–16), funded by the South African National Film and Video Foundation.[6] My decision to make these two films, each spotlighting an African woman filmmaker, arose out of my intense frustration at how overlooked and ignored Black women filmmakers continue to be, in film scholarship and in the film industry, and particularly Black women filmmakers who live on the African continent. As I complete this chapter, the 2024 Sydney Film Festival is gearing up to present an Ousmane Sembene retrospective in June; while Sembene is of course a much-loved legend, it appears that the world's appetite to learn about African filmmakers rarely extends beyond this foundational "Father of African Cinema" figure and certainly not to many women filmmakers. In an article titled "Where Are the African Women Filmmakers?", renowned Ethiopian male filmmaker Haile Gerima laments: "In festival after festival, ninety-nine percent African male filmmakers congregate, parade, discuss, and pass resolutions. At no time, to my knowledge, has there been an agenda that included the absence of African women filmmakers" (2021: 174). While Gerima is correct that the majority of African filmmakers are men, if one looks closer, there *is* also a presence of impressive women filmmakers—and not just the pioneers such as Safi Faye and Sarah Maldoror, who are the only two Gerima mentions in his article.

Lamenting an imagined absence does nothing to rectify it. As Florencia Marchetti says, frustration "fuels a desire to bring stories and injustices to the realm of the visible" (cited in Hennefeld and Horak 2024: 4). Betti Ellerson must be credited for her tireless work to make African women filmmakers visible (see 2000, 2015, 2016, 2020), including through her documentary *Sisters of the Screen: African Women in the Cinema* (2002). Following in her footsteps, I have made *Out of the Box* and *From One Woman to Another* to try to bring visibility to African women filmmakers, in my case by zooming in on two individuals in particular—Kibinge and Selane. I must emphasize that I see my role in making these films as much a curatorial as a directorial one, drawing on my many years of experience as an African film festival founder, director, and curator. Festivals and events, however, are fleeting and fugitive things, too easily forgotten. Consider, for example, Hayley O'Malley's observation that the 1976 Sojourner Truth Symposium, the first Black women's film festival in the world, "left a particularly thin archive" (cited in Hennefeld and Horak 2024: 3). Of course, films too are impermanent, and digital immortality is a myth; however, I feel a deep sense of pleasure when I think about making *Out of the Box* and *From One Woman to Another* freely available to a global audience through our Screen Worlds website after their film festival run, thereby joining

Hennefeld and Horak's "cabal of *feminist archival film curators*" (2024: 1) who are trying to preserve the work of women filmmakers for the future.

My creative work as the director and lead editor of these films also situates *me* as a woman documentary filmmaker, as well as a researcher and curator, engaged in making documentaries outside of my own immediate context, and this aspect of my identity and work is therefore relevant to broader reflections and explorations in other chapters across this volume. Transparency around my relationships to and with people living on the African continent about whom I am writing is a vital element in my attempt to decolonize my work as a white academic based in the UK, since—my friendship with Kibinge notwithstanding—imbalances in power and vast geographical distances require humility rather than hubris.[7] I have written elsewhere about the value of creative practice research through filmmaking, particularly in terms of attempts to decolonize research methodologies (see Dovey 2023a). *Out of the Box* allows Kibinge and her filmmaking community to speak about their own work, in their own voices, with their own expressions and gestures, in a way that I obviously cannot accommodate here, in writing. However, my hope is that a viewing of *Out of the Box*, which has to cover a great deal of ground in its eighty minutes, can also be enriched by reading this chapter, in which I try to provide further insights and information through which to understand and contextualize Kibinge's work, as well as to flesh out certain themes that remain more implicit in the film I have made about her.

It would feel strange in a volume on this topic not to adopt a self-reflexive tone in which I also share some of my own documentary filmmaking experiences, particularly since Kibinge and her community entrusted me to tell their story on film, thus giving me the power to bring my own interpretations to bear on their archive and history. From the very beginning of the project, Kibinge and I established a clear working relationship in which she respected my role as director, but where I frequently consulted her and her community on various decisions related to the pre-production, production, and post-production processes. In this way, we established a balance among the consent that is an ethical requirement in the making of any documentary, the collaboration needed in filmmaking, and the necessity of clear roles and responsibilities, where the director's authority is enshrined.

As Hennefeld and Horak note, "Collaborative curating can . . . take many forms, often affective as much as archival or logistic" (2024: 7). Indeed, my close friendship with Kibinge brought an intimacy to the filmmaking process and, as audiences have noticed and commented on, this intimacy also infuses the aesthetics and form of the final film itself. Our film production team for *Out of the Box*[8] had to pack the principal shooting period into one week—working from morning until night—because of my childcare commitments back in the UK, which Kibinge empathized with, being a mother herself (Kibinge's son Elliot Mwamunga appears in the film—through his own request that I interview him). Notably, my co-producers in Nairobi, the husband–wife team of Christopher King and Maia Lekow, also had a six-month-old baby at the time of the shoot, and so—delightfully—there was a baby on our set for much of the shoot. The editing, back in the UK with my co-editors Remi and Anna Sowa of Chouette Films (also a husband–wife team), did not have to take place under such time pressure, and I spent hundreds of hours on it—cherished hours, since I felt I was spending them alongside Kibinge.

I watched and rewatched the footage we had filmed together—much of it in Kibinge's home. It also involved rewatching Kibinge's films so many times that scenes from them have embedded themselves in my psyche, and often my decisions around which excerpts to use from them were led not only by the rationality of their content and explicit meaning but also by the emotions evoked through music, striking images, and the rhythms of editing.[9]

My desire to make the film about Kibinge and her work stemmed from but ultimately went far beyond my identity as an African film researcher and curator; it also emerged from a profound wish to honor and archive for the future the spirit, charisma, tireless work, and artistic vision of a dear friend who I feel should be celebrated more widely and remembered for posterity. It grew out of a piercing sense of mortality and time passing, and a fear that if we—as women, as friends, as feminists, and as film scholars and curators—do not try to listen to, hold, and tell one another's stories, then they may be lost forever. There was a poignant moment during the filming of *Out of the Box*, in fact, in which Kibinge laments that she never filmed her dear friend Binyavanga Wainaina, the well-known Kenyan writer and founder of the Kenyan literary magazine *Kwani*, before his death in 2019. Although the footage of that moment did not make it into the final version of *Out of the Box*, it became a lodestar guiding the process, constantly reminding me why it was so important to document Judy Kibinge—my much-admired friend—on film. As Hennefeld and Horak stress, to "curate from the archive is to decide whose history matters in the present" (2024: 8); however, if an archive does not exist at all, then we need to create it—and that is what I have attempted to do through the live-action footage in *Out of the Box*. I was delighted that, at the Nairobi premiere of the film on March 1, 2024 (the start of International Women's Month), one of the spectators noted that it was refreshing to have a film made about a living filmmaker. What also made me joyful was that, after that screening in Nairobi, several audience members who are friends or colleagues of Kibinge told me that it had made them realize that they thought they had known Kibinge and her work until they had seen *Out of the Box* and that the film made them want to watch all of her films they had not yet seen and rewatch the ones they had (Figure 2.1).

The making of the film involved the kind of collaboration and intimacy that has long underscored women's filmmaking practices, and the work that women scholars have done to document and archive women's film practices. As Hennefeld and Horak note, in their tenth-anniversary double issue of *Feminist Media Histories*, the "twenty essays included . . . rally for political change by conjuring excluded archives and creating unruly spaces for their readmission in the present," and many of them are "cowritten, collaboratively convened, and collectively voiced" (2024: 2–3). In her chapter "The Many Feminist Histories of Documentary" (in Balsom and Peleg 2022), Teresa Castro asks a poignant question, citing Devika Girish: "because feminist histories are also about joy and companionship, how do we communicate the thrill of collaborative practices and 'the pleasure of being with other women'?" (2022: 56). Filmmaker-scholars Nobunye Levin and Palesa Shongwe have provided a sophisticated, somatic answer to this through the film medium itself, in the breathtaking short film *Reverie* (2023) that they made as part of the *African Screen Worlds* project, and which they describe as being "assembled from film fragments and out-takes from the filmmakers' previous works, and fragments of text and conversation, to reveal a feminist love praxis in the collaborative life of the two filmmakers" (film synopsis).[10] Through this film, they say that "Freedom and pleasure are imagined through the aesthetic and form of states of reverie, where the haptic is also conjured as a further site of freedom and pleasure" (film synopsis).

While *Out of the Box* is very different formally and aesthetically from *Reverie*, as team members and friends, Levin and I were also in conversation with one another throughout the process of making films with Shongwe and

Figure 2.1 Lindiwe Dovey and Judy Kibinge in conversation after the Nairobi premiere of *Out of the Box*, March 1, 2024. © Lindiwe Dovey.

Kibinge, respectively, and I was inspired by the way Levin and Shongwe both practise and theorize the pleasure of their friendship as it manifests through film. While it has been impossible for me to replicate the collaborative pleasure I felt while making *Out of the Box* in writing this chapter, which has been a more solitary activity, I have attempted to draw into it what I have learned through making the film. I try to foreground Kibinge's own words, which is why I have included many long quotes from her, highlighting things that she has said in our conversations—some of which made it into the final cut of *Out of the Box*, and others which can be seen as out-takes.[11] Both the film and this chapter focus on Kibinge's contributions to filmmaking in East Africa, and here I pay further attention to some of the documentaries she has directed as well as to her work as the executive founder and creative director of Docubox since 2013. What this chapter has allowed me to do that the film did not, however, is bring my own subjectivity more explicitly into view, since in the film I did not want to distract from Kibinge and Docubox, whereas here I have more freedom to share my experiences in the "first person feminine" (Heredia et al 2022). This having been said, I do not want my own experiences (especially given my positionality as a white woman) to dominate in a chapter primarily exploring Kibinge's and Docubox's works, so now that I have explained my relationship to the content I am writing about, I want to shift to the third person.

Judy Kibinge, Filmmaker

It is important to note that Kibinge's and Docubox's works have spanned both documentary *and* fiction, and that Kibinge has spoken about the difficulty of separating these modes of filmmaking, even within the same film. In one of my filmed conversations with her for *Out of the Box* about her feature fiction film *Something Necessary* (2013), which tells a story set during the time of the 2007–8 post-election violence in Kenya, she says:

> It was a very uncomfortable film to make. It was an uncomfortable film to show. But what I've noticed is, as time passes, every now and then, someone will request to show it again. . . . And I have a feeling that in time, it'll become . . . a real reflection of that time . . . And I think there's a real truth to it because if you look at the truth, justice and reconciliation sections of that film, they came straight out of a documentary that I'd done. So they were very real. I knew how the TJRC hearings were. I spent tens of hours, spent 100 hours, I don't know how long I spent in those TJRC hearings. . . . And this is where documentary influences fiction and fiction influences documentary. And I think that's why it's a beautiful thing to be interested in both doc and in fiction because they're variations of each other somehow. (pers. comm. 2022)[12]

Kibinge says she feels "so grateful and fortunate to have been able to swing between [documentary and fiction]" because "they really influence each other all the time" (pers. comm. 2020). While foregrounding here films that are conventionally classified as documentary by film festivals and broadcasters, I would like to keep Kibinge's porous conception of documentary and fiction alive, respecting many other women filmmakers' and scholars' restlessness with fixed cinematic definitions.[13] At the same time, I share Julia Lesage and Shilyh Warren's insistence that it is not naïve to take realism seriously (2022). Despite the great diversity of films that Kibinge has directed and supported throughout her career, a common thread running through them is a commitment to documenting Kenyan and East African experiences and histories on screen, grounded in Kibinge's desire not only to represent but also to transform her country and region in positive ways. This having been said, Kibinge also has a strong penchant for magical realism as a mode, as evidenced in *Killer Necklace* (2009) and in her forthcoming short film *Goat*.[14]

Inspiring and undergirding all of Kibinge's filmmaking work is her passion for storytelling through writing and drawing. Writing talent runs in her family, especially on her mother's side; one of her uncles was the novelist and short story writer Leonard Kibera (1942–83). Before becoming a filmmaker, however, Kibinge had an extremely successful, decade-long career in advertising, becoming the first African creative director of McCann Erickson in the East African region.[15] Of her courageous move away from the financially lucrative work of advertising to the precarious world of filmmaking, she says:

> There were so many good things about being in advertising. It was a time where you were creating, but you had the safety of this fantastic salary . . . and getting paid to write and create all these worlds. But increasingly, I found myself really disturbed that I just never saw films on the big screen with . . . any semblance of an Africa that I knew. A lot of the films that you'd hear of getting accolades were just one aspect of the continent. There was a lot of dwelling on the evil dictators and the corrupt politicians. And if it wasn't that, it was the humble village in the middle of a famine. And I was like, where are the cities? I live in a city with millions of other Africans living in similar cities. There is music that globally all young people are hearing, and there are people falling in love and getting hired and having babies and trying on wedding dresses in wedding shops. But you never saw any of that in any of the films that we were looking at. . . . And so I moved. And initially the one thing I got a lot of were invitations to do NGO film work. (pers. comm. 2022)

My conversations with Kibinge have nuanced my understanding and feelings about such NGO films. Elsewhere, I have critiqued with others the problematic overlapping of Eurocentric practices of development aid with filmmaking (Dovey, McNamara, and Olivieri 2013). However, as much as Kibinge has experienced these problematic issues firsthand, she insists that this period of making NGO documentaries also taught her a great deal about the craft of filmmaking before she launched her own production company (Seven Productions) in 2009.

Being commissioned to make NGO documentaries all over the continent also gave Kibinge a very deep and wide-ranging knowledge of Africa, appealing to her natural curiosity about people's realities, a vital quality for any documentary filmmaker. She says:

> Having spent ten years writing up all these commercial worlds [in advertising], it was as if these blinders came off and I was like, "Okay, so this is where I live. These are the villages, the streets, the people, the banks, the sugar factories . . ." It was really wonderful. And it was the perfect sort of segue to making fictional films. Because I feel had I moved maybe straight from advertising into fiction and never had the benefit of diving out to be in these new different worlds, and then coming back again, I think my fiction would be different. (pers. comm. 2022)

Kibinge's motivation for making her fiction films often stems from this reality principle—wanting to give expression to richly textured, heterogeneous African experiences—even if the mode she uses to do this is not always realism. Her directorial debuts were in fiction—with the low-budget rom-coms *Dangerous Affair* (2002) and *Project Daddy* (2004)—and they were hugely popular in Kenya *because* they showed a side of people's ordinary lives (around experiences of dating, love, and family) that had not previously been seen on the screen. Much of her work is deeply rooted in Kenya, where she was born and has lived for most of her life, despite periods of living and studying abroad (in the United States and the UK). It is quite right that Kibinge was awarded the 2021 Lifetime Achievement Award at the Kenya Kalasha film awards and that she was given a Head of State commendation by former Kenyan president Uhuru Kenyatta, when one considers the longstanding, dedicated contribution she has made to documenting Kenyan histories on screen, as well as imaginatively engaging with Kenyan experiences through pushing the aesthetic boundaries of filmmaking.

Kibinge's key documentary films are: *Coming of Age* (2008), *Headlines in History* (2010, co-directed with John Akomfrah), and *Scarred: Anatomy of a Massacre* (2015).[16] What is so striking about watching these films together is how distinct they are from one another (as well as from Kibinge's fiction films) in form and style. Whereas *Coming of Age* explores successive independence governments in Kenya through the eyes of Kibinge as a child and is guided by her own voice-over, *Headlines in History* tells the story of 50 years of the Nation Media Group, founded in Kenya in 1960 by the Aga Khan, through the eyes and voices of the journalists who wrote the headlines for the *Daily Nation* newspaper. As Robin Steedman notes, *Headlines in History* "weaves the corporate history of the media house together with the history of Kenya into a compelling narrative" (2023: 78). With a bold, authoritative, male voice-over and riveting soundtrack, this sixty-minute film holds one's attention like a detective narrative. *Coming of Age*, in contrast, belongs to what Alisa Lebow calls "first-person" filmmaking, which "accentuates the relationship between the individual and the collective, and thus between the personal and the political" (cited in Lesage and Warren 2022: 149); it is as much Kibinge's story as Kenya's story, with a strong dose of her charismatic writing and tongue-in-cheek humor. Mette Hjort describes it as "a subjective take on Kenyan politics, from independence under Jomo Kenyatta, through the Daniel Arap Moi era and the initial period of Mwai Kibaki's regime from 2002 to 2007" (Hjort 2019: 111). Of course, part of the reason for the differences between these films has to do with where the funding came from. *Headlines in History* was a commission by the Nation Media Group itself, so Kibinge and Akomfrah had to navigate that sensitively in their making of the film. In contrast, *Coming of Age* was produced by STEPS International as part of its worldwide "Why Democracy?" initiative and could thus be seen as an NGO film—but it is one in which Kibinge is clearly playing with the very expectations of what an NGO film should be.

Coming of Age had a significant impact on Kenyan audiences. The academic and grantmaker Dr. Joyce Nyairo, who first came up with the idea of a documentary film fund in Kenya, says that it was through watching this film that she realized that, even though Kibinge had been making fiction films previously, she was a master of documentary film form. The Kenyan–German filmmaker Philippa Ndisi-Herrmann says that *Coming of Age* is one of her favorite films by Kibinge because "it's very colloquial, and I think that also represents Judy in a way" (pers. comm. 2022). Ndisi-Herrmann also points to Kibinge's willingness to take risks in speaking the truth, even if that contradicts normative modes of being in Kenya:

> With *Coming of Age*, she says something that a lot of people don't say within Kenyan circles or within Kenyan society . . . Kenyans are very polite and we don't often really say to somebody's face what we think. . . . She often approaches very important subjects head on. (pers. comm. 2022)

Beyond this courageous frankness, whatever mode and form Kibinge selects for each of her films, she often uses her creative work to raise questions about intersectional inequalities in Kenya, frequently with a more explicit focus on class and ethnic, rather than gender, inequality.[17] She says she does not see herself as a particularly "political" person, but she detests, and contests, unfairness (pers. comm. 2022).[18]

Nowhere is Kibinge's frankness, willingness to take risks, and aversion to unfairness more in evidence than in her documentary *Scarred: Anatomy of a Massacre* (2015) about the 1984 Wagalla Massacre of people from the Degodia tribe in North Kenya by Kenyan government troops. As Docubox filmmaker Christopher King says, "it was when I saw *Scarred* that I realised how gutsy Judy is, and also a real risk taker . . . it's such an inconvenient story to take on . . . confronting really difficult truths that have been very buried" (pers. comm. 2022). Docubox filmmaker Pete Murimi started crying in my filmed interview with him for *Out of the Box* as he spoke about what it means that Kibinge had the courage to make *Scarred*:

> Most of us had read about it, but almost no one had decided to document it. The people who were victims, nobody had bothered to go and talk to them. Judy making that film was so important for those people, and I think meant . . . Oh God, I'm getting emotional talking about it because sometimes an injustice happens and nobody cares. And she took that time. . . . To this day, when you ask the people who were affected, that was the most important thing that happened to them. Someone giving them time to listen to their pain. (pers. comm. 2022)[19]

Indeed, when *Scarred* had its first public screening in Nairobi, a row of old men—survivors of the massacre—stood up afterward and saluted Kibinge. She says: "These men who had just lost so much, had carried this thing for decades . . . clearly felt seen that night. So that's the power of documentary" (pers. comm. 2022). Several weeks later, then-president Uhuru Kenyatta issued a formal apology from the Kenyan government for the Wagalla massacre, a result of Kibinge's film (Kimani pers. comm. 2022).[20] If anyone ever requires proof that there is power in cinematic realism and documentary filmmaking, and the potential to transform society through these modes of creative engagement with the world, it is to be found here.

Kibinge made *Scarred* entirely voluntarily and yet says she has never had a "payback for a film greater than that" because of its impact. But it was also the most difficult filmmaking experience she has ever had. The film took her five years to make. She had first read about the massacre in a newspaper in 2002, but she committed to making the film several years after that when listening to an elderly man from the Degodia group speaking about it while she was making a film in North Kenya for the Kenyan Human Rights Commission. She pitched the idea to funders "all over the place," but the only funding she received was US$50,000 from the Open Society, a tiny budget for such an ambitious film. Kibinge explains here how the challenge of making *Scarred* was one of the most significant motivations for her decision to put aside her own filmmaking to found and direct Docubox:

> I think when I see [*Scarred*], I'm reminded more than with any other film how much one needs community, a community of fellow filmmakers around you. . . . *Headlines in History* was for the Nation Media Group. That was different. And I had John [Akomfrah] as a co-director and mentor, I mean, whoa! But [for] this, I really needed a community. I didn't even know where to look for one. And when I look at that film now, I'm like, . . . "How did I do that film without a single lab, without a single mentor?" . . . I think it's very, very strong [but] I think it could have been so much stronger. . . . And even when the film was made, there's so many things I wanted to do with it. I wanted to do a clinic for the women. In the end, I did make DVD sales, take back the money for the women. But I think if I'd realised that there was a bigger way of creating impact with that film, that would have been a great thing. . . . [T]hat film is one of the things that has made me very passionate about Docubox. (pers. comm. 2022)

Translating her own difficulties as an independent documentary filmmaker into compassion for the struggles of East African filmmakers in general—and particularly those filmmakers of younger generations—Kibinge accepted Joyce Nyairo's invitation to found Docubox as a local documentary film fund in

2013, with no-strings-attached funding that Nyairo had raised while working for the Kenyan office of the Ford Foundation. As Nyairo says:

> You see individual genius, but your responsibility is also to institutionalise that genius so that it includes more than one person and so that it has longevity. And the film fund was important for me in that sense. Now, my big fortune was that my [Ford Foundation] director in New York, Orlando Bagwell—he made a film on Malcolm X. So he is himself a filmmaker. So he understood the necessity of people telling their own stories. And he was very, very generous in providing the funds that we needed, approving the things that I was suggesting. And—Judy was the right person for [directing] the documentary film fund. . . . In terms of her training, . . . her experience, . . . her personality. She was what the Ford Foundation needed in that moment. (pers. comm. 2022)

It was not an easy decision for Kibinge to make, however, because she "loves making films" (pers. comm. 2022). But she also recognized that this was "a chance to shape the thing that [she] had needed" because "making films is *so* lonely, and making documentary films in particular is exceedingly lonely"

Figure 2.2 Joyce Nyairo and Judy Kibinge in conversation on the set of *Out of the Box*, Nairobi, February 2022. © Lindiwe Dovey.

(pers. comm. 2020). Kibinge's taking on the role of executive founder and creative director of Docubox in 2013 thus emerged out of a commitment to provide leadership and mentorship to other (particularly younger) filmmakers and a deep desire to transform the dominant documentary film culture in East Africa (Figure 2.2)

Docubox and the Transformation of Documentary Film Culture in East Africa

"A country without documentaries is like a family without a photo album." (Docubox motto)

In 2013, I was delighted to be invited to be part of the first Docubox project selection team, alongside documentary filmmakers I greatly admire, such as Yaba Badoe and Francois Verster. What most struck me in the process were the criteria that Docubox devised for judging the proposals, where our selection team was asked questions such as "Does the film demonstrate the filmmaker's uniqueness of vision and not necessarily follow the traditional issue-based East African NGO documentary format?" and "Is the story both strongly personal and uniquely East African?" As noted above, while Kibinge sees the value in NGO filmmaking, she has been frustrated with how Africans have often not been able to tell their own stories, in their own style, on screen.

In a chapter about the complex relationships between filmmakers of the Global South and human rights filmmaking funded by the Global North, Mette Hjort helps to situate Kibinge's nuanced stance on these issues:

> An independent filmmaker with a primary commitment to the art of film as culture, rather than as a means of direct political engagement, Kibinge does not regret the experience of having been drawn into social justice filmmaking. She does, however, regard the dominance of the advocacy film as imposing unwelcome limits on creative expression and as encouraging a neglect of issues of quality and form. (Hjort 2019: 106)

This is an issue that has especially affected African filmmakers living on the African continent, as I explore in my book *Curating Africa in the Age of Film Festivals* (2015). Ignorance of the diversity and heterogeneity of Africa in the Global North has meant that, until today, Africa continues to be represented as a place of relentless violence and poverty, thereby requiring interventions by the Global North and their footmen. This creates an exhausting vicious cycle from which it is very difficult for African filmmakers to liberate themselves. The problem rests not only in the constraints on filmmakers' creativity; it also resides in the way such filmmaking and film viewing curtail local audiences' understanding and imagination of their own identities and contexts. "You are what you see," Kibinge told a group of young Kenyan filmmakers during a filmmaking masterclass at the Docubox headquarters at Shalom House in Nairobi in February 2022.[21] And she laments,

> If you don't have a broadcaster like Storyville, for instance, that is showing creative doc . . . if you don't have ARTE, where you see more lyrical or creative kinds of documentary, then many people in Kenya begin to think that doc is information-driven, that it's NGO with a message, like "Malaria can be defeated" . . . Quite important work they're doing, but mind-numbing filmmaking. (pers. comm. 2020)

Several scholars have elaborated on how steeped in this kind of documentary film culture East Africa has become, with a high concentration of foreign-led NGOs based in Nairobi in particular.[22] By establishing a completely different set of criteria for the films they fund, support, and screen, Docubox—as Ndisi-Herrmann says—has really "switched up the game" (pers. comm. 2022).[23] Far from only being a film funder, under Kibinge's energetic leadership, Docubox quickly developed into a multi-faceted endeavor and, most importantly, a home for independent filmmakers who need a sense of community and who want to exchange knowledge (pers. comm. 2020). In the year of its tenth anniversary (2023), Docubox described itself as "providing funding, training, and audience expansion resources" and its primary focus as "delivering high-quality content to promote audience growth" (Docubox 2023). In 2014, Docubox initiated its "Starry Nights" open-air screenings in the garden adjacent to its offices in Nairobi (at Shalom House) to build a dedicated audience for documentary films; the screening venues later shifted to PAWA254 and Alliance Française to accommodate larger audiences, before returning to the gardens at Shalom House, with their Halloween, Mzalendo Day (Patriots' Day), and Valentine's "Shorts, Shorts, and Shots" events being hugely popular.[24] Docubox has seen its audience grow from 500, at the origins of their screenings, to over 80,000 regionwide, and the organization has screened more than 300 films, including documentaries and short films (Docubox 2023).

Notably, Kibinge has not introduced identity-related quotas when making decisions about whose films Docubox will fund and support.[25] This has led to criticism from certain quarters, but Docubox filmmaker Maia Lekow (who is married to the Australian filmmaker Christopher King, who has lived in Kenya for many years) emphasizes how inclusive this makes Kibinge:

> One thing I love about Judy is that . . . when it comes to people who are doing great stories and people who are making stuff . . . it doesn't matter what colour you are. It doesn't matter who you are. It doesn't matter where you're from but [that] you're actually here and you've been here for a long period of time. . . . She's so inclusive with no judgment for everybody across the board. (pers. comm. 2022)

Despite Docubox not having quotas, almost half of the filmmakers who have been funded and supported have been women—perhaps unsurprisingly, given Kenya's unusual history of having a female-led film industry (Steedman 2023). In this final section of the chapter, I highlight documentaries made by two women from the first Docubox-funded cohort: Philippa Ndisi-Herrmann and Maia Lekow, who both have Kenyan and German heritage and grew up in Kenya. I initially encountered their work through the proposals they submitted to Docubox's first funding call in 2013, when the selection teams had the difficult task of whittling down 200 proposals to 12 selected projects, each of which was given roughly US$25,000 to kickstart its filmmaking journey. I later came to meet Ndisi-Herrmann and Lekow through curating public screenings of their respective films *New Moon* (2018) and *The Letter* (2019)—both of which I immediately fell in love with—and through holding Q&As with them.[26] Our friendships have developed through further collaborations, conversations, and time spent together.[27] I was particularly fortunate that Lekow and her husband agreed to collaborate with me on my documentary about Kibinge, *Out of the Box*, as co-producers, and through their exquisite cinematography (King was director of photography, and Lekow was part of the cinematography team).

New Moon (dir. Ndisi-Herrmann, 2018) was the first of Docubox's films to be completed, and it won the best documentary prize at the 2018 Durban International Film Festival, one of Africa's leading film festivals. *The Letter* (dir. Lekow and King, 2019), which followed soon after, was Kenya's official submission to the 93rd Academy Awards for best international film and had its world premiere at IDFA (the International Documentary Festival Amsterdam, arguably the most prestigious documentary festival in the world). Although these films are very different in certain ways, there are also some remarkable similarities, which reveal Docubox's philosophies around creative documentary filmmaking and Kibinge's leadership style. Both documentaries took many years to make (*New Moon* took eight years, and *The Letter* took six years), and in both cases, the filmmakers completely changed course from their original proposals. The film Ndisi-Herrmann initially pitched to Docubox was going to explore "the effects of the construction of what was to be Africa's largest port in Lamu, off the coast of Kenya," but it ended up becoming an "observational, poetic and very personal film" about Ndisi-Herrmann's time in Lamu, living with a woman called Raya and her family, and about how that experience "moved [her] towards the Sufi Muslim path" (pers. comm. 2022). Ndisi-Herrmann gives Kibinge credit for allowing her to "divert from the original plan" and to make a film that she felt personally connected to. She says:

> That's one of the remarkable and powerful things about Judy, especially with her behind Docubox, that she adds a flexibility that is very uncommon. And that flexibility to be able to see you as an artist and to be able to say, we support you as an artist; we support your project, but we also support *you* as an artist and what is best for you, that allows us to really blossom and tell even more authentic stories. (pers. comm. 2022)

Lekow, who co-directed *The Letter* with her husband, Christopher King, similarly described to me how Docubox and Kibinge gave them the freedom to let their film evolve away from the original pitch, which was about Mekatilili Wa Mwenza, a historical female freedom fighter in Kenya. For two years, Lekow and King conducted interviews with elderly people in Kenya to learn about Mekatilili, but she says that many of these people said: "Look, we can tell you this lady's story, but there's also the issue now that we're dealing with, which is these elders who are being accused of witchcraft" (pers. comm. 2022). The first translator they worked with, Karisa Kamunga, was shocked when watching the footage because the same thing was happening to his grandmother, and so, Lekow and King started following Karisa's grandmother's journey for the next few years, first building trust and then starting to film in a very gentle, intimate, observational style. As with *New Moon*, the film was in many ways a labor of love, and there were many points at which it seemed as though it would never be completed because of complexities that arose. It was also a deeply emotional experience for Lekow, since the Kamunga family lives in Kilifi County, where her father is from. When it came to screening the film, Lekow and King took the film back to the community, and Docubox supported them with this impact work to use the film to try to effect change.[28]

Ndisi-Herrmann and Lekow are similar in that they bring multiple creative talents to their filmmaking: whereas Ndisi-Herrmann is also a photographer and poet, Lekow is a musician and composer. Ndisi-Herrmann did her own cinematography for *New Moon* (she worked mostly alone on the production of the film) and describes that process as follows:

> I love having the camera in my hands because . . . it's almost like a slipstream you enter. . . . Once it's in your hand you put it to your eyes, the viewfinder to your eyes, and it's almost like you become invisible. You almost melt and blend with the world. . . . And you notice things. I really like noticing subtleties. And I also think you honour each thing, each item, each person, when you're capturing them. . . . You want your eye to be able to reveal something about that person or the energy that you feel in that room. (pers. comm. 2019)

All of Ndisi-Herrmann's films are extremely poetic and are reminiscent of the kind of "cinécriture" (cine-writing) that Agnès Varda engaged in, bringing together the crafts of writing as well as making still and moving images (Smith 2020). Lekow, in turn, comes from a well-known musical family in Kenya and is an acoustic guitarist and singer-songwriter.[29] In the case of *The Letter*, Lekow collaborated with Emmy-winning composer Ken Myhr to develop a beautiful, haunting score for the film with nine original tracks. Ndisi-Herrmann and Lekow each bring their unique creative vision to their work, as Docubox encourages filmmakers to do. While the protagonists of *New Moon* and *The Letter* are women—Ndisi-Herrmann herself and Grandma Kamunga, respectively—the way the films represent these women's struggles and spirituality firmly embeds them within their communities of family and friends, exploring female experiences in intersectional, relational ways.

Love and Rockets

Kibinge and Docubox have worked closely enough with Doc Society (formerly BritDoc), co-founded by the late Jess Search (1969–2023), a legend of the global documentary filmmaking scene, to consider both Beadie Finzi and Jess Search "Big Sisters" and mentors.[30] When Kibinge was in London for work in September 2023, we met up for lunch, and she told me about how, following Search's premature death, Docubox had been inspired by her life and a letter she sent just before her passing—signed off "Love and Rockets"—and emblazoned these words on a neon sign in their Docubox offices. Around this time, Kibinge also sent me a WhatsApp message forwarding Marc Winn's online piece "Imaginal Cells," in which he writes:

> Imaginal cells are the ones that create the incredible process of metamorphosis that occurs when a caterpillar changes into a butterfly. These cells hold all the potential for the future, but initially they act separately, before combining as one to create something incredible that is a great improvement on their previous existence. . . . If we take this as an analogy for society today, it presents an exciting proposition. When systems are breaking down, you can either collapse and die or rise to the challenge of creating something better . . . What if we harnessed this power? What if we worked like imaginal cells—thinking differently from the old ways, working together with others who share our values and principles—to create something wonderful in the world?[31] (Winn 2015)

This concept of imaginal cells gets to the heart of what Docubox has achieved and continues striving to achieve. It also resonates with me, encapsulating my own journey, initially acting separately as an African film researcher, admiring Kibinge's filmmaking at a distance, but then enjoying the close, creative friendship that has evolved between us. I have also had the privilege of feeling that, in some small way, through curating Docubox films and making *Out of the Box*, I have been able to join Kibinge and the Docubox community in working like imaginal cells, trying to create something beautiful in the world together. I am grateful that the editors of this volume have encouraged me to bring my own story and subjectivity into this chapter—something that did not feel appropriate in *Out of the Box*, in which I appear only briefly toward the end. Whereas Kibinge says she loves how that scene of us conversing in the film memorializes our friendship, I am also happy to have had the chance to pay tribute to Kibinge, her professional life, and our relationship in my own words here. The editors have helped me to see that this intimacy is not something to disavow or hide but rather to celebrate openly for the way that it also enables the documenting and archiving of women's film practices.

As I have emphasized earlier, being transparent about my own positionality as a white academic based in the UK researching the filmmaking practices of Black African women, as well as engaging in filmmaking itself as a mode of research, have been vital to my attempts to decolonize my research practices (also see Dovey 2020). Rather than shy away from the absences and aporia of global film archives and scholarship because I am white, I have attempted to learn from Kibinge's "head-on" approach. As Castro says:

> Despite fifty years of debates on what it means to write history, produce meanings, and be the knowing subject, the challenge of feminist historiography remains with us, in particular when tied to our determination to decolonize. For this, there are no magic recipes, no shortcuts, no ready-made methodologies. (2022: 57)

For me, working in friendship and solidarity with Kibinge and Docubox rather than in isolation as an individual academic has allowed me to feel that perhaps I can be both an ally and an author, critiquing and confronting how, so often, "the history of the north excludes that of the south" (Chilean artist Cecilia Vicuña cited in Castro 2022: 43) and how "the anti-colonial liberation movements that swept the Global South were little concerned with toppling heteropatriarchal structures" (Castro 2022: 55). Much work remains to be done, but—through friendships across boundaries and through the "cabal" of feminist archival film curators that Hennefeld and Horak have invited us all to join—I hope that we can not only accomplish it but also enjoy and take pleasure from it at the same time.

Acknowledgments

This research was funded by the European Research Council (ERC) under the European Union's Horizon 2020 research and innovation program (grant t No. 819236—AFRISCREENWORLDS). Many thanks to the ERC, ᴊinge, the Docubox community, and the Screen Worlds collective for ᴊ this research possible.

Notes

1. For overviews of Kenyan film history, and particularly the leading role that Kenyan women filmmakers have played in that history, see Dianga'a (2017), Mango (2023), and Steedman (2023).
2. Kenya won its independence from Britain in 1963.
3. *Killer Necklace* is one of my favorite films due to its rich and multi-layered symbolism; Kibinge also told me that it is her favorite film in her extensive filmography. This was the first time that Kibinge also worked with South African cinematographer Marius van Graan and the first time a RED camera was used in Kenya, and perhaps even in sub-Saharan Africa.
4. For articles that explain and show how academic research is a form of storytelling, and how vital this approach is to decolonizing research methodologies, see Pete (2018) and Vered and Gibson (2022).
5. This kind of continuing conversational approach became central to the methodology of the ERC-funded project "African Screen Worlds: Decolonising Film and Screen Studies," which provided the funding for me to undertake this research about Kibinge (see www.screenworlds.org).
6. These films, along with all the others the project has produced, will be freely available to view on the Screen Worlds website toward the end of the project in 2024/2025: www.screenworlds.org.
7. See Dovey, Agina, and Thomas (forthcoming 2025); Dovey (forthcoming 2025).
8. The key production and post-production team members were: Christopher King (co-producer and director of photography), Maia Lekow (co-producer and cinematographer), Wambui "Bo" Muigai, Emma Mbeke Nzioka, and Remi Sowa (cinematographers), and Ivy Anekaya (production coordinator). I (Lindiwe Dovey) directed the film and co-edited it with Remi and Anna Sowa of Chouette Films. Franki Ashiruka contributed to the editing process, Jyoti Mistry was a consultant for the film, and Tiago Correia-Paulo and BIG PIN provided the score. Chouette Films and the Screen Worlds Collective also helped to produce the film.
9. My making *Out of the Box* was, in fact, the prompt for Kibinge to try to get her own personal archive of the films she has made in better order. This was a

reminder to us both of how fragile and fallible any archive is and of the time, care, and—in some cases—resources required to maintain it.

10 *Reverie* will also be freely available to view on the Screen Worlds website toward the end of the project.
11 For clarity, I have pointed out where quotes from Kibinge—or others—in this chapter also appear in the film. I hope this will allow readers of this chapter and viewers of the film to be able to more easily identify how the two pieces converge and complement one another in different ways.
12 This quote appears in *Out of the Box*.
13 For example, see Minh-ha (2022).
14 There are scenes from the making of *Goat* in *Out of the Box*, to show Kibinge in action on set and also to reveal her return to filmmaking after a decade of generously setting aside her own writing and directing to lead Docubox and support other filmmakers.
15 Creative directors had until then all been white and male.
16 For analysis of Kibinge's films, see Diang'a (2017), Hjort (2019), Mango (2023), and Steedman (2023). My film *Out of the Box* gives equal attention to Kibinge's own filmmaking and Docubox, but—given the time and medium constraints of film—unfortunately cannot offer in-depth analysis of her films.
17 Nevertheless, Kibinge frequently offers powerful commentary on the violence experienced by women through her films. For example, she critiques men's fetishization of female virgins in *Dangerous Affair*; she embeds ironic commentary about prime ministers as "fathers" of the nation in *Coming of Age*; and the scene in *Something Necessary* where the character Anne courageously performs her own abortion compels the viewer to empathize with Anne's pain.
18 Kibinge makes this statement in *Out of the Box*.
19 This scene appears in *Out of the Box*.
20 Martin Kimani telling this to Kibinge appears in *Out of the Box*.
21 This scene appears in *Out of the Box*.
22 See, for example, Diang'a (2016) and McNamara (2016). This is also one of the main themes that arose in my interviews with many filmmakers in *Out of the Box*, for example, Toni Kamau, Lydia Matata, and Emily Wanja.
23 This quote appears in *Out of the Box*.
24 The 2022 Valentine's edition of "Shorts, Shorts, and Shots" appears in *Out of the Box*. These events involve watching short films, wearing shorts, and drinking shots.
25 In the decade of its existence, Docubox has supported more than 150 filmmakers (82 men and 69 women). It has invested more than US$890,000 in film production, with 13 feature-length documentary films, one feature-length

fiction film, and 53 short documentary and fiction films completed thus far (Docubox 2023).

26 Screen Worlds held a live screening of *New Moon* at SOAS in February 2020 followed by a Q&A with Ndisi-Herrmann. Film Africa 2020 and Screen Worlds collaborated to hold an online screening of *The Letter* during Covid-19, followed by a Q&A that I chaired with Lekow, King, Kibinge, and Karisa Kamunga. See https://screenworlds.org/resources/#filmed-events for the latter.

27 My filmed "In Conversation" with Ndisi-Herrmann about her work in general can be accessed here: https://screenworlds.org/publications/beside-the-scenes-a-conversation-with-director-philippa-ndisi-herrmann/

28 Although Docubox supports creative documentary filmmaking rather than conventional NGO message filmmaking, the team does not shy away from using films they have supported to encourage societal change in East Africa. Examples of their impact campaigns include those around the film *Thank You for the Rain* (dir. Julia Dahr, 2017), which led to the construction of a dam serving over 300 families in eastern Kenya.

29 Lekow's father is Salim Abdallah "Sal Davis" Salim, a hit Kenyan musician of the 1960s who also had an international profile. You can listen to one of his songs here: https://www.youtube.com/watch?v=xdiGb7im7JE

30 See https://www.theguardian.com/film/2023/aug/07/jess-search-obituary and watch Jess Search in conversation with Wendy Mitchell here: https://www.youtube.com/watch?v=jm0fGmUtitk

31 See: https://theviewinside.me/imaginalcells/#:~:text=Although%20they%20are%20associated%20with,caterpillar%20changes%20into%20a%20butter fly.

3

Caravan

Rerouting Transnational Feminist Collaboration Networks

Amal Shafek

This chapter introduces the organization Between Women Filmmakers Caravan (for short, Caravan) as an example of transnational feminist solidarity in praxis through documentary filmmaking and exhibition.[1] Founded in 2008, Caravan is an independent initiative based in Cairo, Egypt, which aims to foster a space for Arab women filmmakers to advocate for gender equality. Caravan is by no means the only organization with a focus on transnational film production and exhibition. Women Make Movies (WMM), for example, has been a catalyst for exhibiting films by women from all over the world. However, while WMM focuses primarily on securing exhibition of women's films at international film festivals and in university classrooms in North America, Caravan focuses on dialogue between women filmmakers and their societies on the ground level.

The word "Caravan," in Arabic, *Qāfilh,* indicates the notion of traveling. The concept of a traveling cinema is not new to Egypt. As part of Gamal Abdel Nasser's developmental state project, the Mass Culture Institute repeatedly sponsored the travel of a "culture caravan" from the capital to remote villages and countryside governorates across Egypt. These caravans were often "equipped with a library, a moving stage, audio equipment, and film projectors" (El Khachab 2022). However, the main purpose of the Mass Culture Institute's caravans is to promote a sense of national belonging among the youth of remote areas where even television is rarely affordable to most of the inhabitants. Caravan, on the other hand, deliberately takes a transnational route. While always starting in Egypt, Caravan physically travels to several other Arab countries such as Syria, Lebanon, Morocco, Algeria, and Palestine, then branches out to Latin American countries such as Argentina, Peru, Cuba, Bolivia, El Salvador, and Mexico. Moreover, Latin American filmmakers are invited to come to the Arab world to meet the local audiences, and vice versa for Arab filmmakers. Caravan is a collaboration between women filmmakers mainly from the Middle East and North Africa (MENA) region and Latin America. These two regions are linked by their postcolonial status and their shared belonging to the Global South.[2] Both the MENA region and Latin America have always had a strong presence of women filmmakers at international film festivals. However, in this chapter, I examine how Caravan is a unique space of transnational feminist dialogue where women can speak from a position of equal power, even at the level of speaking in one's own mother tongue.

Transnational feminism has a long history. In "Transnational Solidarity: Women's Agency, Structural Adjustment, and Globalization," Manisha Desai traces the history of women's transnational organizing "back to the middle of the nineteenth century" between women from the United States and Europe (2002: 24). These efforts, Desai illustrates, were the precursor to the United Nations' efforts for supporting women's rights globally. However, as Desai argues, transnational women's activism is not without problems. For example, despite the accomplishments of the UN World Conferences on Women in Mexico in 1975, Copenhagen in 1980, Nairobi in 1985, and Beijing in 1995, these conferences were also "highly contentious occasions" (2002: 28). Transnational feminist collaboration brought to the forefront questions of Western imperialism. Moreover, women from Third World countries "challenged First World feminists' claims that women were universally oppressed because of their gender and that sisterhood was global" (2002: 28). Transnationalism, as Amrita Basu argues, creates a hierarchy of power between the elites who belong to the transnational networks and other grassroots organizations from the Global South who do not have access to these networks (2000: 76). This hierarchy is also reflected in terms of funding, as local nongovernmental organizations located in the Global South often find themselves reliant on funds from the North (Basu 2000: 74). Nonetheless, productive transnational feminist solidarity, Desai concludes, is possible if we are to forge our solidarity based on acknowledging differences and inequalities (32).

Several scholars have written extensively on transnational feminism as theory and praxis (see, for example, Grewal and Kaplan 1994; Mendoza 2002; Mohanty 2003; Moghadam 2005; Khader 2019). However, this rich literature on the history, limitations, and possibilities of transnational feminism has not yet been mirrored in the field of film and media studies. There are some foundational works in this area such as Ella Shohat's edited volume *Talking Visions: Multicultural Feminism in a Transnational Age* (1998); Katarzyna Marciniak, Anikó Imre, and Áine O'Healy's edited volume *Transnational Feminism in Film and Media: Visibility, Representation, and Sexual Differences* (2007); and Patricia White's *Women's Cinema as World Cinema* (2015). Following in the footsteps of the previously mentioned scholars, I aim to contextualize Caravan within the framework of transnational feminism. As a transnational feminist organization based in Egypt and funded mainly by the Basque Country, Spain, how does Caravan navigate the limitations and possibilities of transnational feminism? How are questions of differences and inequalities approached within Caravan? Is it a space of seamless solidarity among women filmmakers or also a potential contentiousness?

I first encountered Caravan in October 2020 through their Facebook announcement of a Q&A with feminist filmmaker Kim Longinotto. I was unfamiliar with Caravan as an organization, but I was definitely familiar with Longinotto, who is considered a canonical figure in transnational feminist film scholarship.[3] White describes Longinotto's work as a "cinema solidarity" (2006), while Belinda Smaill praises Longinotto's work for representing "the cultural 'other' as not outside of, but entrenched in, the complex paradigms of modernity" (2009: 45). However, surprisingly, Caravan picked Longinotto's *Shooting the Mafia* (2019), a film that is a break from her conventional subject matter of featuring disenfranchised women and a break from her strictly observational style. *Shooting the Mafia* features the prominent Italian photographer Letizia Battaglia in a style that combines the observational, the archival, and even fiction. During this virtual event, Longinotto was positioned not as a speaker on behalf of the cultural "other," but as a voice among other women of several languages and styles of filmmaking. Longinotto is known for being a British documentary filmmaker who, according to WMM's website description, "highlights the plight of female victims of oppression or discrimination." However, in this encounter, Longinotto was celebrating the life and work of the Italian Battaglia in a narrative free from any representations of female victimhood. In the Q&A, I asked Longinotto if she has ever considered directing a first-person film, to which she answered that

> this film [*Shooting the Mafia*] was quite personal to me because my father is Italian and a lot of how he was in the family was very much like Letizia's father or her husband . . . the more I discovered about the Mafia, the more I discovered why my father is like that, because he had the same mindset as the Mafia, and it is something that troubled me for a long time.

I add here Longinotto's response at length to highlight the way she positions herself in reference to the subject of her film. I am not suggesting that women are only allowed to make films about topics they have personal attachments to. However, as scholars have pointed out, transnational feminism depends on a practice of reflexive thinking about the differences and similarities that facilitate or obstruct collaboration and solidarity, and Caravan offers a space for such dialogue to take place.

Everything about this event was refreshingly disorienting. There was a promo trailer playing prior to the start of the Q&A, and it featured several clips of the twenty-one films included in the Caravan's film screening program for the year. These films represented different production locations such as Germany, France, Spain, Canada, Cuba, and Greece. Thus, the trailer was a cacophony of different languages featured in juxtaposition to each other in unexpected harmony, but it was also noticeable that Arabic, with varied dialects, was represented with more dominance. Out of the twenty-one films selected, twelve were films from or about Lebanon in the special category titled "Homage to Lebanon" to honor and support Lebanese filmmakers after the 2020 Beirut explosion. When the interview with Longinotto started, instructions on how to use Zoom were given in Arabic, and it was announced that simultaneous Arabic translation was available by clicking on the interpretation icon. This gesture, which seemed so unusual, made me realize that I have begun to take for granted the norm that English is the official language of most virtual events, even if based in Egypt.

Scholarship on transnational feminist filmmaking tends to focus on the power dynamics between the filmmaker and the "others" she features in the film. In contrast, Caravan opens an opportunity for conversations *between* women filmmakers and not necessarily *about* the women depicted in their films. In some ways, all international film festivals offer this opportunity for conversations between filmmakers. However, Caravan is the only initiative I encountered that grants free online admission to the public in addition to providing Arabic interpretation. For the past three years, I have been attending almost all of Caravan's events, and in this chapter, I examine how this organization has engendered a unique space for transnational solidarity based on gender and alternative notions of equality and is also attuned to the specificity of location.

History of Caravan

Caravan is a not-for-profit independent initiative organized by a group of women filmmakers and founded by Amal Ramsis, an Egyptian filmmaker and curator. With a team of seven women, Caravan runs an annual non-competitive festival; a monthly exhibition program; a training workshop for documentary filmmaking open to all women, either with experience in filmmaking or not; and two short workshops oriented toward the development of in-production films by professional Arab women filmmakers. Since 2008, Caravan has been playing a critical role in the development of women's cinema in Egypt and in the Arab world. From 2008 through 2012, Caravan was a traveling festival, but in 2013 it was expanded into the Cairo International Women's Film Festival (CIWFF). Even though CIWFF was gaining momentum and locally growing in terms of scope and popularity, it came to an end in 2018. After the controversial election of President Abdel Fattah el-Sisi for a second term in March 2018, the Egyptian government has been constraining the activities of most non-governmental organizations. Prohibitive regulations, such as Law No. 180 of 2018 on Press, Media, and the Supreme Council for Media Regulation, marked the end of CIWFF and the transition of the Caravan festival back to a smaller-scale traveling film festival. In 2020, Caravan went virtual partially because of restrictions due to the Covid-19 pandemic, and mainly, as Ramsis states, "We wanted to skip [political] restrictions on offline events and at the same time reach more audiences in different countries" (Youssra el-Sharkawy 2021). Caravan's main film screening program will remain virtual until the end of 2024, but it is scheduled to return to traveling offline in 2025 (Figures 3.1 and 3.2).

Figure 3.1 In September 2022, in addition to the regular virtual screening program, Caravan organized a screening event at the International Faire of Rashid Karameh in Tripoli, Lebanon. Image Courtesy of Amal Ramsis.

Inspiration and Funding

The inspiration for Caravan, as Ramsis asserts, came about when her short documentary, *Only Dreams* (2005), was accepted in the third edition of Cine Pobre Film Festival in Cuba in 2006.

During this event, Ramsis noticed commonalities between the sociopolitical and socioeconomic realities of the Arab world and Latin America, which are often reflected in their cinemas. Because of language barriers, however, these two cinemas rarely interact.[4] Ramsis's *Only Dreams* was the only submission from the Arab world, but as she states, "It was not because my film was the best Arab cinema had to offer but because it was already subtitled in Spanish because I directed it while studying filmmaking in Spain."[5] In Cuba, Ramsis was inspired by the idea of Cine Pobre Film Festival, which focused on poor cinema, meaning films with low budget or what Julio Garcia Espinosa coined "an imperfect cinema" (Espinosa 1969). As Ramsis asserts, "That is when the idea of Caravan came about, that we create an open route or channel between Latin and Arab cinemas but from

Figure 3.2 Over three days of Caravan's screening in Tripoli, Lebanon, in September 2022. Featuring three films: *On the Edge* (Leila Kilani, 2011), *Speed Sisters* (Amber Fares, 2015), and *Becoming Whom I Was* (Chang-yong Moon, 2017). Image Courtesy of Amal Ramsis.

women's perspectives."[6] From 2008 to 2012, Caravan was a traveling festival between cities in the Middle East and Latin America. For example, Cairo, Beirut, Amman, Damascus, Gaza, Buenos Aires, La Paz, Lima, Mexico City, Cartagena de Indias, and San Salvador. Every year, about fifteen films (half from Arab countries and half from Latin American countries) participate in the Caravan. However, as Ramsis explains, "Even if the intent is to be a cultural link between Arab and Latin American cinemas, we had to stop by Europe for funding because that is where the money is."[7] In its early years, Caravan was financially supported by the Spanish Embassy in Cairo. The subsequent years were funded by several European and Latin American agencies such as Agencia Española de Cooperación Internacional (AECID) in Spain, the Centro Cultural de España in Buenos Aires, and the British Council in Egypt, among others. These organizations supported Caravan with direct funding for purchasing film exhibition rights, hiring translators for the subtitles from and to Arabic and Spanish, sponsoring filmmakers' travel costs, and providing spaces for film screenings in cities around Latin America and the Middle East.

Among similar initiatives in North Africa and the Middle East, Caravan is unique in combining an emphasis on film exhibition and assisting women's film production through workshops and mentorship. Several other independent film funding and development initiatives exist in the MENA region. For example, Beirut DC in Lebanon, SEMAT in Egypt, Arab Fund for Arts and Culture (AFAC) in Lebanon, and DoxBox (located in Berlin with a focus on Arab filmmaking). With the exception of DoxBox's special program, Mouatheqat—which is a fellowship program for Arab women documentary filmmakers—all previously mentioned initiatives are open to all genders. On the other hand, Caravan's screening events feature only films directed by women, and their workshops are open only to women.

In her survey on women's film festivals in the Middle East, Gönül Dönmez-Colin refers to the gender-specific struggles women filmmakers in the Middle East face to practice their trade. Women's film festivals, Dönmez-Colin asserts, are crucial spaces of solidarity and valuable exchanges of experiences (2014). Dönmez-Colin's article is followed by a list of nine women's film festivals in the MENA region compiled by Stefanie Van de Peer. It is challenging to study film festivals in the region since, as Dina Iordanova and Van de Peer point out, the MENA region is "an area that alternates between the vibrant and the volatile" (2014: XXIV). Indeed, by now, at least three of the nine festivals compiled in 2014 have already evaporated.[8] It is clear then that the stability and continuity of Western international film festivals, either dominant or periphery festivals, is a luxury the MENA region cannot afford.

Precarious economic conditions are not the only obstacle threatening the existence of Arab film festivals. Even a wealthy Arab country like the United Arab Emirates decided not to maintain its not-for-profit Dubai International Film Festival (DIFF), which ran between 2004 and 2017.

However, that is by no means the end of the DIFF model. In fact, the festival made a comeback in 2022 under the name META Film Fest. In her analysis of DIFF, Kay Dickinson reads this festival along the history of Dubai as a port city and looks at the trading practices within the festival's model. As Dickinson observes, "Just as Dubai amassed key infrastructural elements like ports, airports and an airline before extending outwards, so too has its entrance into the film industry progressed not with a national body of film works, but a network for dissemination: an international film festival" (2016: 124). To promote its goods globally, DIFF brands itself as a neutral space of dialogue between cultures and a hub of free trade. However, the neutral ideological position of DIFF is at odds with the political nature of most Arab films. As Dickinson points out, "A survey of what DIFF has screened over the years will unequivocally present an attention to those registers. As such, how the festival frames that politics is telling" (2016: 139). Indeed, how any festival frames its content is telling. In the following section, I read the stories that are told by Caravan's framing of its content and how that framing has engendered transnational feminist collaboration.

Caravan's Politics

Caravan is not dissimilar to the older Arab film festivals, such as Carthage Film Festival (JCC) or Damascus Film Festival, where politics are discussed not in the name of an exchange of balanced views from around the world but with a clear declaration of political resistance to global Western hegemony. However, due to Caravan's scale and mode of organization, the closest framework applicable to it is what Viviane Saglier calls a "not-yet festival" (2020: 127). In reference to the Palestinian film festival, The Days of Cinema, Saglier celebrates the "not-yet" status of the festival and of the Palestinian film industry in general. As Saglier argues, what has been "mistaken as symptomatic of Palestine's 'not-yet' temporality" (2020: 143) is indeed the way in which the Palestinian film industry produces its own time and space, which "does not conform to European ideals of stable film festivals" (Saglier 2020: 143). Similarly, Caravan produces its own time and space in paving a new route of transnational circulation. The timeline of this festival and its scope and activities are almost constantly transforming to circumvent the challenges imposed on the institution by local and international circumstances.

Over the years, Caravan's Egyptian fanbase has grown, and as Ramsis speculates, "We succeeded in attracting the attention of locals because all the films have Arabic subtitles, all screenings are free of charge, and we strive to invite filmmakers to meet with the audience after film screenings."[9] Indeed, even the Cairo International Film Festival does not offer Arabic subtitles for its foreign film selection. This phenomenon might seem strange; what country does not care to offer subtitles in the local language of its own film festival? However, as Chihab El Khachab observes in his anthropological study of the contemporary film industry in Egypt, the industry imagines the local audiences to be divided by class. There are two types of films that are produced for two different types of imagined audiences: the so-called "commercial" films are made with a popular *(sha'bi)* audience in mind, while "artistic" films are made with the international film festival crowd in mind (El Khachab 2021: 185). As El Khachab asserts, "the broad classist contrast between 'popular' and 'festival' audiences is naturalized among industry insiders" (2021: 189). In contrast, Caravan, which by 2013 was CIWFF, insists on imagining the *Sha'bi* audience to be capable of digesting "artistic" films. Despite the political turmoil in Egypt after the 2013 military coup, as Ramsis asserts, people came to the theaters eager to see what Caravan brought to them because they had already gained the local population's trust that the film selection would be thought provoking and, quite simply, linguistically accessible. It is worth noting that the festival started its screenings on November 16, 2013, only three days after the end of a national curfew. Nonetheless, all the festival venues located in downtown Cairo were at full capacity.

Funding has always been scarce for Caravan, especially since the festival does not receive any fiscal support from the Egyptian government. The main source of support, as Ramsis reports, has always been the Spanish Embassy in Cairo.[10] However, in 2013, this funding stopped due to the escalation in the European economic crisis. To overcome this obstacle, Ramsis applied for a partnership with the Culture, Communication, and Development Fund (KCD), and together, they received funding from the Diputación Foral de Bizkaia in the Basque Country. In a private conversation the author had with Ramsis, she elaborated that she chose the Basque regional government because of its clear stance on the issue of the Palestinian occupation. Likewise, Ramsis asserts, Caravan has a strict policy of boycotting any collaboration with the Israeli government and filmmakers. To illustrate this point, Ramsis shared with me that in 2017, the festival canceled the participation of a Turkish film after it was initially accepted and even after the Arabic subtitles were completed because they discovered that one of the film's crew members is an Israeli citizen. Despite my sympathy for the intentions behind this decision, I initially read it as a sign of the limitations of transnational collaboration. This identity-based restriction assumes that individuals are fixed in their presumed political leanings. When I reached out to the Israeli filmmaker, Shelly Grizim, for a comment on this encounter, she stated in a text conversation with the author that rejecting the film even after the team's proposal to remove Grizim's name foreclosed an opportunity to build bridges instead of walls.[11] While I share Grizim's frustration with the situation, it is perhaps necessary to consider how we have arrived at this point of a failed transnational dialogue. In other words, why is transnational feminist collaboration so greatly challenged by the question of Palestine?

Transnational feminism has a long history in Egypt, and Palestine has been a central cause for Egyptian feminists. For example, as Margot Badran points out, in 1936, the Egyptian Feminist Union (EFU) led by Huda Sharawi "responded to the call from the Arab Women's Committee of Palestine . . . [and sent] the League of Nations to support the Palestinian women's demand to end Jewish immigration" (1995: 225). By 1939, after attending the 13th Conference of the International Women Suffrage Alliance in Copenhagen, "the EFU was consumed by the Palestine question and the increased Jewish immigration connected with the spreading fascism in Europe" (Badran 1995: 216). The question of Palestine is not only central to Egyptian feminists; as Desai states, the two most heated issues at the UN's World Conferences on Women in Mexico City (1975) and Copenhagen (1980) "were, first, whether Israel was racist in its relationship to Palestinians, and second, the role of the West in perpetuating neocolonial strategies" (Desai 2002: 28). The struggle for Palestinian liberation remains a focus of contemporary transnational feminism. In 2001, a collective of Arab and Arab American women activists drafted the paper, "The Forgotten '-ism': An Arab American Women's Perspective on Zionism, Racism, and Sexism," which "was originally written for the United Nations World Conference against Racism in Durban, South Africa" (Naber, Desouky, and Baroudi 2016: 98). While this paper was distributed during the Durban conference, it did not represent the official stance of the conference, which removed the term "Zionism" from its official documents (Naber, Desouky, and Baroudi 2016: 98). During the 2014 annual conference of the National Women's Studies Association (NWSA), over 1,000 NWSA members signed a petition in support of the Boycott, Divestment, Sanctions (BDS) movement (Sarah Benton 2016). And in 2021, The US-based Palestinian Feminist Collective (PFC) declared their pledge that "Palestine is a feminist issue" (PFC: 2021). This pledge is also clear in its call to boycott

Israel. BDS is a continuous area of debate between pro-Palestine feminists on one side and pro-Zionist feminists on the other. This is an area where reconciliation between two fundamentally opposing views is impossible. However, it is important to note that BDS calls for the academic boycotting of Israeli institutions and not individuals. As Nadje Al-Ali asserts, "There is still much confusion about what BDS means in practice when it comes to individuals as opposed to links with institutions. My personal view is that we should do everything possible to collaborate more and work with Israeli colleagues who are critical of their government's policies toward Palestine" (Simona Sharoni et al. 2015: 661). Nonetheless, it is difficult to navigate the terrain of BDS within cultural activities such as film festivals. This is a gray area where Caravan is unable to lead as an example of transnational feminist collaboration between Israeli and Arab women filmmakers. While the incident of rejecting the participation of an Israeli woman filmmaker exemplifies a limitation of transnational collaboration within Caravan, the organization's commitment to the Palestinian cause, which I will explore in detail, is a clear example of transnational solidarity.

The tensions around the Palestinian–Israeli conflict are highly visible on the international film festival circuit as well. For example, on November 15 at the 2023 International Documentary Film Festival Amsterdam (IDFA), protesters against the ongoing bombing of Gaza held banners with the slogan "From the river to the sea, Palestine will be free" (Rizov 2023). In response, the conference issued a statement condemning the slogan. Several filmmakers such as Basma al Sharif, Maryam Tafakory, and Jumana Manna withdrew their films from the festival in protest of the handling of the situation and the failure of the festival to call for a ceasefire (Rizov 2023).

In contrast to the ambivalent position of IDFA on the political conflict in Israel/Palestine, Caravan made it publicly clear where they stand. On October 17, 2023, Caravan posted a statement on their Facebook page in Arabic and English stating, "Between Women Filmmakers Caravan stands today, as always, exclusively and without equivocation, with the Palestinian people and the Palestinian resistance against the Zionist occupying enemy" (Caravan 2023). When Hamas attacked Israel on October 7, Caravan was coincidentally featuring the Palestinian docu-fiction *Foragers* (Jumana Manna, 2022) for their October 2023 screening program. After the subsequent Israeli bombardment of Gaza, Caravan changed their screening program for

November and December and announced a special program under the theme Children of Palestine as Portrayed by Palestinian Women Filmmakers. This special event featured four documentaries by Palestinian female filmmakers Mai Masri and Azza el-Hassan. Masri's films, *Children of Shatila* (1988) and *Frontiers of Dreams and Fears* (2001), were featured at Caravan for the first time. However, el-Hassan's films, *News Time* (2001) and *3CM Less* (2003), were previously featured at Caravan in 2010.

In her introduction to this special program, Ramsis states Caravan's conscious decision to rewatch el-Hassan's work alongside Masri's to grasp the history of Palestinian cinema through the eyes of Palestinian women filmmakers (Caravan 2023). Reflecting on the choice to focus on Palestinian children, Ramsis states that rewatching these four films troubles her more now that she is a mother (Caravan 2023). Moreover, because of the brutal attack on Gaza, Ramsis was asking if it is even possible to make films now, and to whom we are making them, considering, in Ramsis's words, "the shameful indifference of most international film festivals and their audiences" (Caravan 2023). In the Q&A with el-Hassan, she reflects on her journey with the making of *News Time* and *3CM Less,* which were both filmed during the Second Intifada (Palestinian revolts against Israel between 2000 and 2005). She states that after finishing these two films, she became outraged with the political turmoil in Palestine and the Arab region in general and decided to refrain from making films in or about Palestine. As el-Hassan says,

> we Palestinians had this feeling that if only the world knew about our predicament, they would surely sympathize with us, and see the conflict from our perspective. However, now at the age of social media, images are available, and information is easily attainable and maybe that is a liberating moment for Palestinian filmmakers so we would let go of the obsession to tell reality. (Caravan 2023)

What I would like to highlight here in the words of Ramsis and el-Hassan is the practice of self-reflexivity. In a space of mutual respect, both women can think freely about their position in the world and their ways to navigate the struggles they find themselves entangled in. In this incident of transregional dialogue between an Egyptian and a Palestinian filmmaker who share the same ideology, it is worth noting that for the Q&A with el-Hassan, four aspiring Egyptian women filmmakers were invited to join this roundtable discussion.

Promoting an intergenerational dialogue and knowledge sharing is one of the strong feminist features of Caravan. In a similar fashion, in 2020, Caravan invited Masri to offer a virtual masterclass.

Caravan's clear agenda on the question of Palestine is not a new development. For example, through Caravan's 2020 program, I watched Dahna Abou Rahme's *Kingdom of Women* (2010), which features the stories of Palestinian women in refugee camps in Lebanon, and Nabiha Lutfi's *Because Roots Don't Die* (1977), which documents the Tel Zaatar Massacre of Palestinians in Lebanon. Via the 2021 program, I was first introduced to the work of Annemarie Jacir as Caravan featured her 2012 feature film, *When I Saw You*. Jacir is often credited as the first Palestinian woman director to shoot a feature film, *Salt of the Sea* (2007).

In 2022, Caravan started a program titled Carte Blanche in which every month, an invited woman filmmaker has the freedom to highlight the work of another woman filmmaker from anywhere in the world. Even in this collaborative curation model, Palestine remained part of Caravan's narrative. Lebanese filmmaker, Eliane Raheb used her Carte Blanche to call attention to Sandra Madi's *Saken* (2014), which is a delicate documentary on an elderly Palestinian *fedai* (soldier) who was severely injured during the 1982 invasion of Lebanon. Moreover, Ula Tabari invested her Carte Blanche in the uplifting and energetic documentary *Speed Sisters* (Amber Fares, 2015) featuring the all-women car race team based in the West Bank. Based on the clear ideological statements Caravan issues alongside the organization's curatorial choices and collaborative networking with Palestinian filmmakers, Caravan is without a doubt a space where Palestine as a feminist issue is affirmed. However, with the restrictions on the participation of any Israeli filmmakers, the framework of transnational feminism is unable to expand beyond the limits of a transregional space of the MENA region. I lament this limitation because I admire the potential of Caravan for fostering intergenerational and interregional dialogues between women filmmakers. However, we cannot read this omission as solely a failure of Caravan to foster transnational collaboration. Ultimately, there is a glaring lack of literature on Israeli women's cinema featuring films that are critical of Israel's policies toward Palestine. Nonetheless, such films do exist, for example, in her reading of Elle Flanders's *Zero Degrees of Separation* (2005), Terri Ginsberg considers this film a "cross-generational/cultural queering of Israeli/Zionist history" (2016: 8).

In their most recent initiative in support of the visibility of films from and about Palestine, Caravan published on their Facebook account a link to a virtual catalog titled "Palestinian Cinema Guide." Similar initiatives by organizations and individuals have proliferated since October 2023 in response to the Israeli attack on Gaza. For example, in April 2024, the fifteenth edition of the Arab Film Festival in Berlin (ALFILM) dedicated its program to Palestinian cinema. Moreover, Arab cinema streaming platforms such as Aflamuna also sponsored free virtual access to Palestinian films. What distinguishes Caravan is combining the free virtual exhibition of Palestinian films with English subtitles and subsequently featuring Q&A sessions with the filmmakers moderated by several prominent women filmmakers, researchers, and film scholars.

This model of film viewing is a form of transnational feminist collaborative knowledge production. However, given the highly charged political nature of the Palestinian–Israeli conflict, engaging in this transnational feminist dialogue requires nuanced listening. The political act of talking and listening is one of the strongest features of Caravan. In the following section, I will contextualize Caravan's transnational feminist model within Arabyya epistemology.

Arabyya Epistemologies and Egyptian Feminism

The rise of a new understanding of gender politics in Egypt has been influenced by global feminist movements, for example, the #MeToo movement, but it is also critically aware of the local specificities of the current moment in Egyptian history, the intersections of the postcolonial conditions, and the new post-2011 revolution realities. Even though the revolution has failed to bring about any sustainable reforms in Egypt's political system, it nonetheless brought women back into the public sphere. Egyptian feminists have always participated in the public sphere, but they also paid a high price for their participation.

This type of feminism is theorized in Manal Hamza's *Women Resisting Sexual Violence and the Egyptian Revolution: Arab Feminist Testimonies* (2020). In this book, Hamza argues that "Arabyya epistemologies are focused on reading and resisting the intersecting nexus of militarism, neoliberalism and capitalism, Islamism, settler-colonialism, and heteronormativity oppressing the bodies of Arabs in different geographical contexts" (Hamza 2020: 10).

Moreover, Hamza asserts, the act of giving testimonies, in Arabic *shahada*, is how Egyptian women "resisted repression and theorized their experiences of gendered violence as they were seeking social justice" (2020: 3). In this book, Hamza analyzes the *shahadat* of Egyptian women about their experiences with state-sanctioned sexual violence and points out the similarities between Arabyya and Chicana feminist thought "as both are anti-colonial and critical feminist epistemologies" (2020: 12). Either in novels, in activism, or in film curation activities such as Caravan, Arabyya epistemologies are evident. Two methodologies of Arabyya feminism, as Hamza points out, are "shahadat and Haki" (2020: 13). *Shahadat* is the plural of testimony in Arabic, and *Haki* means storytelling or conversation. These two techniques, as Hamza asserts, are tools for collecting data and for preserving and continuing Arab women's oral history tradition.

I argue that Caravan uses Arabyya epistemologies to assert Arab women's existence in the public sphere of filmmaking in Egypt. The films featured via Caravan document Arab history as seen and told by Arab women. The spaces created for unstructured discussions following each film are similar to Haki tradition; they provide an open conversation between women with an invitation extended to women all over the world. This transnational Haki adds the extra labor of translation, which I believe is crucial in asserting that no one language is to be falsely taken as the natural language of feminism. Moreover, the organization's effort to make Arabic the main language of communication is also indicative of their class-oriented ideology. Proficiency in English and other Latin-based languages in Egypt is a marker of socioeconomic privilege.

As I have argued, Palestine is a central issue to Arabyya epistemologies and to Egyptian feminism as seen via Caravan. However, beyond Palestine, there is also a focus on Third Cinema and on the criticism of the gendered predicament of global capitalism. Examples of films that are critical of the gendered effects of global capitalism are Jewel Maranan's *In The Claws of a Century Wanting* (2017) and Julia Roesler's *Marina* (2018). The former is a documentary that sheds light on the harsh lives of port workers in the Philippines, and the latter is a fictional reenactment of a collective of real stories of migrant domestic workers in Germany. In reference to Third Cinema, Caravan featured several films in alliance with this theme. For example, *The Hour of Liberation Has Arrived* (Heiny Srour, 1974), which featured the Dhofar rebellion in the Arabian Gulf, and *El Futuro Es Nuestro* (The Future Is Ours, Virna Molina and Ernesto Ardito, 2014), which tells the story of a group of revolutionary teenagers who were kidnapped and killed in Argentina in 1976 during the Socialist Revolution. In a conversation between Virna Molina and Arab Loutfi, the latter gives *shahada* (testimony) to her experience watching this film and relating it to the 2011 Revolution in Egypt (Caravan 2022). As Loutfi states, "watching this film gives me hope that we might one day break the shackles of dictatorship and see our youth free" (Caravan 2022). Loutfi, who is a prolific Lebanese–Egyptian filmmaker and activist, used Caravan to relate her own pain of surviving the Civil War in Lebanon and participating in the 2011 Revolution to the experience of watching *El Futuro Es Nuestro* and discussing it with the filmmaker in the presence of a public audience. However, it is crucial to note that Caravan's open discourse of collaborative knowledge production is not a space of neutral or liberal exchange of ideas between women filmmakers transnationally. This conversational and relational space is unproductive if participants are not fully committed to anti-colonial struggles or at least willing to comprehend these struggles from the perspective of their initiators. In May 2024, Caravan featured Loutfi's provocative documentary *Tell Your Tale, Little Bird* (2007), which features interviews with seven Palestinian female guerrilla fighters who participated in several airplane hijackings in the 1970s organized by the Popular Front for the Liberation of Palestine. The Q&A, moderated by the Palestinian filmmaker Ula Tabari, was preceded by a short trailer highlighting some key points in the intersection between gender-based struggles and the national liberation project from the perspective of Palestinian women at a specific point in history. The trailer starts with a scene orienting the viewers to the space and time of the interviews featured in the film, the city of Amman in the winter of 1993. The following scene shows Laila Khaled, one of the most well-known Palestinian female hijackers, recalling her memories of the demonstrations she participated in as a young woman in support of the Algerian anti-colonial struggle and in protest of the murder of Patrice Lumumba. Similarly, Tabari's questions to Loutfi contextualize these seven women's armed struggle within the historical moment of their generation growing up during the events of 1948 (the Nakba) and the aftermath of the 1967 war. In Loutfi's answer, she weaves herself as part of this generation and explains how her personal life and subsequently her activism have been shaped by her belonging to this generation and their political struggle for liberation. The conversation between Tabari and Loutfi frames the logic of Palestinian militant activism from the perspective of the lived experience of Loutfi's generation, which includes the subjects of *Tell Your Tale, Little Bird*. Moreover, the film's narrative, which weaves together the different stories of the seven retired militant women, invites the viewers to think about the political rationale behind the women's actions at a specific historical moment and to refrain from seeing them as exceptionally heroic or villainous characters.

Conclusion

The testimonies, stories, and conversations taking place within Caravan are Arabyya epistemologies in praxis. The insistence on creating an accessible space financially and linguistically sustained Caravan's operations in the MENA region and beyond for over a decade. I read Caravan as a space of transnational solidarity based on the common politics that foster coalitions between women filmmakers from around the world who share the common goals of fighting imperialism, colonialism, and the material inequalities of global capitalism. However, while I argue that Caravan is a model of transnational feminist film culture, it is also challenged by the politics of the contemporary moment. The hypersensitivity of Caravan to refrain from any collaboration with Israeli filmmakers is at odds with the liberal understanding of transnational feminism and even stands in contradiction to the guidelines drafted by the BDS movement. While I see this identity-based restriction as a limitation of the transnational feminist model of Caravan, it is not difficult to see where this distrust originates. A survey of the recent scholarship on transnational feminism from the perspective of scholars from the Global South reveals the stark reality of the failed attempts at transnational solidarity between the Global North and South.[12] For example, in "Catastrophic Aid: GBV Humanitarianism in Gaza," Rema Hammami criticizes the politics of gender-based violence (GBV) in the context of Gaza in the aftermath of Israeli military operations in 2010. Hammami convincingly argues that the humanitarian GBV in Gaza is "highly selective, raising the more fundamental question of what the 'care' in this context actually accomplishes" (2023: 352). In a situation where women are in desperate need of shelter, food, education for their children, and work for their husbands, consciousness-raising and advocacy for gender equality are at best insufficient. Moreover, Hammami is critical of the humanitarian framework and sees it as complicit in the catastrophization of Gaza. For Hammami, GBV operations in Gaza are a performative act that reduce Palestinian women to victims in need of rescuing from their own cultural ills. In this highly charged political moment that we are witnessing, combined with the divide over what Palestinian solidarity should look like and what freedom of Palestine means to both Palestinians and Israelis, it is hard to imagine a productive transnational feminist model that is free of contentions. However, we should continue to strive to build metaphorical bridges despite our differences as feminist filmmakers committed to the pursuit of justice for all, though I also understand that this might be futile to some while the everyday lives of Palestinians are catastrophically affected by imprisonment within physical walls.

Notes

1 Arab and Latin American countries are diverse in terms of ethnicity and geographical locations; however, their cultural bonds are intertwined through both regions' ties to Moorish Spain. Moreover, in recent history, the relationships between the two regions strengthened as they were both involved in the rise of the South–South Cooperation for Development in the 1970s. For more on the political and economic relations between the MENA region and Latin America, see *The Arab World and Latin America: Economic and Political Relations in the Twenty-First Century*. Ed. Fehmy Saddy 2016. London: I.B. Tauris, and *The Middle East and Brazil: Perspectives on the New Global South*. Ed. Paul Amar 2014. Bloomington: Indiana University Press. And in terms of my use of the term "Global South," I echo Alfred J. Lopez and Ricardo Quintana-Vellejo's definition of the term as "not a geographical designation but an ontological one. It constitutes the mutual recognition by the rest of the planet's population of its shared condition on the margins of the neoliberal dream: modernizing but not yet modern, developing but never quite developed—forever becoming" [Alfred J. Lopez and Ricardo Quintana-Vellejo, "Introduction: Cardinal Points and 'Hilly Sand'," in *The Routledge Companion to Literature and the Global South* (London: Routledge, 2024), xiii].
2 Belinda Smaill has written extensively about the work of Kim Longinotto. See, for example, "Women, Pain and the Documentaries of Kim Longinotto," in *The Documentary* (London: Palgrave Macmillan, 2010).

3   Amal Ramsis in conversation with the author, December 2021.
4   ibid.
5   ibid.
6   ibid.
7   The three discontinued festivals are: Shashat Women's Film Festival, Palestine; The Cairo International Women's Film Festival, Egypt; and Arab Women's Film Festival, The Hague, The Netherlands.
8   Amal Ramsis in conversation with the author, December 2021.
9   ibid.
10 Shelly Grizim, in correspondence with the author, March 2023.
11 See, for example, Abu-Lughod, L., R. Hammami, and N. Shalhūb-Kīfūrkiyān, eds. 2023. *The Cunning of Gender Violence: Geopolitics and Feminism*. Durham: Duke University Press; Razack, S. 2022. *Nothing Has to Make Sense: Upholding White Supremacy through Anti-Muslim Racism*. Minneapolis: University of Minnesota Press; Shehabuddin, E. 2021. *Sisters in the Mirror: A History of Muslim Women and the Global Politics of Feminism*. Oakland, California: University of California Press; and Alsultany, E. 2022. *Broken: The Failed Promise of Muslim Inclusion*. New York: New York University Press.
12 Even though Caravan occasionally features fiction films, the organization is predominantly focused on documentary films. Out of the sixty films exhibited from 2020 to 2023, only a dozen were fiction. Moreover, one of the main activities of Caravan is the Creative Documentary Workshop, an event dedicated to training aspiring female filmmakers on the theories and practices of documentary filmmaking.

Part II

Rereading Public and Private Connections through Documentary

4

Feminist Animated Documentary

Ways of Confronting Violence against Women

Shilyh Warren and Christine Veras

This chapter focuses on short, animated films by independent international women artists that confront forms of violence against women. The films selected here span from 2019 to 2021, a short period of three years that was nonetheless remarkable in terms of the growth of social movements for women's rights and the increase in awareness about violence against women. From the #MeToo movement and the Covid-19 pandemic to changes in laws concerning reproductive rights in the United States, Europe, and Latin America, twenty-first-century women have experienced drastic impacts on their basic human rights, sometimes for better, sometimes for worse. Notably, increasing numbers of women animators have embraced feminist perspectives on issues of global concern—a growing tendency that has seldom been investigated. In this chapter, we make the case that animation plays an increasingly important role in both mainstream and independent filmmaking among women interested in foregrounding and exploring non-fictional issues relevant to global feminisms.

For example, *My Year of Dicks* (2022), written and created by Pamela Ribon and directed by Sara Gunnarsdóttir, created a major sensation when nominated for an Oscar for best animated short in 2023. The film revisits Ribon's desperate mission to lose her virginity to one uninspiring guy after another as a fifteen-year-old growing up outside Houston, Texas, in the early 1990s. Each of the film's five chapters is created in a distinct visual style inspired by pop culture and art movements with references that range from Impressionism to horror and gothic to anime, depending on the "dick" of the moment. Although the film did not ultimately win the Oscar, it put feminist animation on the mainstream map, raising public awareness of the common yet unseen struggles and anxieties of a teenage girl. That same year, *Turning Red* (2022), a feature film directed by Domee Shi for Disney Pixar Studios, also helped raise awareness about puberty and menstruation in a major mainstream film, perhaps for the first time. In Europe, *Granny's Sexual Life* (2021), one of the shorts we will analyze here dealing more directly with sexual violence against women, co-directed by Urška Djukić and Émilie Pigeard, won the César Award—the National Film Award in France—for best animation short. These breakthroughs indicate a growing tendency among women in animation to reveal deeply personal and gendered experiences as well as growing appreciation from global audiences. Our interest is in exploring how this feminist trend manifests more specifically in animated documentary, arguably one of the most dynamic areas of investigation in documentary studies over the past two decades.

At the center of our study are four short works, *Carne* (2019), *Awakening the Goddess* (2020), *Granny's Sexual Life* (2021), *and KAM* (2020), that speak to contemporary trends at the nexus of feminism, animation, and documentary. In *Carne* (Flesh, Brazil/Spain, 2019) by Camila Kater, testimonial interviews are presented using different tactile techniques of animation, offering women's perspectives on their bodies as they change in different stages of life. In *Awakening of the Goddess* (India, 2020) by Debjani Mukherjee, a cacophony of women's voices in three different languages creates an oral tapestry that testifies to the collective experience of abuse women often face in public. Animation of and on the actor's body creates a confrontational parallel between women's violence and the representation of the goddess. *Granny's Sexual Life* (Slovenia/France, 2021) by Urška Djukić and Émilie Pigeard manifests a complex relationship between form and content, sound and image, fact and fiction, and selves and collectives in its exploration of women's sexual oppression in Slovenia in the early twentieth century that still resonates. *KAM* (Turkey/Australia, 2020) by Zeynep Akcay embraces experimental techniques, such as long-exposure photography and pixilation animation, creating a visual explosion that welcomes reflection on political attempts to control and contain the female body. In these works, which we classify as feminist animations, women's bodies reclaim agency, space, liberty, and mobility in the public sphere, generating forms of aesthetic resistance and solidarity that remind us of the expansive political and critical possibilities generated by animated documentaries.

Feminism and Animation and Documentary

Our goal is to shed light on an overshadowed category we call "feminist animated documentary" and thus create new links between documentary, feminist, and animation studies. Scholarship that focuses on the intersection of feminism and documentary has expanded since the publication of *Feminism and Documentary* (1999), edited by Janet Walker and Diane Waldman. In their introduction to that field-defining volume, the editors note that the nexus of the two terms was previously characterized by "omission" (1999: 4). Feminist studies and documentary studies operated in parallel despite their overlapping concerns—about political impact, the ethics of representation, Eurocentrism, and the way that geopolitics shape relations between filmmakers and filmed subjects. In turn, animation studies, despite being a younger field of study dating from the late 1980s, has seen significant growth as a result of "the influence of post-modernism on Media Studies," observes Maureen Furniss (2016: 3). Scholars and pioneers of the field, such as Furniss and Jayne Pilling, welcome the connections between animation and feminist studies. In recent years, more specific contributions by Annabelle Honess Roe (2013), Jonathan Murray and Nea Ehrlich (2019), Nea Ehrlich (2021), Cristina Formenti (2022), and others have also investigated the intersection of documentary and animation studies. Yet overall, scholarly attention to gender and feminist politics in documentary (animated or otherwise) has lagged dramatically compared to feminist analyses of fictional productions.

Despite contemporary contributions, including Lisa French's *The Female Gaze in Documentary Film* (2021) and the twin volumes *Female Authorship and the Documentary Image* (2018) and *Female Agency and Documentary Strategies* (2018), edited collections by Boel Ulfsdotter and Anna Backman Rogers, few scholars have engaged with questions at the intersection of *animation*, documentary, and feminism. Recently, Slava Greenberg observed that feminist animation—"its themes, aesthetics, styles, and creation—has scarcely been interrogated" as a subgenre of either women's animation or feminist filmmaking (2020: 72). However, the history of animation certainly encompasses women animators who center feminist perspectives on issues of global concern, including oppression, sexual violence, and the gendered impact of war and political violence. Greenberg draws attention to a handful of animators like Finnish-born and London-based artist Marjut Rimminen, whose feminist animations date back to the 1970s, as well as Ruth Lingford, Signe Baumane, Shira Avni, Marjane Satrapi, and others. Several of these artists deal explicitly with armed conflict, war, sexuality, and sexual violence, such as Rimminen's *Some Protection* (1987), Lingford's *Death and the Mother* (1997) and *Little Deaths* (2010), Avni's *from Far Away* (2000), and Satrapi's *Persepolis* (2007). By way of defining feminist animation, Greenberg observes that the feminist animators at the heart of his study "center the viewers' attention on timely feminist issues and amplify feminist subjectivities" (2020: 75).

Contemporary thinkers are indebted to Pilling's edited book and DVD collection, *Animating the Unconscious: Desire, Sexuality and Animation* (2012), which brought early light to this discussion, asking a question that continues to intrigue us: "why and how animation is so appropriate a medium for such subject matter" (2). Pilling and the contributors to the volume were among the first to focus on short "auteur" or "art" animations that explore sexuality and desire from a feminist perspective. For Pilling, a number of factors led to the growth of animated documentaries, such as "a general shift in auteur animation culture that has seen more from the universal to the more particular; the influence of feminism; the emergence of a specific animated documentary film; and a much more frequent use of the human, rather than 'cartoony' or anthropomorphic, voice, i.e. one that confers a sense of a real person speaking their own experience" (2012: 4). From the vantage point of 2012, Pilling produces a moment of reflection in the field about the intersection between feminism, animation, and sexuality—a legacy that influences our approach in this chapter.

In their exhibition of feminist non-fiction, *No Master Territories*, and companion scholarly volume, *Feminist Worldmaking and the Moving Image*, Erika Balsom and Hila Peleg foreground the notion of "feminist worldmaking." The authors write that to "engage in wagers of worldmaking is to refuse the *status quo*, to reject the authority of received frameworks of intelligibility, to clamor to bring the new into being" (2022: 23). In a plurality of aesthetic forms, thus, including animation, we venture, feminist documentary propels both the critiques and idealisms of feminist discourse, exposing and illuminating the politics of gender and sexuality across sites of difference and uneven power relations. In this chapter, we ask what animation contributes uniquely to the audiovisual and, specifically, non-fiction project of worldmaking as identified by Balsom and Peleg. Feminist documentary animation, following Greenberg, encompasses animated films that maintain a tie to reality and seek to amplify and advance issues of concern to feminist publics; they are both "flights of fancy and the imagination" and "associated with truth" and the real, to invoke Nea Ehrlich and Jonathan Murray's irreconcilable differences at the heart of animated documentary (2020: 3).

In *Documenting Gendered Violence* (2016), editor Heather McIntosh identifies the issues that come to the fore in documentary regarding gender-based violence: how to represent the unrepresentable, how to avoid re-victimizing survivors, how to empower and contribute to healing, and how to create meaningful impact on audiences to mobilize change. The volume does not include contributions on animation; however, we forward the claim that animation is well suited to address representation, ethics, and impact because of the unique ways that animation envisions forms of reality that are impossible to capture, for example, unfilmed events of the past, dreams, fantasies, emotions, memories, and trauma. As Debjani Mukherjee, one of the filmmakers featured in this chapter, observes, "The animated form provides the power to visualise and depict the images that are not always visible, the historical events that exist in memory alone, the vulnerable emotions that resonate in the heart, the thoughts that whisper in the mind and the images that creep up in dreams. This form speaks to the violence, preserving the anonymity of the victims yet raising their voice" (2020: np). Feminist animation activates and re-enlivens personal recollections, gives shape and form to traumatic experiences, and produces new possibilities for the recognition of shared experiences of sexism and gendered violence, therefore helping to imagine a collectivized reckoning and path to transformative justice.

Women in Animation

Traditionally interpreted as the professional field of animation, the animation industry is a term connected to practitioners who work for major entertainment studios, helping to create animated feature films, short films, interactive experiences, and advertisements, among other related work that belongs to the mainstream media. However, independent studios and individual creative practitioners have historically found ways to tell their own stories alongside the animation industry. Animation and film festivals provide a significant platform to distribute and exhibit independent creators and offer them a venue for public access and engagement. Of course, the democratization of the internet has also played a major role in facilitating access to and visibility for independently produced animation films. In a way, animation festivals democratize the relationship between independent creators and the audience and facilitate the connection between independent creators and the mainstream industry. Therefore, the animation industry gains a broader context and meaning when these independent creators are included, and the films we analyze here belong to this broader context. The feminist animations here are intensely focused on matters of sexual abuse, oppression, and violence. Consistently, independent filmmakers like those at the center of our study remain true to their voices, embracing creative freedom and portraying subjects that matter to them personally.

As in every other creative field, the opportunities for women have been growing in animation. In 2019, the Women in Animation Association joined forces with Stacy L. Smith, founder of the USC Annenberg Inclusion Initiative, to assess the state of representation in the industry, creating what the film critic Carlos Aguilar called "the first-ever inclusion in animation survey" (2019: np). In their industry census, they aimed to evaluate women's participation and the state of inclusion in the animation industry. Pledging to change the industry and to reach 50/50 by 2025, the association has been the longest supporter of women in the field, locally and internationally.[1] The results are publicly available and can be summarized as a confirmation of what we have historically known: women are significantly underrepresented in the industry.[2] However, the survey provides in-depth quantitative and qualitative data and has pointed out the challenges women experience as inclusion efforts are growing in the animation industry. Nonetheless, the results also indicate the uphill battles women face, which include a male-dominated and male-centric culture that persistently undervalues women with distorted claims, such as presuming that there is less female interest in the field despite the large numbers of women in animation schools. The research also raises awareness about the adverse challenges faced by women of color in the animation industry, namely, tokenization and isolation.

This data, despite analyzing the context of the animation industry in the United States, resonates with the experiences shared with us by international independent women animators. The four films investigated in this chapter were originally part of an event organized in collaboration with the Women in Animation student club at the University of Texas at Dallas titled "Animated Perspectives: Violence Against Women," where the authors met in 2022. Christine Veras curated the screening at the event to showcase international animations created by independent women directors working on experimental animation techniques that discuss violence. Focusing on independent women directors was a straightforward criterion as, expanding upon the results above, more women succeed in creative leadership positions in the independent filmmaking scene than in the traditional animation industry. Additionally, we wanted to increase the outreach of these films and expose our students to these unique perspectives on the subject. Because of Veras's background as a traditional experimental animator and scholar, it was important for her to search for films that had a tactile appeal or that were produced with alternative animation techniques, such as drawing on paper, clay on glass, scratching directly on film, stop-motion puppet animation, and pixilation, among others. The haptic response elicited by those techniques connects us with the handmade nature of traditional animation production. Mukherjee, for example, describes the connection between the processes of handmade animation and the content in films about violence as sharing an emphasis on viscerality (2020: np). In terms of modes of production as well, animated films that reflexively foreground their time-intensive, hands-on techniques potentially stress the fact that processes of healing and recovery similarly take significant time, space, and endurance. The final criterion of having the animations addressing topics related to violence against women, in many ways, responds to the growth of violent actions that have been curtailing women's rights globally in the twenty-first century.

The in-person screening event was followed by a panel discussion that generated meaningful insights and conversations that we took up and explored in more depth in this chapter. We decided that the first step in our research would be to conduct interviews with the directors and animators. Interviews have played a central role in feminist documentary filmmaking and scholarship since the 1970s when women around the globe began to insist that the personal was political. Early feminist documentaries from that period regularly centered on the voices and experiences of ordinary women rather than the patriarchal experts that dominated previous non-fictional work. Two of the films under investigation here similarly depend on interviews with ordinary women and feminist activists. The research expanded as we interviewed each of the directors to add their perspectives. The key questions that we asked them to discuss were: (1) the inspiration for the work; (2) whether they considered their animation a documentary; (3) whether they see their work participating in the documentary tradition of creating social awareness and inspiring change; (4) what they think about the term "feminist animation" and if they believe the term describes their work well; and (5) their hopes for audience outreach.

Each of the films we analyze centers on the experiences women face in private and public spaces constructed around patriarchal logics that devalue, demean, restrict, and control women's bodies, freedom of expression, and potential for self-actualization. Violence is a persistent element of these experiences, whether in the form of physical or emotional abuse and neglect or individual or collective manifestations. According to the United Nations (UN), "the availability of data on violence against women and girls has improved considerably in recent years," which allows researchers to grasp closer numbers worldwide to assess this global issue. In its online information page about "Facts and Figures to End Violence against Women," the UN provides fourteen facts about such violence supported by data, ranging from technology-facilitated violence to trafficking and genital mutilation, including violence against women in the public sphere, to name a few.[3] Our findings and the analysis of each of the films presented here reinforce our sense that animation has much to offer to global documentary scholarship and discourse, especially as it concerns the possibility of ameliorating the injustices faced by women and gender minorities around the globe.

Camila Kater and *Carne* (2019)

In Brazilian director Camila Kater's debut short film *Carne,* the focus is on the psychic and physical harm women endure because of social and political demands on their bodies. Body politics have long been a core concern of feminist politics and women's filmmaking. In *Carne,* five diverse women reflect on their relationships with their bodies in relation to societal pressures and expectations. At the beginning of the short, over a black screen, a voice-over remarks, "No woman lives in her own body." Throughout, the film interrogates this notion: the way that women's bodies often seem to belong to others—to society, to spouses, and to children, but also to capitalism—and in the service of the demands of others. What does it mean to live in a body that is not your own and, of course, is only yours? Kater uses the metaphor of *carne* or flesh to subdivide the film into five chapters, each titled after familiar terms used to describe the cooking temperatures of meat: raw, medium rare, medium, medium well, and well done. By creating parallels between women's bodies and terms of preference for cooked flesh, Kater draws our attention both to the idea of preference and to the objectification of women's bodies. For whom do women manipulate their bodies? How do external pressures and preferences determine women's sense of worth and value?

The progressive nature of change also comes to the foreground in *Carne*, which pairs each cooking temperature with a stage in women's lives: childhood, puberty, adulthood, postmenopause, and aging. At each of these stages, women face the realities of biology, but even here the film is careful to acknowledge that race, gender, and sexual expression produce diverse experiences of embodiment among those who identify as women. From the outset, Kater knew she wanted to create an animated film with subchapters that would feature unique profiles based on real women's experiences. Her goal was to create an expansive, intersectional film that would cover significant bodily transformations that many people who identify as women share throughout their lives. The interview subjects were either personal connections or women in the film crew—all women—found through research or personal contacts on social media. Each of them narrates an experience from a particular stage of life. The film thus combines documentary interviews with various animation techniques to achieve the familiar and urgent goals of social-issue documentaries: to give voice, to raise awareness, and to bridge the personal with the political and the individual with the collective.

The first chapter, "*Crua*," or "Rare," centers on Raquel Patrício, who tells the story of growing up fat under the scornful eye of her mother, a nutritionist. The animation, by Kater herself, features a ceramic plate on a tablecloth, which we view from overhead. Centered in the frame, the plate serves as a canvas on which the painted drawings come to life while the tablecloth changes in the background. A vibrant exchange emerges between the animated paintings on the plate and the pattern and color shifts in the background. As a formal device, the plate also limits the frame, hinting at the constriction of choices girls experience beginning at a young age: eat this, play that, look pretty. The ceramic plate, like the porcelain doll that appears later in the segment, is aesthetically pleasing but also fragile, easily broken under the weight of external pressures. Each segment of *Carne* features formal choices that evoke poignant themes—in this case, constraint, vulnerability, damage, and the challenge of self-actualization.

The second chapter, "Medium Rare," which focuses on puberty and menstruation, features animated watercolor paintings by Giovana Affonso with narration and experience by Larissa Rahal. In the first image, a spot of red paint bleeds into the white page, spreading, in Kater's words during an interview with the authors, to create "an uncontrollable form."[4] Conversations and pressures from school friends reappear here, as well as the mother. In this case, however, the mother is supportive and kind, guiding her daughter through an extraordinary change. Even when Rahal discovers that her mother has taken photographs of her first stained undergarments, the daughter is understanding. Menstruation makes her feel connected to generations of women throughout history in a positive, beautiful way. The watercolor paintings center on a young girl floating in white space who matures as she rotates on screen. As the chapter concludes, a series of women with varying body shapes and skin colors appear and disappear, signaling a connection between them.

The third chapter, "Medium," created in motion graphic digital 2D animation, centers on a Black trans woman, Raquel Virginia. The color palette is grounded in a warm brown color, and heavy line drawing dominates the graphic style animated by Flavia Godoy. At stake is the vulnerability of the Black trans body and the responsibility she feels to mitigate the discomfort and fear others experience in response to her. Virginia describes the challenge of controlling energies that she does not necessarily know how she generates. In one series of images, the body becomes a steak on a rotating spit on television screens—the narrator points to the hypersexualization of Black women's bodies, obvious in the discrepancy between their screen appearances: they never appear as regular women on telenovelas, but they gyrate and dance during carnival. The television screens seem to glitch with the competing demands and energies until a woman breaks out of one of the screens in boxing gear as if menacing the status quo. In another section, the voice-over describes the fact that transwomen are at the bottom of the social pyramid. On screen, a woman is closed in by three lines in the shape of a triangle. The soundtrack includes the sounds of heavy metal objects, giving the lines a sense of weight as they begin to fold in, crushing on the figure at the center. She is increasingly squeezed by the lines that eventually collapse on her completely.

The film also celebrates bodily change and offers a positive message, especially about aging. Embracing change and physical signs of aging in a culture obsessed with youth and beauty does not come readily to most women. Hence, the final segments of the film stage a feminist reclamation of the phases of life in which women often feel invisible, damaged, or disregarded because of their age. Animated by Cassandra Reis, "Medium Well" employs clay as a screen on which to manipulate changing images of women. Clay, like the body, is sensitive to temperature, moisture, and time, changing in ways parallel to women's bodies through perimenopause and menopause. Significantly, this chapter is told from the perspective of Valquiria Rosa, a woman who describes herself as a lesbian without children. In voice-over, she describes the work of fighting medical professionals for the right to keep her uterus when her doctors tell her that she might as well remove it. The chapter is a celebration of the new life inaugurated by menopause.

The final chapter, "Well Done," draws out the connections between celluloid and human skin and features Helena Ignez, a star of Brazilian cinema from the 1960s, animated directly on film stock by animator Leila Monsegur. Monsegur applied paint to a film strip from *A Mulher de Todos* (1969). In the film, Ignez plays a character who dreads aging. Yet, in her voice-over, Ignez seems at peace with her aging body, which she describes as a borrowed, material gift that she cares for, and which houses her "eternal and infinite" spirit.

Carne emphasizes forms of discursive and epistemic violence—the oppressive norms about beauty, health, and desirability that women face in the home, school, medical establishment, and the media. Yet Kater's film also helps us understand how ideas and stereotypes take hold of women in both psychic and physical ways and sometimes lead to violence from those who feel threatened (as Virginia describes). Each of the chapters is linked by the theme of transformation, which occurs in stages or chapters of the body as it ages. This transformation is initiated by social and collective experiences and leads

Figure 4.1 Debjani Mukherjee, *Awakening the Goddess* (2020) reproduced with the permission of Debjani Mukherjee (left). Camila Kater, *Carne* (2019). Reproduced with the permission of Camila Kater (right).

the women to see themselves in a new light, empowered and stronger than they started (Figure 4.1).

Debjani Mukherjee and *Awakening the Goddess* (2020)

Debjani Mukherjee commits to both documentary and animation as forms of creative social protest. In step with the long history of documentary filmmaking, Mukherjee aims to create films that have a social impact and raise awareness about pressing issues, especially those that affect women and social and ethnic minorities. Before making *Awakening the Goddess,* Mukherjee worked in Myanmar as an animation mentor at the Yangon Film School (YFS). Founded by Lindsey Merrison, an Anglo-Burmese filmmaker, YFS provides media training, especially in documentary filmmaking, for young people in the country's former capital (2020: np). They made a series of animated films, which she describes as ethnographic, each with its particular style: sand, textiles, hand painted. This experience focused on raising awareness about the ubiquity of rape as a political weapon in times of war, which resonated with her own experience. But these were her students' films; she also felt she needed to make a film of her own. Similar to Camila Kater, Mukherjee describes her inspiration as an idea, a reaction to the difficulties she had both heard and experienced that she needed to "get out of her system."[5]

For Mukherjee, animated documentaries offer the possibility of going beyond the literal articulation possible in more traditional documentary films and in filmed interviews, for example. Putting the camera in front of people in a traditional filmed interview setting creates barriers, discomforts, and eruptions of performance that animation can liberate because of the various ways that animation goes beyond the restricted qualities of the real. Mukherjee appreciates the way that animation provides the ability to traverse the physicality and materiality of spaces and bodies, to move beyond the physical reality into the realm of emotion and affect, into shame and anger, for example, which are both prominent in *Awakening the Goddess*.

Awakening the Goddess is as much a confrontation with the sexism that pervades women's lives as a utopian response to it. Her initial inspiration was to use the human body as a canvas since so many ideas about gender, the body, and value are literalized by the human figure—written on the body. The short film opens with a voice-over on a black screen. "You don't know your body is very inviting. Your gestures are very inviting." Slowly, the nude torso and head of a woman fade into view. She looks over her shoulder, her right hand covering her heart. As her hand moves, frame by frame, down toward her breast, hand-written words are slowly revealed: PRUDISH, AUNTY, ASKING, BITCH, SLUT. The central visual image in the film is the woman's body, which is slowly layered with paint and markings, serving as a canvas that will make visible and legible the gendered demands and degradations of a sexist society. In *Awakening the Goddess*, Mukherjee imagines the revolving body as the cinematic manifestation of the sense, no doubt familiar to many women, of being surrounded and invaded by damaging ideas about the body.

In the audio track, several women in three languages, Bengali, Hindi, and English, share their personal experiences with sexual harassment and physical and verbal abuse, including childhood sexual abuse and rape. The collage of voices, which Mukherjee composed from excerpts sent to her by various women, builds into a tense chorus, intensified by the accompaniment of a percussion crescendo. To create the soundscape, Mukherjee sent out a call on social media for women to send her audio recordings. She asked them to record one moment in their lives when they had been put down, made to feel bad, or experienced something that had made them angry and left them with a need to speak out. She assured volunteers that they would remain anonymous. The seven women who responded recorded themselves in the comfort and privacy of their own homes and revealed an openness that transmitted a special kind of intimacy, the kind only possible when you are speaking to yourself or a trusted friend. The soundscape that results is an audio collage of those shared experiences—as unique as they are familiar to many women in India and across the globe.

Throughout the animated film, markings continuously build upon each other on the woman's body. The initial text is soon joined by a dark mass of squiggles, a blot of dark confusion, which grows as the woman's body rotates and finally transforms into black handprints that soon cover her back, which now faces the camera. "The touch of his fingers . . . the next step was rape." A replication of a barcode appears on her cheek, indicating the objectification and commodification of the woman's body. She applies red lipstick, manifesting the cinematically familiar image of a sexualized woman preparing her image, but this is not a simple neoliberal vindication of "the choice" to be sexy. The lipstick soon smears and comically (or tragically) covers her chin and cheeks. Patterns of red lipstick bars show up on her cheeks, forehead, and neck. The tone shifts from an erotic moment of performance to a sudden danger zone. Warning: "Drums and women are meant to be beaten up."

As the film nears its conclusion, a transformation takes place. Patterns of interlocking triangles, reminiscent of the sign for toxic waste, cover her torso, then her face, gradually filling in the negative space with more black paint, which eventually covers her entire torso and face.

"You provoke me and then you get beaten up." Over the black paint, her lips remain painted. Three yellow lines appear on her forehead and then chest. Yellow hands materialize on her arms, chest, and then her neck. She contorts as if choking, but in fact, she is transforming. The lips disappear into the black paint, and with wide eyes, she sticks out her tongue and raises the palm of her hand, covered also in orange paint. Wind blows back her hair, wild. She has become the goddess Kali in a transformation, which, according to the text on screen, "symbolizes the voice within. It pervades all boundaries of caste, class, race, religion and gender."

In the end, Kali is a metaphor, Mukherjee says, for the ways that the demure Indian woman (a damaging stereotype, she insists) can remove that outer layer of the body—"the skin that is scarred and marked and abused by other people."[6] For Mukherjee, Kali's emergence signals a moment of protest and manifests the tension between the important range of female goddesses who are worshiped and the reality that ordinary women are demeaned in a society that is often sexist and misogynistic. Kali comes into that mythological circle by protesting and raising her voice.

Mukherjee appreciates and anticipates the way global audiences may interpret the work in their own ways, informed uniquely by their context. Even the goddess Kali can be interpreted in different ways. For the same reasons, she feels it is also not necessary to translate every single word. For Mukherjee, what matters is the visualization and possibility of protest, which for her is a transnational gesture—all societies around the globe experience, to varying degrees of possibility, social protest. Women are not merely passive receivers of misogyny and abuse; they have the capacity to react, respond, protest, and change the material reality that oppresses them.

Thus, Mukherjee embraces the word "feminism" to describe her work. "Even though I dream of a humanist society, I feel the need for such a community of women who make films despite all odds, speak about 'women' and give voice to the unspoken."[7]

The film is dedicated to her daughter and by extension future generations of women. She had taken her infant daughter on the original trip to Myanmar, which inspired *Awakening the Goddess*. Despite her work guiding activist animated film projects, she felt helpless listening to the stories of the women she interviewed and deeply concerned about the future her daughter would inherit. She observed that the film is a way of preparing her daughter for an uncertain future, but one likely to continue to evidence traces of the gendered violence that has affected so many women we all know. Her message to her daughter, and to all of us, is to be like Kali. Keep your voice. As a filmmaker, Mukherjee is neither helpless nor voiceless. In her feminist animations, she hurls her voice into the world and encourages others to do the same.

Urška Djukić and Emilie Pigeard and *Granny's Sexual Life* (2021)

Granny's Sexual Life (2021) is an animated documentary directed by Urška Djukić and Émilie Pigeard, based on the anonymous testimonies collected by Milena Miklavčič in her book *Ogenj, rit in kače niso za igrače* [Fire, Ass, and Snakes Are Not Toys]. The book was published in Slovenia in the 1970s and does not yet have an English translation. The author claims to have interviewed more than 2,000 women in their eighties and nineties about their sexual experiences as young women growing up in rural Slovenia. *Granny's*

Sexual Life is narrated by four older women, who share memories inspired by testimonies from the book. The short film shines a light on the youth and intimacy of these women, who could be our grandmothers. The directors invite viewers to reflect on these women's experiences from a relatively recent past through humor, shock, and a clever combination of fiction, documentary, and animation.

The film starts with the voice of an older woman over a black screen saying in Slovenian, subtitled in English, "I grew up in a time when a woman's greatest virtue was that she was quiet and didn't speak when it wasn't expected from her." Fade in, and a series of old black-and-white photographs framed on women's hands—frozen in time capturing what appears to be their wringing hands—are displayed one after another. The association between the voice and the images invites us to reflect on what we hear and what we see, helping us situate the voice and the image in time and space, and contextualizing what we are about to experience. The transition of every new photograph is accompanied by a subtle, bouncing, intriguing sound interruption. Feet of men and women, as sections of the same images, appear next. Then, a crackling sound, suggesting an old slide projector, introduces a new sequence of images: extreme close-ups of men's mouths. In the fourth image of that sequence, the sound of a woman's laughter is mixed with the sound of a child humming, while a drawn mustache appears on the man's face. The image then transitions to a childlike drawing style of animation, with a little girl seated on a chair drawing on top of photographs in what appears to be a humble Christian house as revealed by the cross on the wall and the image of a farm from the window. From the outset, the film moves between techniques drawn from documentary, live-action, and animated filmmaking to bring to life a very real history of women's sexual oppression and violence.

Bookended by sequences that use documentary photographs, *Granny's Sexual Life* tells most of its story through hand-drawn animation. The children's drawing-like style is a trademark of Émilie Pigeard's animations. It was her scribbled, smeared cartoon technique that caught Djukić's attention when they met in Sicily at the Magma Short Film Festival. Pigeard was launching her debut short animation *Encore un Gros Lapin?* (Big Bunny Again?, 2016). Pigeard stretches, moves the characters, and creatively transitions from one scene to another. In *Granny's Sexual Life*, the characters are made from basic shapes. The minimalist environment is surrounded by asymmetric forms, and the lines are jagged. There are always signs of smudging to reinforce that the drawings are not clean. However, the seemingly naive representation allows Pigeard to create a universe of her own. A robust woman contained inside a house doing her daily chores while waiting for her husband to arrive, phallic tree shapes, and soldiers wearing testicular hats all reinforce the visual metaphors and suggest the survival strategies and solutions these women had to find to survive their inescapable fate. Perspective, space, proportions, and other standard drawing concepts are broken as the animation twists, expands, and shrinks to reconstruct itself in a new scene.

Djukić also realized that sound could be a very powerful strategy for engagement with the content of the film, particularly in moments when it could be hard to use images to portray the violence of some of the experiences. In the story, one of the women is questioned by the priest about why it has been two years since she was last pregnant. Tormented by the church and the social pressure, the narrator insists that she would never have denied her husband's pleasure (that was never an option). The screen becomes dark, and each woman narrating the story remembers how painful the intercourse was and how their pleasure was never considered. They were forced to submit to their husbands' desires. The scene continues in the dark with only the sounds of a door creaking, male grunts and groans, followed by heavy breathing, reaching a climax. The scene lasts one minute, and for the audience, it may feel too long and unbearable to listen to, but we immediately understand what is happening to the character, and even though we are powerless in this situation, the surprise of that moment forces us to reflect on women's sexual violence. For some, it may even bring back painful memories. After seeing the film and the black screen rape scene at a public screening, the author of the book, Milena Miklavčič, told Urška Djukić how powerful and accurate that scene was. For her, listening to these sounds in the dark references many children's experiences at the time as sound witnesses of the violence their mothers endured.[8]

The film opens and closes with the same photographs. But when they reappear in the end, we see the faces of the women whose hand gestures we were previously introduced to. There are no smiles, just deep, sorrowful eyes looking back at us. The images displayed in the film do not correspond to the women whose stories have been shared in the film, although they may serve as documentation of behaviors and demeanors of the past. They were selected by

Djukić from a photographic archive in Slovenia of women and families from the same period as the stories.

Djukić ended up choosing images that were all taken by the same photographer or photographic company. Traditionally, photographs certify reality and endow a film with a documentary quality. However, in the short, the most realistic images are fictional, and the animation, although stylized and playful, poignantly represents the reality expressed in the women's testimonies from the book. The film connects fact and fiction to bring attention to issues that are still happening today. On the other side, animation, which is typically categorized as fiction, was the element most directly connected to the documentary aspect of the film, illustrating the experiences narrated.

Since most interviewees were by then deceased, Djukić hired actors to read a selection of stories she had edited from the book. One of those actors was a ninety-two-year-old actress who also shared her personal story when recording the audio. In the end, four women and two voice actors (one male and one female) played the roles. The animation helped to enhance the emotion and added a humorous element to some of the scenes, representing forms of violence that would be unbearable to watch in live-action. In terms of dramaturgy, Urška Djukić believes that the playful balance between unburdening the audience with humor compensates for the times when she burdens them with the cruel reality of these women's experiences, as in the black screen rape scene. For her, the film portrays a documentary topic through fictional representation. Djukić and Pigeard do consider the film a feminist animation. However, they believe the term is still taboo. They are proud to help give voice to the repressed and hope that the film will bring awareness to sexual violence against women, a pressing reality for many women worldwide.

During our interview, Djukić shared a story about an elderly man who watched the film in Slovenia and was radically opposed to it, saying that it never happened that way. She suggested he read Milena Miklavčič's book, and after some time, he read the book and returned to her to apologize, becoming a defender of women's rights. The film was shown in numerous festivals worldwide and has been awarded and acclaimed by audiences, demonstrating that a local and specific, well-told story can have a transnational appeal (Figure 4.2).

 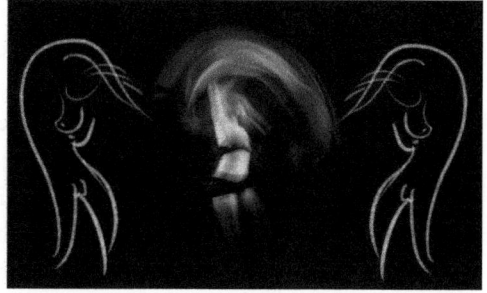

Figure 4.2 Urška Djukić and Emilie Pigeard, *Granny's Sexual Life* (2021). Reproduced with permission of Emilie Pigeard (left). Zeynep Akcay, *KAM* (2020). Reproduced with permission of Zeynep Akcay (right).

Zeynep Akcay and *KAM* (2020)

The opening sound of howling in *KAM* leads us to witness a fictitious ritual. Over a black background, a live-action woman appears photographed in sequential-long exposure movements, framed and retained in a box made of white lines. Breathing heavily, she will soon break free from those framing lines. Energized, she floats in space, while animated white lines drawn over her image change into different shapes as she dances. The drumbeats of ritualistic sounds set the animation's pace. She breaks into a celebratory power dance to release herself.

As the Turkish filmmaker and scholar Zeynep Akcay, animator of *KAM*, shared in her interview with the authors, the film allows the character power to explode, dance, and celebrate the festive energy that, for Akcay, is part of the Turkish spirit.[9] In the director's words, "Kam, which means 'shaman' in old Turkish, was conceived as a response to the rise of conservative and misogynist official discourse in Turkey, and it features a woman's fierce dance."[10] As Zeynep Akcay explained in her article about the film, the piece was created as the director's response to the growing oppressive discourses around women's rights in Turkey and worldwide:

> According to Didem Unal Abaday (2020), the rise of right-wing populism in Europe and over the world, especially in recent years, has brought a new wave of "familialist, pronatalist and anti-feminist" (2020) discourses in politics. Such discourse praises the family and positions women as the primary ones responsible for maintaining its functioning; encourages married women

to give birth; and limits access to birth control and reproductive freedoms. The same patterns are easy to spot in contemporary Turkey, where the conservative turn in politics is becoming increasingly authoritative and misogynist. Starting with restrictive regulations against abortion, the aggressively sexist politics of the ruling Justice and Development Party under Recep Erdoğan have recently culminated in Turkey's withdrawal from the Istanbul Convention, the world's first binding treaty to prevent domestic violence, despite the country being one of the first signatories on 11 May 2011 in Istanbul. (Amnesty International, 2021; 2021: 70)

Although grounded and inspired by an oppressive reality, this piece may initially be seen as the most disconnected from traditional documentary practices among the works presented here. The animated film in itself does not include voice-over, interviews, data, images, or any explicit reference to gender politics or nation. However, if we consider, as Honess Roe puts it, that in a documentary, "it is more interesting to ask what aspects of reality are being conveyed, and how that is being done [instead of representing reality]" (2013: 22), Akcay's work fits as a creative response to the collective feelings and grievances of women for centuries. Additionally, if we consider that documentaries document and share "truth," her film tries to reconnect with a truthful relationship with the world, calling for change even if the call is not direct. The vibrancy and energy of her visuals, combined with the music, communicate something more intrinsic and primal, resonating with audiences. As Akcay puts it: "In this film, besides watching the spectacle of transformations and interplay of 'contour' and liminal representations, the viewer also witnesses a visceral expression of the potency of female anger in rejecting any fixed form/identity" (2021: 70). In one way or another, we have all experienced such anger, and Akcay attempts to represent those feelings as physical transformations incorporated into the character's body at each metamorphosis. The dancer, aided by the animation, sets her body free in ways one could not achieve in reality. In transforming from a wolf to an eagle to a naked woman wearing a shaman headpiece, the dancer reconnects with the shamanic energies of pagan rituals that unapologetically celebrate the body and beauty of being a woman.

By animating long-exposure still images, Akcay tries to capture the moment of rupture when the woman breaks into dance, an explosion of her anger and rebellious spirit. Ironically, this celebratory dance is made of static images that burst into flashes of color and smeared shapes, creating unique animated movements in a combination of long-exposure pixilation and 2D animation. The technique allows the dancer (Sevinç Baltali) to float in space, suspended mid-air, sometimes with multiplied limbs and body parts that can no longer be confined to one body. These combined techniques amplify the dancer's movement, reinforced by the overlapping animated lines, suggesting a reconnection with a powerful female essence that plays, dances, and changes in and out of the dancer's body. These white lines also mark the director's interference with the original material, animating on top of the long-exposure sequential photographs. They add character and meaning to the dancer's expression, moving and mutating around her as a mischievous spirit finally set free.

In a way, the film visually encourages the viewer to restore a connection, allowing the woman to find and reconnect with herself. For Akcay, the visceral feeling the film inspires has a feminist and feminine energy. There is an ambiguous relationship between the line drawing and the dancer until a point when the drawing possesses the dancer and sets her free to express her anger and joy. In *KAM*, the animation allows the dancer to portray her inner truths, also as an extension of the animator's intentions, adding layers of expression and meaning to the piece. The female vocals of Amolvacy, an underground group from New York, in their song *ho-ho-kus,* add sonorous weight to the piece and help define the animation's timing. Akcay mentioned, "the song, which features explosive female vocals, was chosen especially because of its modern interpretation of tribal themes," reinforcing the ritualistic nature of the piece, reconnecting with something old yet still relevant today. For Akcay, *KAM* can be interpreted as an activist animation or even a feminist animation. It is also a collaboration between two women (her and the dancer) expressing their feelings in their unique way. Her films have no dialogue as she aims for accessibility to a transnational global audience.

From readings in anthropology, Akcay discovered the *liminal transformation* concept associated with tribal societies and rituals on the threshold between old and new, which translates well to the metamorphosis concept in animation, where, visually, a character or shape can change into another. Dance is very important in these transformational rites of passage as the movement expressed by a dancer reflects and expresses the observation of their surroundings. It connects us back to nature and the observation of animals, replicating their movements and rituals, helping us to make sense of the world around us in a way that our primal ancestors did. Dance celebrates and reconnects us with such rituals. While the meaning of those rituals may have lost its original message, expressing ourselves through dance is still a performance represented in Akcay's film as an embodied animation. Yet, *KAM* is, for Akcay, more contemporary and, in many ways, more punk, which is a culture that she relates to. Seeing the film through the lens of punk culture allows us to identify with its rebellious nature, often associated with a non-conformist view of society, celebrating individual freedom over societal norms and regulations that reinforce injustices.

Conclusion

Though each of the shorts analyzed here is unique, together they announce a surge of new creative and scholarly work in animation by socially engaged international women creators who invite the public to critically reflect upon forms of gendered and sexual oppression that persist in both local and global contexts. As Formenti sustains, "Although it is just a little more than two decades since it began receiving scholarly attention, the animated documentary can thus count today on a vibrant and growing body of literature" (2022: 3). This expansion of scholarship on animated documentaries mirrors the proliferation of films produced in the genre, which reinforce the power of animation to *represent the unrepresentable* and thereby establish a visceral and emotional connection with the audience. They share, expand upon, and literally draw the different manifestations of oppression and violence endured by women across the globe in the hope that awareness will inspire change and contribute to healing the traumas of the past and those we anticipate in the future. As optimistic as this interpretation may be, interviews with the animators and analyses of their work lead us to believe that feminist animation definitely has a social impact on artists, collaborators, audiences, and the industry and thus the potential to contribute to feminist worldmaking, both materially and conceptually. Over twenty years ago, Sandra Law ascertained, "until recent decades, the animated female images that were available to female audiences were those that existed in the mind's eye of their predominantly male creators" (1997: 67). Today, feminist animators create art that engages with the power of the real to expose the gendered oppression women continue to face around the globe. They also create representations of women who find ways to resist, respond, and rebuild and thereby reclaim their narratives and their subjectivity. As Sharon Couzin reveals, "what is important at this point in animation is to recognise the significance of women artists who take risks in creating work which radically intrudes on conventional forms, traditional 'plots,' especially for women, and conventional expectations from cinema" (1997: 81).

In feminist animation, women's bodies crack, break, explode, fly, take up, and transform private and public space, producing expanded possibilities and new forms of feminist worldmaking. This playful and poignant "fictional" representation of emotion, memory, trauma, and hope creates visually engaging and impactful non-fictional experiences for global audiences. At a time when there's a sense of uncertainty about the future viability of documentary, animated documentaries, "small and strange," may be the future of the form (Kohn 2023: np).

Acknowledgments

The authors express their gratitude toward the animators and directors who kindly offered their time to discuss and share their animated documentaries. We would also like to acknowledge the generosity of Annabelle Honess Roe and Julie Ann Crommett, who provided valuable feedback on earlier versions of the text, leading to its final version. Finally, we extend our thanks to the students from the Women in Animation UTD student club, who partnered with us and engaged in discussions in 2022 during the event that laid the foundation for this article.

Notes

1. They recently signed an agreement with UNESCO to support global gender parity and inclusion in animation. More information is available at: https://womeninanimation.org/wia-unesco/
2. The Increasing Inclusion in Animation report is available at: https://assets.uscannenberg.org/docs/aii-inclusionanimation-201906.pdf
3. Article from United Nations Women, available at: https://www.unwomen.org/en/what-we-do/ending-violenceagainst-women/facts-and-figures#notes

4 Camila Kater (animator) in an online conversation with the authors on April 20, 2023.
5 Debjani Mukherjee in an online conversation with the authors on April 25, 2023.
6 Debjani Mukherjee in an online conversation with the authors on April 25, 2023.
7 Debjani Mukherjee in a personal communication with the authors via email, April 26, 2023.
8 Animators in conversation with the authors online on April 17, 2023, with Émilie Pigeard and on May 4, 2023, with Urška Djukić.
9 Zeynep Akcay in conversation with the authors online on April 26, 2023.
10 Ibid.

5

Affective Relations and First-Person Enunciation

Daughters/Filmmakers Reformulate the Latin American Documentary

Lorena Cervera

As Julianne Burton notes, "nowhere have the manifestations of documentary been as multiple and their impact so decisive as in Latin America" (1990: 6). Even though Burton was referring to the corpus of documentary films produced as part of the film movement known as the New Latin American Cinema in the 1960s and 1970s, since then and especially since the turn of the millennium, the Latin American documentary has continued to expand. This phenomenon is not unique to the region. In the twenty-first century, documentary industries across the world are providing new funding opportunities, training programs, and distribution and exhibition channels. As a result, the number of commercially released documentary films has increased significantly (Chanan 2007). Alongside this, there has been a call to diversify these industries. Within the Latin American context, some organizations have approved measures and policies that seek greater gender parity in the allocation of resources and funding, which in turn has enabled more women to access directorial and other roles (Ivanov et al. 2021).[1] However, often, women filmmakers do not wish to be pigeonholed as such in an attempt to resist confinement. And the study of documentary cinema in the region seldom incorporates a gender perspective, with few notable exceptions that have, nevertheless, shown an "aware[ness] of the dangers of ghettoising women and their work" (Martin and Shaw 2017: 2).[2]

If the history of film is mostly written without gendered nouns despite being predominantly dominated by male directors and written by male critics and scholars, why should the study of contemporary documentary cinema be gendered? This chapter builds on the idea that looking at Latin American documentary cinema through a gender lens brings into focus a corpus of films that, despite its importance, has been sidelined. For instance, recent publications on Latin American documentaries pay little attention to films directed by women or other marginalized (gender) identities for the matter.[3] And those works that look primarily at films directed by women rarely acknowledge whether and, if so, how the director's gender identity informs the making of films. By incorporating a gender perspective into the analysis of contemporary Latin American documentary cinema, I am not claiming that women—understood as a socially constructed gender identity open to ongoing change and contestation (Butler 1990)—make essentially different films, as already pointed out by Lisa French (2021). However, as with any artistic practice, a filmmaker's gaze is informed by experiences that are, inevitably, traversed by their gender as well as other traits of their identity. Furthermore, the exploration of how a filmmaker's gaze is situated within a given context and nurtured by specific experiences is particularly relevant in the analysis of contemporary Latin American documentary films.

In the last decades, Latin American cinema has turned toward stories that foreground personal experiences, intimate spaces, and affective relations in what B. Ruby Rich referred to as a "shift from 'exteriority' to 'interiority'" ([1991] 1997: 281).[4] This shift was accompanied by a change in the mode of enunciation, as pointed out by Beatriz Sarlo. Although writing more broadly about cultural texts, Sarlo employed the concept of the *subjective turn* to refer to the prominence of autobiographic accounts in the telling of the tragic events that shaped the history of Argentina in the 1960s and 1970s. These lingering memories are ideologically and conceptually rearranged in cultural artifacts written or produced not by those who directly suffered the violence perpetrated by or under the authoritarian regimes of the time, but as perceived by their children (2005).

Similarly, Marianne Hirsch uses the concept of *postmemory* to "characterize the experience of those who grow up dominated by narratives that preceded their birth, whose own belated stories are evacuated by the stories of the previous generation shaped by traumatic events that can be neither understood nor recreated" (1997: 22). Drawing from these ideas, within the field of documentary, several scholars have used the term *postmemory* to refer to the growing corpus of films directed by the children of disappeared militants, the so-called "second generation" (Lazzara 2009; Nouzeilles 2005; Page 2005; Ramírez 2010; Tadeo Fuica 2015; Llanos 2016). These films are preoccupied with the convulsive events of the 1960s and 1970s, but unlike the militant films of the time, they deal with the emotional residue of these violent decades as felt and perceived by themselves and their families.

Many *postmemory* documentaries are, as Bernardina Llanos contends, directed by the daughters of disappeared fathers/militants.[5] These films, she argues, mobilize affect "to explore the subjective dimension of postmemory" (2016: 244) while also contesting the "metanarratives based on the revolutionary ideal of the 'New Man'" (p. 248). Expanding Llanos's observation, in this chapter, I analyze three debut films that are enunciated from the daughter/filmmaker's perspective and are constructed, more broadly, around the figure of the father. Agustina Comedi's *El silencio es un cuerpo que cae* [*Silence Is a Falling Body*] (Argentina, 2017) unveils family secrets related to her late father's dissident sexuality; Ana Isabel Bustamante's *La asfixia* [*Asphyxia*] (Guatemala, 2018) traces her father's disappearance at the hands of the Guatemalan state while her mother was pregnant with her; and Mercedes Gaviria's *Como el cielo después de llover* [*The Calm After the Storm*] (Colombia, 2021) constructs a family portrait in between a daughter's love for her father and a filmmaker's aspirations in a male-dominated industry.[6] Somehow still entangled in the patriarchal ideologies that regard the legacy of the father as more valuable, these daughters/filmmakers also confront this legacy by pointing to the difficulties of being women within the family, in the film industry, and in society at large. Drawing from the works of cultural and documentary theorists such as Marianne Hirsch, Judith Butler, and Alisa Lebow, in the following analyses, I contend that these films are part of a feminist genealogy of documentaries that put the emphasis on the situated self to interrupt long-lasting silences, master narratives, and dominant regimes.

Agustina Comedi's *El silencio es un cuerpo que cae* (Argentina, 2017)

When Agustina Comedi was born in 1986, her father bought a handheld camera and became an avid amateur filmmaker. He recorded family holidays,

Sunday meals, and Agustina's school shows, among other scenes extracted from those special moments in a family's life. He even recorded the fatal moment in which he fell from a horse, an event that caused his premature death in January 1999. *El silencio es un cuerpo que cae* is made mostly out of his footage. These home movies construct a seemingly ideal portrait of an Argentinian family formed by a father (Jaime), mother (Monona), and daughter (Agustina) who are also presented in terms that stress their bourgeois status, as an awarded lawyer, a successful manager of the family estate, and an outstanding student, respectively. However, Agustina re-uses this footage not as a way of "solemnizing and immortalizing the high points of family life" (Bourdieu 1990: 19), but to look at what lies below the surface and to uncover her family secret. In this analysis, I focus on how the director employs different formal devices to reframe the meaning of these home movies and facilitate the journey of understanding her father's sexual identity.[7]

El silencio es un cuerpo que cae opens with a sequence of shots of Michelangelo's David in the Galleria dell'Accademia during a family trip to Italy in the mid-1990s. Jaime's shaky hand zooms in and out, admiring the details of the sculpture with inquisitive movements. His curious observation of David's carved body is interrupted—through Agustina's editing—by a shot of herself as a child rigidly posing next to her mother and below the sculpture. In the shot, she notices the camera and half-smiles. This moment captures the distance that inevitably exists between the person behind and those posing in front of the camera. Agustina and Monona appear in planes, in hotel rooms, and on the streets of the numerous cities they visited during their holiday trips. In these images, mother and daughter perform their gender roles "through corporeal signs and other discursive means" (Butler 1990: 173), that is, through the choice of clothing, poses, and gestures. As the cameraperson, Jaime is always out of frame. His absence from this social reality, in which each gender identity is constructed through repeated social performances, implies a resistance to fully fit into what those images convey. At the same time, it serves as a projection that fulfills society's expectations for heteronormativity. The idea of Jaime as an outsider is stressed through several other scenes in which the camera—held by him—is always looking at a performance from the position of the spectator. Agustina includes several shots of Disneyland shows. One of them captures the part of *Little Mermaid* when Ariel renounces being a siren in order to fit into the outside world as a way of allegorically referring to Jaime's life, who had to renounce his sexual identity to fulfill his desire to become a father (Karrer 2022: 205).

Unlike the revolutionary hero's *macho*-masculinity foregrounded by the figure of Ernesto "Che" Guevara—the Argentinian "New Man" who took part in the Cuban Revolution in 1959—the director's father was queer, and his first sexual and romantic relationships were with men. When at forty, he married Monona to have a child, he kept his bisexuality a secret. Even though Argentina had its democracy restored in the 1980s, Argentinian society was still ruled by heteronormative values. In the film, this context is presented through a series of scenes that illustrate some of the misconceptions that perpetuate stigma toward non-normative sexual identities. One of them captures a school visit to the zoo. Here, Agustina's teacher makes misleading claims about mating rituals as a way of normalizing heterosexuality among animals. Another scene shows how homophobic jokes were widely accepted and laughed at. Such hostile social environments forced the need to hide non-normative sexual orientations, and as the film implies, the social pressure to fit within a heteronormative regime led to the premature loss of the director's father, who died from a fall while riding a horse in front of his friends and family (Figure 5.1).

Agustina only learned about her father's bisexuality a few years after his death when one of his old friends told her: "when you were born, something in Jaime died." This sentence appears written on the screen, and in voice-over, she also says it twice, replacing the "you" with "I." These types of poignant statements punctuate the documentary throughout and are utilized as poetic contestations that interrupt the long silence around non-normative sexual identities. By resorting to a mode of address that is articulated by the filmmaker's first-person enunciation, the film "ruptures the illusion of objectivity so long maintained in documentary practice and reception" (Lebow 2012: 5). Instead, it points to the constructedness of non-fiction films, particularly home movies and how they reproduce certain types of gender performances but conceal others.

Agustina's first-person enunciation interweaves the disparate traits of Jaime's identity. She holds conversations and conducts interviews with relatives who depict him as a family man—who was, nevertheless, perceived as different—and with Jaime's friends, who talk about his involvement in Córdoba's gay scene. They also reveal how they were brutally persecuted by the police

Figure 5.1 *El silencio es un cuerpo que cae* directed by Agustina Comedi © El Calefón Cine 2017. All rights reserved.

during the dictatorship years and were marginalized by leftist comrades who regarded, as Agustina's voice-over points out, gay militants as part of a deviant bourgeoisie that undermined the revolutionary spirit.[8]

To sum up this analysis, in Latin American post-authoritarian countries, new trends in political art broke away from the codes and conventions of 1960's and 1970's militancy to put the emphasis on the vulnerability of the body through an exploration of pain and desire (Polgovsky Ezcurra 2019). *El silencio es un cuerpo que cae* joins these efforts by positioning the intimate and affective as political. Agustina reveals her family secret, and while addressing the loss of her father, she also makes a poignant political statement through both content and form. Reframing her childhood's moving images, she interjects some of the impostures of this well-established middle-class practice. As Hirsch contends, family images often attempt to provide a sense of cohesion, but when incorporated into new cultural texts, they can also expose absences and invisibilities, including "the passions and rivalries, the tensions, anxieties, and problems that have, for the most part, remained on the edges or outside the family album" (1997: 7). By reframing her home movies within twenty-first-century discourses on sexual orientation and gender identity, Agustina points to how these images, despite being extracted from everyday life, construct a fictional narrative and manufacture social performances as dictated by heteronormative regimes that, although still prevalent, can be contested and dismantled.

Ana Bustamante's *La asfixia* (Guatemala, 2018)

Ana Bustamante's film is also constructed around the loss of her father, even though she never met him. Emil was disappeared by the Guatemalan State in 1982 amid the Guatemalan Civil War (1960–96) while Ana's mother was pregnant with her.[9] In *La asfixia*, she visits the locations that her father inhabited and looks closely at the images that capture his existence as if traces of him could be sensed in these spaces and materials. As a first-person documentary, Ana becomes an on-screen vehicular character that guides the narrative. Alisa Lebow states that first-person films "'speak' from the articulated point of view of the filmmaker who readily acknowledges her subjective position" (2012: 1) but nuances that the use of the first person is inherently social as it expresses commonality and interrelatedness (3). Similar to other documentaries directed by the children of disappeared militants from different Latin American countries, Ana appears in the film processing the "irreparable sense of personal loss" (Llanos 2016: 248). However, unlike other *postmemory* documentaries, such as the Argentinian *Papá Iván* (María Inés Roqué, 2000), she does not condemn her father's involvement in the struggle against authoritarianism or his absence from family life. Instead, she instrumentalizes the making of this film as a way of coping with intergenerational trauma and of strengthening the bond with her mother.

For Hirsch, "postmemory is a powerful and very particular form of memory precisely because its connection to its object or source is mediated not through recollection but through an imaginative investment and creation" (1997: 22). *La asfixia* avoids recreating traumatic events and, instead, embraces a poetic use of the visual language that enables an attitude of playfulness. Many of the images included in it are not literal or illustrative of events but figurative or expressive of affections and emotions. The film begins with the burial of a sea turtle in the Guatemalan seashore. The director's voice-over reveals that the corpse of a sea turtle reaching the shore is extremely rare. In most cases, it falls to the sea floor and decomposes. This opening scene serves as a metaphor to account for what escapes representation, that is, for the burial that her father—a lecturer in veterinary science who funded a rehabilitation center for sea turtles—never had (Figure 5.2).

Ana also experiments in the editing to suggest or imply how she felt undertaking such an endeavor. She shows upside-down landscapes to hint at the current state of Guatemala and adds backward effects to signal its regression. She conducts interviews with relatives, attorneys, and other militants in order to find information about her father's disappearance. Her authorial position is asserted through voice-over interjections and editing techniques. For instance, some of the interviewees are, at times, purposely silenced in the editing to avoid including those details that she is not ready to process or does not want to remember. In voice-over, she responds to their discourses with poignant comments that unravel her discontent with the little progress made to find out the whereabouts of her father, even ten years after the legal case was opened and nearly forty years since his disappearance.

Unlike the other two films analyzed in this chapter, *La asfixia* does not include home movies. Accessing cameras in the 1980s was possible only for those from privileged backgrounds. Even though the director's family was

Figure 5.2 *La asfixia* directed by Ana Bustamante © Nanuk Audiovisual 2018. All rights reserved.

part of the bourgeoisie, in the midst of a civil war, documenting daily life was never an option as this footage could be used against them. The film, though, includes some photographs extracted from the family album. They show the Bustamante family prior to her father's disappearance. They also show the director as a fatherless child living with her mother and sister as de facto political exiles in Mexico. The scarcity of family images that can act as tangible memories of her father's existence is contested with an insistence to try to find a moving image of his participation in the resistance during the war.

Ana looks closely at recordings of two historical events where he might have been present: a miners' march and a militant's funeral. In the film, she interacts with this footage—pausing, rewinding, and zooming in—trying to sense him. Her desire to find a trace of him takes her to those locations that Emil inhabited. She goes to the family house where he grew up. The rusty vehicles accumulated on its premises point to the decaying state of something larger. Little remains of the dairy farm that it used to be, but family memories are brought alive in the encounter with her relatives. She also visits the police station where his father and many others were allegedly tortured and killed, only to find out that what once was a place of horror, today is rented out for parties. The frivolity of this reuse hints at the general attitude toward this historical episode. Even though her images fail to show what happened to her father, they achieve something larger, to create an emotional state that seeks a reaction against the spiral of apathy and stagnation toward the country's long-lasting unresolved conflict.

Hirsch contends that second-generation survivors inherit, in one way or another, their parents' trauma, which can unfold in overwhelming and painful burdens (1997). In *La asfixia*, this inherited trauma is rooted not in her father's disappearance per se, but in what her mother felt on that day, a sudden incapacity to breathe, which Ana also experiences. Mother and daughter travel together and hold conversations about issues they have never addressed before. The process of making this film is primarily employed as an opportunity to break her mother's long silence and to deal with painful memories, loss, and intergenerational trauma. This aim is set through a scene that returns to the moment of the disappearance. Instead of imagining and reenacting what might have happened to her father, Ana shows what her mother was doing: cooking a birthday cake for her cousin. Thus, even though *La asfixia* is constructed around the figure of the disappeared militant father, the film's focus is to create a safe space for mother and daughter to be able to speak about traumatic memories. By doing so, Ana defies those patriarchal imperatives that regard the legacy of the father as more valuable and, instead, chooses to look after the difficulties endured by her mother. Despite the emotional upheaval of embarking on a creative project of this kind, the process of filmmaking makes plausible the act of healing for both of them while also pointing at how the brutality of war lingers in the realm of emotions.

Mercedes Gaviria's *Como el cielo después de llover* (Colombia, 2021)

Víctor Gaviria is recognized as one of Colombia's best-known film directors. His films portray different types of violence that take place in Medellín's most deprived communities and are performed by non-professional actors.[10] When his daughter Mercedes decided to become a filmmaker, instead of following in her father's footsteps, she decided to build a career of her own, away from his shadow. After moving to Argentina, she attended film school and began working in sound production. Living abroad gave her the distance to think about her debut film, *Como el cielo después de llover*. This documentary draws a family portrait at the crossroads between a daughter's love for her father and a woman's aspirations in a male-dominated industry. In this analysis, I focus on how the director employs different formal devices, including video diaries, the behind-the-scenes footage from two of her father's films, and her family's home movies, to establish her own filmmaking approach while also contesting the legacy of her father.

Como el cielo después de llover opens with several scenes of Mercedes off-screen recording wild tracks and atmospheric sounds in different locations in Argentina. These images and sounds introduce her as the director of the film while performing her usual job, that of the sound recordist—a so-called below-the-line role within the hierarchy of film production. The way Mercedes introduces herself breaks with the idea of the film director as the primary creative agent of a film, as auteur theory claims. But, paradoxically, by positioning herself as "a user of signs rather than a sign-object" (Butler 1990: 66), she asserts her own authorial voice. However, she does not establish herself as "a center of absolute plenitude and power" (Butler 1990: 159). Instead, she positions her place of enunciation as intrinsically traversed by gender dynamics as well as her upbringing, experiences, and decisions. Employing the form of the video diary, she shows instances of her daily life: the piled books and plants in her flat, the journeys in the subway, and the streets of Buenos Aires. In voice-over, she speaks using the first person to introduce her family, first her mother and then her father. Through on-screen texts, she reproduces fragments of their digital correspondences that promptly shift to the conversations she holds with her father about her role in the shooting of *La mujer del animal* [The Animal's Wife] (Víctor Gaviria, 2016), a film about domestic violence.

Mercedes appropriates the family's home movies—shot by Víctor—to develop her own audiovisual approach. By doing so, she is somehow acknowledging that her father has been key in the development of her fascination for filmmaking while also departing from the epicness of his filmography. These tapes, she says, contain what remains of her childhood memories. Unlike in Agustina's film, Mercedes's home movies are not representations of the high points in a family's life, but everyday moments that capture the complicity that exists between father and daughter. Patricia Zimmermann notes that home movies occupy a contradictory place, as they reproduce conservative values of middle-classness and consumerism, but also offer resistance and hope (1995: ix). *Como el cielo después de llover* also occupies a contradictory place. Mercedes attempts to construct a family portrait but faces opposition from her mother and brother. She refers to her mother's unsettled role within the family and shows her brother's insistent rejection of being filmed. They do not share a fascination for filmmaking and refuse to take an active role in Mercedes's film. She also addresses the marks that others left on her and confesses her feelings of jealousy and confusion when the young actors from the lower classes that rehearsed at her house called her father "dad Víctor." Throughout the film, Mercedes seems to realize that the only way to get close to her father is by obeying his requests, especially by letting him direct. In the home movies, as a little child, she willingly follows Víctor's directions, combing her hair, singing lullabies for her new-born brother, or posing as he dictates (Figure 5.3).

In a different moment of the film, Mercedes includes a series of shots from the behind-the-scenes footage of *La vendedora de rosas* [The Rose Seller] (Víctor Gaviria, 1998)—the film that turned her father into an internationally

Figure 5.3 *Como el Cielo después de llover* directed by Mercedes Gaviria Jaramillo. © Gentil 2021. All rights reserved.

acclaimed film director. She chooses the moment in which a young actor refuses to perform for him, despite his insistence. He becomes increasingly frustrated with her lack of obedience and storms out of frame in anger. This moment offers an insight into a side of Víctor that diverges from the descriptions that others provide. While family members insist on his great sensibility, these other instances unveil the violence of his responses when someone questions his authority. He is shown as a complex man who can navigate social boundaries and seems to be equally comfortable amid poverty in Medellin's shantytowns as enjoying middle-class comfort in the family's holiday home. This hypocrisy is also contested by Mercedes as she struggles to accept his entitlement to film stories that he has never experienced, particularly those related to sexual violence against poor women. Mercedes constructs then a portrait of her father that is ambiguous, paying tribute to their loving relationship, but also, as Thomas Matusiak notes, revealing her unease about how he unapologetically embraces the figure of patriarchal authority (2022).

Even though the film continuously slips into the role of Víctor as a father and film director, she also pays attention to her mother. One of the most haunting moments is when Mercedes reads the ending of a diary that her mother wrote to her before she was born. The last sentence says, "you cannot live like this." Mercedes's mother is referring to the difficulties of living in the shadow of her husband, of being the wife of an absent companion, about whom she constantly worries.

Víctor's absence from domestic life is briefly acknowledged by Mercedes in a voice-over, who states that even when he was at home, he kept himself busy writing scripts or holding heated conversations on the phone with colleagues. She implies that their tumultuous relationship changed her mother irreversibly. In the film, Mercedes listens to her mother's advice and refuses to live under the shadow of her father. By doing so, she is resisting to reproduce those patriarchal values that have governed the family and the film industry and embraces hope for the possibility of formulating new ways of filming and caring.

To conclude, the three films analyzed in this chapter—*El silencio es un cuerpo que cae*, *La asfixia*, and *Como el cielo después de llover*—are emblematic of a shift within documentary practices and discourses in Latin America. What characterizes this shift is the use of the first person to tell stories about vulnerability, pain, and desire as experienced by the filmmakers and their families. Even though these types of films began being made in the last decades of the twentieth century, since the turn of the millennium, many of them are directed by women. What has also changed is that some of these films are articulated, specifically, from the daughter/filmmaker's perspective. As with *postmemory* documentaries, this positionality enables the revisiting of past events that revolve around the figure of the father and whose traumatic effects still linger in the realm of emotions. Yet, looking at these films through a gender lens brings into focus how the daughter/filmmaker's perspective also mobilizes a gender identity to interrupt long-lasting silences around patriarchal ubiquity and heteronormative regimes. Creatively enunciated through a situated gaze nurtured by particular personal experiences and affective relations, which are inevitably traversed by gender dynamics, these films subvert conventions of audiovisual representation. They are part of a feminist genealogy that confronts the imposibles and hypocrisies that continue to undermine women's ever-evolving roles within the family and society. That is, they challenge a legacy that sidelined women's contributions and, by so doing, inscribe their overlooked experiences within the history of film.

Notes

1. For instance, the Ibermedia Program recognizes as a priority the need to promote the active participation of women within the film industry in a twofold manner: by providing financial incentives to those projects that include women and by incorporating more women into their own structure (Berrendo Pérez et al. 2023: 422). In Argentina, the National Institute of Cinema and Audiovisual Arts (INCAA) also approved a gender policy that aims at both reducing asymmetries and promoting participation and equal access for women (Cunha da Cruz and Ciotti 2022). However, changes in government are jeopardizing the progress already made. Similarly, there is an ongoing discussion about having quotas for women's films as well as for those films made by Afro, indigenous, and LGBTIQ+ filmmakers, in film festivals across the region.
2. See, for instance, Lesage (1990); Martin (2012); Cumaná and Lord (2013); Llanos (2016); Bossay and Peirano (2017); Cervera (2022).
3. Among the most recent publications on Latin American documentary are Haddu and Page (2009); Foster (2013); Traverso and Wilson (2013); Navarro and Rodríguez (2014); Arenillas and Lazzara (2016).
4. B. Ruby Rich expands, "in place of the explicitly and predictably political, at the level of labor or agrarian struggles or mass mobilization, we often find an attention to the implicitly political, at the level of banality, fantasy, and desire, and a corresponding shift in aesthetic strategies [which has] opened the field to women" (Rich [1991] 1997: 281).
5. Some of the *postmemory* documentaries directed by the daughters of disappeared fathers/militants focus on stories from Argentina—María Inés Roqué's *Papá Iván* (2000), Albertina Carri's *Los rubios* (2003), and Natalia Bruchstein's *Encontrando a Víctor* (2005); Chile—Alejandra Carmona's *En algún lugar del cielo* (2003) and Macarena Aguiló's *El edificio de los Chilenos* (2010); and Uruguay—Maiana Bidegain's *Secretos de lucha* (2007). The themes of disappearance, absence, militancy, and the father–daughter relationship are also explored in films made by women in other Latin American countries, including Susana Barriga's *La ilusión* (Cuba, 2009), María Fernanda Restrepo's *Con mi corazón en Yambo* (Ecuador, 2011), Marcia Tambutti Allende's *Allende mi abuelo Allende* (2015), and Carolina Arias Ortiz's *Objetos rebeldes* (Costa Rica, 2020).
6. Debut films are complex and revealing as they tend to be crafted with great care, motivation, and risk, albeit also with a certain level of inexperience. The first film allows the trying out of an audiovisual language that, if well received, might become part of a filmmaker's distinctive style. However, many filmmakers

only manage to make one film, as funding opportunities shrink afterward and a filmmaking career solely in directing is, in many cases, financially unsustainable.

7   To avoid confusion, I use the first names to refer to each family member throughout the analysis of the three films.

8   Over these years, a brutal dictatorship known as the Dirty War (1976–83)—backed by the United States-led campaign Operation Condor—tortured, imprisoned, and killed between 9,000 and 30,000 people in an attempt to erase socialist, left-wing, and Peronist ideas.

9   The Guatemalan Civil War was an extremely violent conflict between leftist organizations and the government that led to the disappearance of 45,000 people and the killing of more than 250,000 people, in what is considered a genocide against the Mayan population. In 2013, the former dictator Efraín Ríos Montt was found guilty of genocide in the trial against the perpetrators of the war. Yet, a few weeks later, this decision was overturned by the constitutional court. Ríos Montt eventually died in 2018 without having entered prison. Unlike most of those who were disappeared or killed during the war, Ana Bustamante's father was a middle-class university lecturer who belonged to the intellectual community formed at the University of San Carlos that actively opposed the country's authoritarian turn.

10 Until the ratification of the peace agreement in 2016 and for the most part of the second half of the twentieth century, Colombia suffered from what is known as the Colombian conflict, which refers to the unofficial war between drug trafficking organizations, guerrillas, the paramilitary, and the Colombian government. As a result of the violence perpetrated in different parts of the country over these decades, there were large displacements of people, particularly toward the main cities, which led to the rapid expansion of shantytowns and other informal settlements in Medellín and Bogotá.

6

Politicizing Familial Space

Women's Post-Fukushima Documentaries as the Creation of Counterpublics

Wakae Nakane

A massive earthquake struck the Tohoku region of Japan on March 11, 2011. Not only did the unprecedented scale of the quake bring about destructive damage to vast areas of northeastern Japan, but the resulting tsunami also led to the disastrous accident at the Fukushima Daiichi nuclear power plant, which caused large-scale radioactive contamination.[1] Among the series of events occurring in the triple disaster of the earthquake, the tsunami, and the nuclear meltdown, the radiation has presented peculiar difficulties due to the long-lasting dangers posed by its contamination. As Jean-Luc Nancy points out, nuclear catastrophe "remains the one potentially irremediable catastrophe, whose effects spread through generations, through the layers of the earth" (Nancy 2014: 3). The large-scale and erratic spread of radioactive substances affected people's lives both spatially and temporally even beyond the legally mandated evacuation orders and relocation.[2] At the same time, we have witnessed the rising discourse of *tojisha-shugi* or "affected party-ism," which has been accompanied by the counter-productive attempts to delineate victims and non-victims of the disaster, resulting in a deeper social divide.[3] What's more, the complicated historical legacy of Japan's nuclear policy further divided public opinions and reactions to the accident, which hindered the formation of the public consensus necessary to re-evaluate Japan's nuclear power policy in the aftermath of the disaster.[4]

Fukushima's nuclear catastrophe has also posed representational challenges. Radiation is invisible and odorless, and it cannot be detected by human senses, yet it gradually affects the ecosystem, including human bodies. Radiation lacks the violently spectacular aspect of other catastrophic incidents or an easily discernible body count, whose sensationalistic effects are favored by the mainstream media. Much of the mainstream coverage factually relied heavily on representing devastated coastal landscapes, the people's mourning over the deaths of their loved ones, and the reports of the death toll, which eventually counted up closer to 20,000, including missing people. In addition, although the accident debunked Japan's nuclear safety myth, the government's continuous adherence to prolonging nuclear power operations pressured the obedient mainstream media to underplay the gravity of the situation. The representation of radiation, in this sense, requires different aesthetic strategies, which go beyond the mainstream media's emphasis on the immediate and representable devastation of the tsunami to include the slower process of radioactive violence and its complicated relationship to technology, politics, economy, and history.[5]

Disillusionment with the mainstream media propelled many independent filmmakers to assume responsibility for giving a fuller account of Japan's post-catastrophic situation, with rising awareness of the tensions between private lives, the sociopolitical sphere, and the historical legacies of postwar Japan.[6] One of the noticeable phenomena is the active participation of both professional and non-professional filmmakers, who began documenting themselves, their families, and their communities in the distressed aftermath of 3/11.[7] This proliferation of the first-person style is also associated with the increased participation of female filmmakers, which is remarkable considering the male-dominated film industry's continuous devaluation of women's contributions and their artistic agency. This form of participation, which blurs the line between professionals and amateurs, is interestingly conditioned by the fact that many of them started to record the situation they faced without the intention of making publicly released films. The process of recording in these cases occurred organically, and some of the footage would eventually be turned into films. These films are, in this sense, the result of the ubiquitous presence of recording equipment in our everyday lives and the ways people use it to grapple with the enormity of the situation, which is beyond our capacity to comprehend.

What is remarkable here is the way these documentaries direct our attention to the dialectical relations between the private and the public spheres by revealing the intermingled relations between individual affectivity and the nature of discursive mutual consensus conventionally associated with the public. As Jonathan Kahana argues, "Every encounter with documentary produces a similar connection, or tension, between the singular and the universal" (Kahana 2008: 8). These documentaries precisely capture the singular nature of everyday experience and connect it to wider social concerns by strategically accentuating the inseparable connections between the private and the public.

These first-person documentaries' dialectical representations of public and private life remind us of the longstanding debate on the gendered dichotomy of the public and the private spheres in feminist scholarship. As Seyla Benhabib illuminates, this conceptual division presupposes a corresponding delimitation of the private with the feminized attributions of naturalness and immutability (Benhabib 1992: 13). This binary logic has not only been abused to exclude women from activities in the public sphere, such as opinion formation and decision-making on matters of common interest, but also has devalued the political and emancipatory potentials of the private sphere. Of course, the private sphere can still operate repressively to confine women within dominant societal norms, but its generative potential in its dialectical relations to the public should not be dismissed.

It is noteworthy that many women filmmakers creatively problematize the public/private division and the devaluation of the latter. That is where first-person documentation has served as a critical space for feminist praxis, mirroring the global trend of so-called post-vérité documentaries. There, women filmmakers have actively disrupted the myth of documentary objectivity and impartiality by foregrounding subjective and affective qualities of the personal. This tradition is precisely concomitant to the feminist critique surrounding the public/private. Women's post-Fukushima documentaries are, in this sense, worth examining for drawing our attention to the underrated lineage of women's image-making as well as rethinking the intricate connection between the civic sphere and individual life.[8]

This chapter examines two post-Fukushima first-person documentary films, Tomoko Kana's *A Lullaby under the Nuclear Sky* (*Lullaby* for short, 2016) and Miran Oura's *The Road Home* (2017), to address the following mutually related queries: how do their aesthetics of the personal and their radical rethinking of the public/private binary tackle the difficulties of representing Fukushima? How do they deal with *tojisha-shugi* or "affected party-ism"—the social division between the victim and non-victim concerning the radiation? How have the nuclear catastrophe's intermingled relations to the political, social, and economic been negotiated through cinematic representation?

In *Lullaby*, after interviewing residents in the immediate aftermath of the catastrophe in radioactively contaminated areas of Fukushima to which access had been restricted, the filmmaker discovered that she was pregnant. Centered around her experience of pregnancy and her constant anxiety regarding the potential effects of radiation, she presents her body as having become inextricably intertwined with the sociopolitical situation surrounding the nuclear disaster. In *The Road Home*, the filmmaker, who was forced to evacuate from her hometown in Fukushima after the accident, scrutinizes the concept of a "disaster survivor" by continuously trying to have conversations with her family, especially with her father, who works for the Tokyo Electric Power Company (TEPCO).

One of the aims of the chapter is to clarify an important aspect of the feminist aesthetics of the personal by connecting the question of documentary subjectivity to the discussion on the public sphere and the political media ecology.[9] By doing so, this chapter argues that their shared strategy of disrupting the public/private division creates an alternative public sphere for dialogue that foregrounds the material connectivity of bodies (*Lullaby*) and familial spaces (*The Road Home*). The feminist emphasis on corporeality, familial space, and connectivity beyond geographical distances creates an essential basis for us to think and act in a post-disaster society, in which the illegibility of the connections between individual lives and their political, technological, and social contexts has been a concealed source of anxiousness and helplessness at a moment already defined by endless uncertainties and crises.

Representing the Maternal and the Network of Mothers: *A Lullaby Under the Nuclear Sky*

Lullaby is a documentary film directed by Tomoko Kana, who discovered her pregnancy after holding interviews as a journalist in affected areas in

Fukushima in the weeks following the meltdown, where access had been restricted due to radioactive contamination (Figure 6.1).

Although the threat of radiation made her anxious for her baby's health, she decided to record her pregnancy, childbirth, and childcare experiences. In her voice-over commentary throughout the film, *Lullaby* narrates her experiences both as a journalist and as a mother, culminating in the scenes where she gives birth to her son. Despite its self-financed production format, the film drew relatively wide public attention across Japan and abroad: the film was first shown at the Busan International Film Festival in 2014, which was followed by further international circulation at film festivals. The film was also theatrically released in 2016 in Japan at independent movie theaters and followed by numerous self-organized screening events.

What distinguishes *Lullaby* from other post-Fukushima documentaries is its foregrounding of the gradual shift from the filmmaker's position as an impartial journalistic observer into an inextricably affected individual (*tojisha*) through her maternal experience. According to film critic Ryo Hagino, many post-Fukushima documentaries made immediately after the disaster shared similar formal traits of what he calls "the narrative of arrival" (Hagino 2013: 114) as a cliché of the travelogue or ethnographic film. These documentaries often begin with the scenery viewed from a car window as the filmmakers approach areas struck by the quake. These traveling scenes are

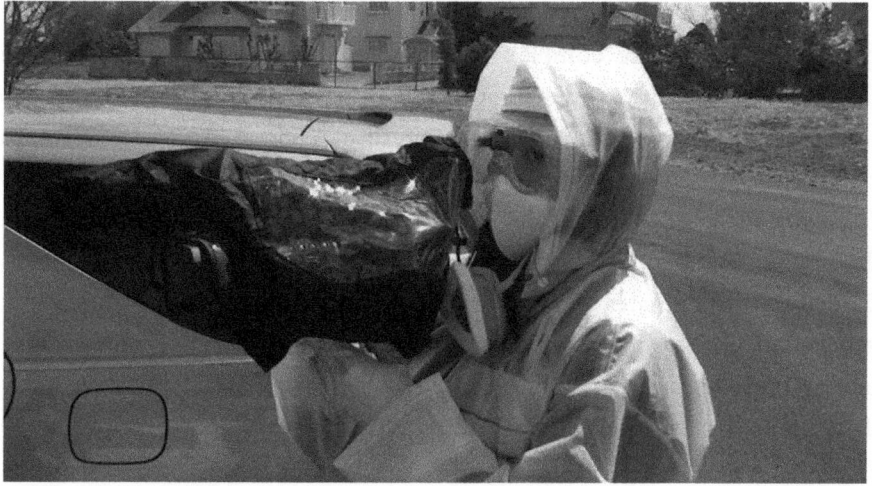

Figure 6.1 *A Lullaby under the Nuclear Sky* by Tomoko Kana. © Horizon Features 2016. All rights reserved.

then followed by the filmmakers' "arrival" at the areas, where they witness and document the affected lives of people and the disastrously changed landscape. A considerable number of these documentaries have portrayed the disaster as something geographically and psychologically distanced from the site where they have everyday lives. The documentary film *311*, directed by Tatsuya Mori, Yoji Matsubayashi, and Takeharu Watai in 2011, exemplifies this category. The film's production was propelled by the filmmakers' journalistic urge to document the scenes of the affected sites. The resulting film consists of a series of devastated landscapes, including areas wiped out by the tsunami, piles of rubble, and a school gymnasium used for placing victims' bodies. "The narrative of arrival" here is endorsed by the observational ethnographic mode through which the filmmakers place themselves as outsiders to the event. For instance, there is a scene where one of the filmmakers approaches a search party to shoot found bodies, and a person throws a wooden block toward the filmmaker, deterring them from approaching and shooting them. This transgressive approach to documenting the disaster is conditioned by the strong delineation of the self and the other. At the same time, the film is reliant mostly on the spectacular scenes of the total destruction of the affected area. The issue of radiation is communicated only through the ominous sound of the Geiger counter, which is activated when they are near the restricted area, which has also become one of the widely used conventions among post-Fukushima documentaries.

Conversely, what is consistent in *Lullaby* is the way it situates the filmmaker within the complex sociopolitical structure surrounding the nuclear disaster. The sequence at the beginning of the film is similar to that in other films using "the narrative of arrival" as it revolves around her journalistic report about Fukushima. However, the difference between *Lullaby* and other documentaries already appears in these initial scenes. The voice-over commentary accompanying the scenes on her way to Fukushima accentuates her socio-historical embeddedness in the situation, especially concerning the sense of guilt she feels for not knowing that the electricity generated in Fukushima was sent to the Greater Tokyo Area. The voice-over mentions, "I realized that my life has been supported by the nuclear power plant in Fukushima. I am also responsible. I should not look away from the situation as an aggressor." This contemplative commentary reveals the city's exploitative treatment of the rural areas, which most urban dwellers had been ignorantly enjoying up until the moment of the fatal disaster.

This sense of responsibility and guilt is, however, gradually replaced by the fear concerning her potential exposure to radiation, which tactically bridges the distance between Fukushima and Tokyo through Kana's emotive and physical reactions. There is a scene, for instance, where she falls ill for an unknown reason soon after discovering her pregnancy. Her voice-over reveals her concerns about her baby's potential exposure, saying, "What have I done? The radiation is imperceptible. I even became scared of breathing." Her maternal experience signals the shift in her experiences of the nuclear disaster. The issues concerning Fukushima start to invade her everyday life beyond the geographical distance or the public/private distinction. The foregrounded sense of fear and anxiety communicates the undetectable nature of radiation by human senses and its threat to her vulnerable maternal body.

The importance of representing the connectivity between her material corporeality and the larger social situation here, however, lies not only in her attempt to represent the intangible nature of radiation but also in its creation of new forms of networks, which mediate and speak for others who share fears of radiation exposure, whose risks have been understated by the mainstream discourse. At first, the familial kinship represented as her emotional ties to her husband, enables her to express her anxiety, pain, and fear at a very personal level. For example, the caretaking nature of the relationship is foregrounded in multiple scenes, where the camera is exchanged from Kana to her husband. Here, the husband sometimes responds to her by gently stroking her back, with the camera in the other hand. The camera's presence in their intimate familial relationship functions as a basis for her expression of fear at a subjective level.

However, her feelings are not only personal but also mediate and speak for others' experiences beyond the familial relationship. By using documentary footage from an internet source, the film displays the massive demonstration taking place in front of the prime minister's office in Tokyo, which condemned the government's negligence and inappropriate response to the nuclear accident. It is said that at its largest, approximately 200,000 people joined the demonstration despite the mainstream media's general dismissal.[10] The film places specific emphasis on one participant with tears in her eyes as she accuses the government of its decision to raise the acceptable level of radiation in schoolyards in Fukushima to a much higher level compared to the international standard. In the sequence, Kana adds her voice-over commentary: "She is also fighting for my child." Here, the emotional expression of the mother's anxiety and rage at the demonstration site resonates with the filmmaker's own emotions. As is clear from this example, fear and anxiety as bodily sensations function as a starting point for the construction of a network of people sharing a public, affective response.

The way Kana audio-visually constructs a connection between herself and other participants in the demonstration reminds us of Alisa Lebow's discussion on the plurality of first-person documentaries. Lebow suggests those documentaries are both "singular" and "plural" at the same time, for as she puts it, "despite the fact that we believe it to express our individuality, it nonetheless expresses our commonality, our plurality, our interrelatedness with a group, a mass, a sociality, if not a society" (Lebow 2012: 3). Kana's relational selves represented here show the emotive connectivity among mothers and all those who share concerns for the unknown risks of radiation exposure.

The nature of the network is closely connected to the shift in the convention of social movements in post-Fukushima society. According to sociologist Mika Morita, there are three important factors to consider regarding the conditions of the social movement after the Tohoku earthquake: the populace in Tohoku, the local government, and the mothers (Morioka 2014: 177–200). By contrasting the passivity of local people with the dysfunction of local governments, she emphasizes the important role women play in social movements, who, with concerns about the risk of radiation to their children, have started to actively participate in or organize various social movements across Japan. *Lullaby*, which foregrounds mothers and motherhood, precisely represents this shifting strategy in social movements and increasingly centralized agencies of mothers in post-Fukushima society.

Lullaby not only shows alternative possibilities for private/public dynamics by emphasizing the emotive aspects concerning the fear of radiation but also literally created an alternative public. It should be noted that various screening events of post-Fukushima documentaries have taken place, and they construct networks in physical spaces. As for *Lullaby*, after its theatrical release, self-organized screenings by volunteers have constantly been held. Sometimes accompanied by lecture events that encourage interaction among participants, these screenings have constructed networks involving activists, filmmakers, and members of the general public.

The construction of this alternative public sphere reminds us of Nancy Fraser's discussion of subaltern counterpublics. According to Fraser, subaltern counterpublics are political spheres that emerge as a counter to the official public sphere, and these are the arenas "where members of subordinated social groups invent and circulate counter-discourses to formulate oppositional interpretations of their identities, interests, and needs" (Fraser 1990: 67). The concept is therefore beneficial to understanding the ways these independent documentary filmmakers attempt to create alternative models of public expression and political activity by exposing issues conventionally associated with the intimate sphere and feminine corporeal activities such as pregnancy. The way in which *Lullaby* affectively creates counter-discourse against the government's underplaying of the health risks of radiation aligns with Fraser's conception of subaltern counterpublics at both textual and physical levels through the film's emphasis on the radiation's threat to vulnerable children and her own maternal body.

However, the counterpublics that textually and materially emerge in and from *Lullaby* might look somehow singular and unified in their opinions on the matters at hand. Although we should acknowledge the importance of the film's creation of counterpublics where people can build their community based on shared ideas and emotions, it is also true that the complications faced in post-Fukushima society are derived from the very difficulties of having conversations beyond the polarized social divisions. Open communication is considered difficult, especially in the context of Japan's traditional emphasis on social harmony and conformity. Although it is important to secure the space where one shares opinions and emotions, this can occur at the expense of debate and vigorous discussion capable of penetrating into mainstream discourse or staking a position in the inhospitable terrain of mainstream media and political discourse. It is essential for realizing the full potential of cinematic counterpublics to activate the possibilities of that terrain as a discursive space for dialogue among people from differing political or social grounds. How, then, is it possible to actualize liberatory spaces for expressing diverse and sometimes contradictory opinions and perspectives in order to eventually create an alternative consensus? To address this issue, this chapter will turn to *The Road Home* that presents the nascent attempt to transform the unconfrontational and conciliatory domestic sphere into the dynamic site for dialogues.

Transforming the Familial Space into the Dialogic Site of Communication: *The Road Home*

While *Lullaby* focuses on the potential for the creation of counterpublics starting from the filmmaker's private experiences and tactically disrupting the public/private divide, *The Road Home* shows the filmmaker's constant trial of utilizing conversation to overcome differences within the familial dynamic. *The Road Home* is a film that was made in 2017 by Miran Oura, who was forced to evacuate from her hometown in Futaba city in Fukushima after the disaster when she was in high school. The film chronicles the story of her family in the years following the disaster and exposes their confused and fractured sense of belonging after being forced to abandon the house where all their familial memories reside (Figure 6.2).

As Oura continuously scrutinizes her situation of being labeled a "disaster survivor," the film traces a subtle shift in the familial relationship. She completed the film with the footage she continued shooting years after the incident while she was a film student in Tokyo. After its exhibition at the Pia Film Festival in 2017, the film traveled the festival circuit, including the Yamagata International Documentary Film Festival in 2017, and was screened

Figure 6.2 *The Road Home* by Miran Oura. © Miran Oura 2017. All rights reserved.

at small showings and arthouse theaters. Compared to the technical maturity of *Lullaby* and its coherent anti-nuclear power narrative, *The Road Home* might appear to heavily rely on the tropes of a coming-of-age story revolving around miscommunication between children and parents. Despite the seeming naiveté, however, Oura's film is worth paying attention to as an attempt to create a space for discussion that involves facing others who do not share the same opinions, which challenges the closed, conciliatory, and suppressive nature of the private sphere from the inside by advancing the feminine voice in the home. The home's paradoxical role to reinforce patriarchal norms and to open the possibility of feminine agency outside of public mechanisms of control, the shaming of feminine "unruliness" or the dismissal of women's hysteria high among them, is at the core of the film.

This is well represented through the filmmaker's attempts at having conversations with her family members, who do not share her concerns and ideas, especially with her father, who works for TEPCO. The film's constant display of her uncomfortable feelings with being labeled as a "disaster victim" seems to come not only from her frustration with the mainstream media's monolithic representations of the victims but also from her family's complicated social status owing to her father's employer. However, unlike *Lullaby*, the film seems to be hesitant to show the filmmaker's direct political opinions except for some subtle displays of Oura's disillusionment with the government-led promotion of nuclear power. Rather, what seems consistent in the film is her sense of avoidance from being aligned with any political activism. There is one scene, for instance, where she encountered a large rally in Tokyo in 2015, which was against the passing of the militaristic 2015 National Security Bill, and the intertitles confess Oura's rootless and alienated feelings being among the protesters, thus revealing her distance from political activism, sharing a common sense of distance from politics expressed among a majority of Japanese youths.

However, there is the alternate potential for the creation of a counterpublic in her attempts at entering into conversations with her family members: the overcoming of the problem of dis/miscommunication. It is noticeable that the film consistently shows Oura's hesitation to initiate an honest conversation with her family members. Her voice-over commentary throughout the film shows that the family lacks the ability to communicate honestly and share their authentic thoughts and feelings.

Although most of the film revolves around Oura's hesitation to start a conversation with her father over the issue of nuclear policy, toward the end of the film, there appears one sequence where she awkwardly initiates the conversation with her father. However, her father exhibits his reluctance to talk over the issue by stating, "Let's not talk about that." Holding a camera in her hand, Oura continues to question her father, and that eventually results in her bursting into tears over the refusal of her father to have a discussion with her. In the following sequence, Oura and her father blame each other for the lack of transparent and honest communication. Toward the end of the film, however, nothing extraordinary happens. Rather, what we observe is the subtly changing familial relationship that reveals the filmmaker's grief over her failing attempt to communicate with her family members.

Although the film never shows whether or not the conversation between her and her father reaches some reconciliation, it succeeds in showing the subtly changing relationship and the importance of trying to speak with people even if they have differing opinions. At the very end of the film, we hear her conversation with her mother on the phone. Here, Oura says, "We, my family, are very much taking care of each other, so that's why we try not to talk about things that might hurt each other." The following scene shows the intertitles on the screen, "there are many things in our family that we can never understand, but there are more people in the society who we can never understand. I do not want to pretend that I do not realize the distance that emerged between me and my father. I want to empathize with the words and feelings of the ones I care about." Here, by exhibiting the rupture and emotional conflict caused by the unexpected result of the nuclear disaster, the film still shows the attempts to bridge the gaps between family members. Although the film does not show the resolution, it documents the filmmaker's ongoing attempt to transform the familial space from one of conformist oppression to a space where honest opinions can be shared.

The attempt to create a discursive space within the familial space, where normally uniformity of opinion reigns, reminds us of the importance and responsibilities of paying attention to the process of communication in the counterpublic. Robert Asen emphasizes the discursive (as well as non-discursive) quality of counterpublics, asserting that "emergent publics cannot articulate all possible perspectives in public debates without asserting a dubious discursive totality that presumes knowledge of the need and interests of others prior to discursive engagement" (Asen 2000: 441). Although his emphasis on the communicative aspect of the counterpublic is a criticism aimed at the sometimes oppressive tendency of a singular, consensual public sphere, his discussion of the importance of the discursive and communicative aspect of the public sphere holds strong relevance in the devastatingly divided post-Fukushima society. It would also be a necessary process for a counterpublic to serve as a space for different opinions to be exchanged in order for it to disrupt the logic of the homogeneity that conditions the oppressive nature of the public sphere. In this sense, Oura's filmic attempt shifts our attention not only to the nature of counterpublics but also to the actual process of opening up the closed and unconfrontational private sphere and transforming it into a dialogic space of heterogeneity. This can be precisely aligned with the longstanding feminist strategies of renegotiating the divisions of the private and the public by questioning the closeness and exclusiveness of the domestic sphere, which has been conventionally dominated by the paternal order in the tradition of the modern family.

The significance of Oura's attempt to create a discursive and dialogic space within the familial sphere becomes more evident when comparing it with *Lullaby*. Even though Oura's attempt does not seem very successful in terms of creating a truly functional space for open dialogue, in the sense that it fails to advance their communications or achieve any shared consensus, her attempt shows political significance in a context where social division becomes increasingly severe. Actually, as sociologists have pointed out, many communities have been divided not geographically (by forced evacuation) but emotionally over the issue of radiation.[11] The resulting consequence is the inert discussion among each member of a section or society with the aim of avoiding conflicts. *Lullaby* displays the capacity of the documentary to engage in public dialogue for creating social change as an anti-nuclear movement, and it has the power to make the audience recognize themselves as part of a political movement. On the other hand, in *The Road Home*, we cannot see the filmmaker's intention to create any significant social change related to a particular political ideology. Rather, what we see is the very difficulty of constructing a discursive space. Still, it opens up the possibilities and responsibilities for us to try to create a space for productive dialogue among people. The film in this sense initiates significant changes in the unconfrontational and closed familial space by the methods of documenting the confrontation and the following subtle shift in the familial dynamics.

Conclusion: Cinematically Mediated Counterpublics

"It required a lot of courage for me to make a film about my family."[12] With this remark, Miran Oura opened the Q&A session that was held after the screening of *The Road Home* at the Yamagata International Documentary Film Festival in 2017. As a film student when she started the film, she made up her mind to face her family with a camera in her hand. "It consequently revealed the problem of my family that every one of us was reluctant to share what we were thinking about the series of incidents caused by the earthquake." This remark reveals the particular difficulties of disrupting the harmonious and conciliatory familial space by bringing in the "untouchable" issue concerning the nuclear disaster. However, at the same time, the camera's intervention in the closed domestic space bears subtle political significance as it shows the potential of problematizing the unconfrontational stagnancy of the private sphere and transforming it into a dialogic site for future political transformations through the emergence of an assertive, or even questioning, female voice.

Mainly analyzing two documentary films that deal with issues surrounding post-Fukushima Japanese society, this chapter examines how first-person documentary practices by female filmmakers function as forms of political and critical intervention against the backdrop of post-Fukushima society. The chapter clarifies that in Tomoko Kana's *Lullaby*, the representation of her experience of pregnancy, giving birth, and child-raising functions as a basis for the network, which mediates and speaks for others' feelings, in this case, the anxiety of radioactive contamination. At the same time, the film not only shows the construction of a network on the textual level but also has a significant link with post-Fukushima social movements, especially in terms of women's (mothers') active participation in the political arena as participants in demonstrations and the organization of political events, which can be considered to be "counterpublic."

On the other hand, Miran Oura's *The Road Home* portrays the subtly changing familial dynamics with an emphasis on Oura's relationship with her father. The chapter illuminated her attempts to have a conversation with someone who has a dissimilar opinion. By doing so, the film shifts our attention to the steps necessary for the process of creating a heterogeneous counterpublic. The film does not go so far as to show the connection between the familial space and the actual sociopolitical surroundings. However, the way she initiates the dialogue attests to the prescriptive function of documentary intervention in the post-Fukushima society, where increased social division has further intensified interpersonal polarization. This act of reforming the private sphere is precisely aligned with feminists' longstanding attempts to achieve a more egalitarian private/public sphere by activating their dialogic potential.

Both documentary films politicize familial space in highly diverse ways from each other. As examples of feminist praxis within personal documentaries that tactically disrupt the clear division between the private and the public, these two documentaries show crucial possibilities of film media as the networking bases to create alternative public spheres: *Lullaby*'s emphasis on maternal connectivity of bodies foregrounds the ties between individual affectivity and public while *The Road Home* problematizes the repressive stagnancy of the private sphere by activating the communicative action within the sphere. At the same time, both documentaries exemplify the importance of women's participation in post-Fukushima filmmaking, in terms of both the significance of women's involvement in media creation and their contribution to rethinking the intricate connection between society and individual life, especially in times of crisis and anxiety. The rapid onset of ecological, economic, and political catastrophes on a global scale no longer allows us to ponder upon any single incident. In reality, societal amnesia regarding Fukushima already seems to prevail in Japan, contributing to the renormalization of the situation: despite international criticism, contaminated wastewater has been released into the ocean, and the safety myth surrounding the operation of nuclear reactors across Japan has been gradually reestablished. In such a situation, it is all the more necessary to remind us of the importance of connectivity beyond the public and the private, sociopolitical, economic, and cultural, a series of relationships that are highlighted through their reorientation in these two documentaries.

Notes

1 The contamination triggered by the worst nuclear disaster since Chernobyl in 1986 is a continuously serious problem that requires the highest level of attention and maintenance. The responsibility of the government and the Tokyo Electric

Power Company (TEPCO) for this incident is still been interrogated by angered people despite the unbelievable result of the former TEPCO executives being found not guilty of criminal negligence in September 2019.
2 Approximately 150,000 people were forced to evacuate from the affected area following the government's decision. It is also said that around the same number of people in the Tohoku and Kanto regions voluntarily relocated due to health-related concerns.
3 Regarding social divisions after the nuclear accident, see Yotsumoto and Takekawa (2016).
4 Those who benefited from the nuclear power policy in the formation of the so-called nuclear power village (*genshiryoku mura*) are rather reluctant to criticize the government's incompetence regardless of whether their ways of living were affected by the accident.
5 It is important to remind us that there has been a lineage of representations of nuclear disaster in postwar Japan following the devastating destruction of Hiroshima and Nagasaki by atomic bombs. Although some films (mainly commercial) represented the fear of internal exposure to radiation, such as *Black Rain* (Shohei Imamura, 1989), most of the films focused on representing the spectacularized violence of atomic bomb explosions and the total destruction of cities.
6 Scholarship on cinematic (and other artistic) representation of Fukushima, the issue of radioactive contamination, and the anti-nuclear activism includes Iwata-Weickgenannt (2016), Marciano (2012), and DiNitto (2014).
7 Since 2011, some institutions have launched the activity of restoring and exhibiting materials related to the memory of the disaster. Among them, the Yamagata International Documentary Film Festival in Yamagata and the Center for Remembering 3.11 in Sendai are functioning as hubs for archiving and exhibiting these works related to the disaster from both amateur and professional filmmakers. The biannual film festival, YIDFF, continues to feature the entry titled "Cinema with Us," exhibiting the documents and testimonies of 3/11. As the Sendai Mediatheque has already tried to seek the way to cooperate with citizens by lending the citizen filming equipment and processed the audiovisual materials as part of their archive, the Center for Remembering 3.11 expanded the potential of methods for collaborating with citizens. In their archival activity, the Center lends filming equipment to the participants, prepares a studio equipped with editing tools, and provides technical support to the participants.
8 Although the chapter places specific focus on the intersection between the first-person mode and women's documentary revolving around familial relations,

we can also see women's documentaries on the topic that use diverse ways of expressions, which include Masako Sakata's *Journey without End* (*Watashi no owaranai tabi*, 2014), Hitomi Kamanaka's *Little Voices from Fukushima* (*Chisaki koe no kannon*, 2014), Mizue Furui's *Mothers of Fukushima: Eiko and Yoshiko* (*Itatemura no kachantachi: tsuchi to tomoni*, 2016), Mayu Nakamura's *Alone in Fukushima* (*Naoto hitorikkiri*, 2015), and *Alone again in Fukushima* (*Naoto imam o hitorikkiri*, 2020).

9 The first-person aesthetics of feminist cinematic practices have been vigorously and variously discussed mainly in documentary scholarship. The relevant academic literature includes Michael Renov (2004), Alisa Lebow (2008), and Kiki Tianqi Yu (2018).

10 The organizer of the anti-nuclear demonstration in Tokyo announced that the demonstration that took place in July 2012 had 200,000 participants. See Yoshitaka Mori (2013: 30).

11 A lot of research has been done on the social division in post-Fukushima society, including Tanaka, Hunahashi, and Masamura (2013).

12 Oura's remark, the paper cites here, is based on the notes I recorded at the Q&A session on October 26, 2017.

Part III

Reimagining Documentary Activism

7

Iranian Women's Biographical Documentaries as Sites of Recognition and Advocacy

An Ecofeminist Reading

Najmeh Moradiyan-Rizi

Biography has a long history within literary and cinematic contexts. Yet, the dominant biographical approaches have focused on the lives and achievements of male individuals, thus offering "the 'great man' theory of history: the belief that history is 'made' by the inspired acts of outstanding individuals, whose genius transcends the normal constraints of historical context" (Allen and Gomery 1985: 53). Within this male-driven biographical context, as Susan Mann Trofimenkoff contends, "An occasional queen, saint or female 'first' might be allowed to slip through the net of exclusivity but their presence among the Great Men merely accentuates their own marginality and even more so that of the entire female population which they do not represent in any case" (1985: 2). A feminist biographical approach thus attempts to not only challenge the dominant and essentialist biographical trends but also to reframe and reconstruct the sociocultural standpoints by presenting women as active social agents. In fact, the feminist biography has an ideological and political objective: its "purpose may be as simple as uncovering a past that has been denied women . . . or it may be as complex as exposing the patterns of patriarchal society in order to be able to change them" (Trofimenkoff 1985: 4).

Emphasizing the significance of feminist biography within a documentary filmic context, this chapter foregrounds the unprecedented rise in Iranian women's biographical documentaries on women's lives and experiences since the late 1990s that has occurred in tandem with various sociopolitical, technological, and environmental changes in contemporary Iran. In doing so, it aims to showcase how these biographical acts become an activist tool for recognizing women's lives and their contributions to the public and the environment, while also undermining patriarchal traditions and norms. I am particularly interested in those biographical documentaries that present their feminist perspective in tandem with environmental activism, films that I call biographical ecofeminist documentaries. How do these works connect biographical recognition to acts of advocacy for women and the environment? How do these films challenge the binaries of private/public, self/other, and nature/culture?

Women documentarians have paid close attention to the notion of the "personal is political," interrogating it within their films in various forms in order to self-consciously center women's voices and experiences. As Kristin Lené Hole and Dijana Jelača (2019) explain, two common approaches in this regard have been autobiographical and biographical documentaries. In the former, the filmmakers turn their camera to their own personal lives to explore identity, family history, and at times, national memory and sociopolitical issues as they intersect with personal experiences. In the latter, women documentarians have focused "on politicizing the personal stories of others, or rather, conveying large-scale historical events through the intimate experiences of those whom history often forgets" (Hole and Jelača 2019: 184). In the same vein, "Critical ecofeminism is rooted in a relational standpoint that illuminates inequalities from the personal to the political—ecological, economic, sociopolitical—promoting just and equitable relations by raising questions such as, who benefits, and who pays?" (Gaard 2017: 19).

This chapter similarly indicates how Iranian women's biographical ecofeminist documentaries draw from the lives of other women to advocate for larger societal transformations, particularly regarding women's status and environmental protection. These documentaries also stem from the activist commitments of the documentarians themselves, for whom the documentary provides a useful and active site for recognition and advocacy. In what follows, I first offer a brief historical overview of biographical documentaries and environmental conditions in Iran until the 1990s. I then discuss major sociopolitical and technological changes in the country since the late 1990s that have not only prompted a surge in women's biographical documentaries and environmental activism but also provided a ground for the interaction and convergence of biography and environmentalism within biographical ecofeminist documentaries. Finally, I provide close readings of two biographical ecofeminist documentaries: *All My Trees* (*Hame-ye derakhtan-e man*, 2015) and *Poets of Life* (*Shaeran-e zendegi*, 2017).

Biographical Traditions and Environmental Conditions in Iran: A Brief History

Biographical traditions in Iran developed within a masculinist context in which the lives of male individuals, often from upper classes and higher social ranks, were spotlighted. As Michael Craig Hillmann writes, "In the authoritarian, patriarchal Iranian environment, biographies other than the approved lives of kings, their representatives, and other establishment father figures might not have a place" (1990: 34–5). Within this context, William L. Hanaway (1990) points to some influential and popular biographies including biographies of Abolqasem Ferdowsi, the great poet of Persian epic poetry, and Imam Hussein, the third Shiite Imam. According to Hanaway, "For the most part, this sort of life writing conforms to the view of biography as an example or model of moral and didactic value for readers" (1990: 60). Interestingly, within a cinematic context, one of the early examples of a biographical film can be seen in Abdolhossein Sepanta's *Firdausi* (1934), which was "based on the life of the eleventh-century poet Abolqasem Ferdowsi and re-created parts of the mythical and paradigmatic battle of father and son—Rostam and Sohrab—from Ferdowsi's epic poem *Shahnameh*" (Naficy 2011: 222). Within a documentary context, "newsreels documenting the royal court and works by foreign documentarians who came to record the country's heritage and development" (Atwood 2016: 66) dominated the early decades of the twentieth century. In the 1960s and 1970s, ethnographic documentaries became a dominant practice aiming to record ways of Iranian life rather than the lives of specific individuals. According to Hamid Naficy, in terms of content, the major trends in the ethnographic documentaries of this period include religious culture and rituals, tribes and tribal migration, and indigenous technologies, such as underground irrigation tunnels known as qanat (2011: 101–13). Before the 1979 Islamic Revolution, biographical documentaries that present parts of individual lives with a more focused perspective can be seen in Parviz Kimiavi's short documentary *P like Pelican* (*P-e mesl-e pelikan*, 1972) and his feature-length work, *The Stone Garden* (*Bagh-e sangi*, 1976), both of which depict the lives of isolated men living at the margins of society.

It was during the 1979 Islamic Revolution and its immediate aftermath that biographical documentary found a special significance. As Naficy mentions, "The upheavals of the revolution and its aftermath affected individual lives tremendously, making them more interesting as film subject" (2012a: 109). Yet, regardless of the active participation of women in the Revolution, and the fact that the event immediately changed women's sociopolitical conditions—including "elimination of women from the judiciary, segregation of women in public spaces, such as buses, sports grounds, beaches, and the campaign to impose the veil" (Najmabadi 1991: 69)—the state-sponsored biographical documentaries of this period primarily focused on male figures, such as Jalal Al-e Ahmad, Ali Shariati, Mehdi Bazargan, and Ayatollah Taleqani (Naficy 2012a: 110–13). The emergence of biographical documentaries with more inclusive approaches and more diverse topics had to wait until the late 1990s.

Since the 1979 Islamic Revolution, similar to the state of Iranian women's lives, the Iranian environment has also faced drastic changes and challenges. Prior to the Revolution, "the parliament approved the creation of the Game and Fish Department of Iran" in 1967, directed by Eskandar Firouz (Laylin 2018: 2). Firouz's efforts ultimately transformed the organization into the Department of Environment (DOE) in 1971. While at this time Iran saw rapid modernization and the growth of industrial factories and automobiles, the DOE managed to accomplish some major tasks including, among others, the creation of "six wildlife reserves and thirty-five protected regions . . . in order to safeguard endangered species and threatened ecosystems" (Yarshater Center 2020). The sociopolitical upheaval of the 1979 Revolution, followed by eight years of the Iran–Iraq War (1980–8), pushed environmental concerns to the margins while exacerbating environmental degradation. The "DOE suffered greatly from minimal budgets—and from incompetent, and sometimes corrupt, management" (Laylin 2018: 3).

The decade after the war saw rapid (re-)construction and road building, population growth, dam building, well digging, deforestation, desertification, as well as continued inefficient agricultural methods, thus putting the environmental condition in a critical state. Currently, "Iran overall ranks sixth in the world in terms of greenhouse gas emissions, according to the Global Carbon Atlas, having more than doubled CO_2 emissions in the past two decades"

(Scollon 2023). Paradoxically, or perhaps as a result of the environmental crisis in post-revolutionary Iran, there has been a growing awareness since the late 1990s regarding environmental issues facing the country that reflects itself in both grassroots activism and environmental documentaries. Some of these documentaries have used the lens of biography to highlight women's efforts and contributions to environmental protection and education. The following section underlines various changes in contemporary Iran since the late 1990s that have contributed to the transformation of biographical documentary and environmental activism, prompting the emergence of biographical ecofeminist documentaries.

Women, Environmentalism, and Biographical Documentary in Iran Since the Late 1990s

In 1997, Mohammad Khatami, a reformist cleric, was elected president with overwhelming support from Iranian women and youth, initiating a period of social and political transformation that came to be known as the Reform Era (1997–2005). Civil society, the rule of law, and human rights discourses formed major tenets of Khatami's presidential campaign and administration. As Leila Alikarami argues, prior to 1997, "the term 'civil society' was rarely used in public discourses in Iran. Any existing NGOs (non-governmental organisations) were primarily focused on economic development. During Khatami's administration, however, civil society emerged as a force in the country" (2018: 65). A considerable impact of encouraging the involvement of citizens in society showed itself in areas related to environmental activities, women's status, and documentary filmmaking. The mushrooming of various cultural, environmental, and women's NGOs was one of the manifestations of civil society aiming to provide a ground for ordinary individuals' involvement in society. Khatami also appointed Masumeh Ebtekar as the first female vice president and the head of the DOE. During her tenure, the DOE "was restructured, leading to the launch of the National Action Plan for Environmental Protection . . . In 1998 the Public Participation Bureau was founded within the Department of Environment to assist environmental non-government organisations (NGOs) and encourage participation" (Fadaee 2018: 145).

During Khatami's two-term presidency (1997–2005), the "Department of Environment claimed that the number of environmental groups reached 640 across the country whereas it has only been around twenty before this period" (Fadaee 2016: 19). Furthermore, given the popularity of Khatami among women and youth, "these two groups became the main advocates of the newly empowered institutions of civil society including the environmental movement" (Fadaee 2016: 18). In addition to being active members, young women assumed leadership roles within these NGOs, thus significantly contributing to the enhancement of environmental awareness and women's status within Iranian society. As Simin Fadaee writes, "Most environmentalists of the 1990s and the 2000s were highly educated and some of them had spent part of their education and life abroad. Many were from the politically conscious strata of the middle class who had spent part of their lives as political and social activists engaged in various issues" (2016: 19). Their environmental activism was thus entangled with larger efforts for progressive sociopolitical and gendered transformations.

Women's sociopolitical participation was further enhanced through the establishment of city councils. "[T]he first-ever city council elections [were] held in February 1999," with the goal of transferring "some administrative authority" to local councils (Osanloo 2009: 42). As a result, "Some 5,000 women were given a chance to run for 220,000 local council seats in cities, towns, and villages across the country. Nearly 300 women were elected to the local city councils" (Monshipouri 2016: 7). These transformations provided women with a more active role in the public sphere and also with the opportunity to discuss and reflect on women's status and contributions through the documentary medium.

The considerable increase in the number of women documentarians in the late 1990s and early 2000s was part of a larger revival of documentary filmmaking in Iran facilitated by sociopolitical openness and technological advancements. Significantly, the Iranian Documentary Filmmakers Association (IRDFA)—*Anjoman-e mostanadsazan-e sinemay-e Iran*—was officially established in 1998 as the first domestic documentarians' guild within the House of Cinema (*Khaneh Sinema*), which is the Iranian alliance of motion picture guilds, in order to support the rights of documentarians and promote the documentary film culture. According to Naficy, IRDFA's "membership grew from 41 to 115 by 2005" (2012b: 3). As such, the recognition of documentary and documentary practice at this time became a crucial ground for the rise of documentary filmmaking, especially among women.

Technological advancements also played a pivotal role in the rise of documentary practice. Smaller and lighter, yet higher quality, video cameras, video editing software, online sharing, and streaming websites all provided a more affordable and accessible production and distribution experience for documentary filmmakers. As Blake Atwood states, "In May 1993, Ali Larijani, the minister of culture and Islamic guidance, announced that the ministry intended to lift the ban on video technology. . . . However, it was not until Khatami's presidency that video achieved widespread popularity and became associated with the ideals of democratization that marked the use of video around the world" (2016: 100). Democratic aspirations and civil engagement thus became crucial elements for encouraging documentary production on social, gender, and environmental issues as a form of grassroots activism. Furthermore, Fadaee points out that "technological changes, particularly satellite television and the internet, played an important role in raising and shaping environmental awareness and activity in Iran. From the late 1990s to the present the number of articles and reports on the environment in newspapers has increased. . . . Many campaigns, projects and demonstrations became possible only through the use of [social] media for spreading information" (2016: 19).

Within this climate of social transformation, documentary emerged as a quintessential medium of expression, allowing documentarians to reflect on various conditions pertinent to women's lives and the environment. In fact, since the late 1990s, "[A] profound change has occurred in how Iranians perceive the relationship between humans and nature, and their relationship with the state" (Fadaee 2012: 93) and with each other. This new recognition of the self, the other, and the environment has also impacted the biographical approaches in documentary. In this regard, Omid Balaghati asserts, "The portraits of famous figures, marginalized and outcasts, or hot and sensitive subjects, have been substituted by [the portraits of] ordinary individuals and their micro lives" (2016: 67). The new biographical works primarily choose as their subject matter ordinary individuals or important but less-known figures, and present some specific aspects of their lives. Through micro-level explorations, these biographical documentaries investigate larger societal issues, connecting the private to the public, the personal to the political, and the individual to the society. The narration and presentation of micro-lives have become a form of social critique and identity exploration within the physical and natural world. These new representational possibilities in biographical documentaries, along with the exacerbation of the environmental crisis, have prompted a surge in both biographical documentaries on women's lives and environmental documentaries.[1] Some documentarians have also converged these two trends in their biographical ecofeminist approaches as a way to recognize women's lives and gender and environmental advocacy, examples of which include Mojtaba Mirtahmasb's *Lady of the Roses* (*Banoo-ye gol-e sorkh*, 2009), Rakhshan Banietemad's *All My Trees* (2015), Mahnaz Afzali's *Mother of the Earth* (*Madar-e zamin*, 2017), and Shirin Barghnavard's *Poets of Life* (2017).

By the end of Khatami's presidency in 2005, the official attempt at reform fell short of its promises, resulting in the disenchantment of many supporters. As Rebecca Barlow and Shahram Akbarzadeh argue, "The reform movement's choice of strategies failed adequately to take into account the contextual constraints they would face. While Iran's constitution exhibits republican aspects, it very clearly bestows ultimate authority upon the most learned Islamic jurist (the Supreme Leader, or *Vali Faqih*) over elected politicians" (2018: 10, original emphasis). Within this context, Khatami's administration failed to enact some of its progressive goals, especially regarding women's rights and status. Significantly, the administration "failed to get the Guardian Council to ratify the UN Convention on the Elimination of All Forms of Discrimination Against Women (CEDAW)" (Atwood 2016: 119).

During the subsequent presidency of conservative Mahmoud Ahmadinejad, and particularly after his disputed second-term election in 2009, the crackdown on women's rights and environmental activists intensified, which also severely restricted the NGOs' activities. The "Department of Environment was restructured and the Public Participation Bureau was dissolved" (Fadaee 2016: 20). Yet, progressive grassroots activism and efforts could not be stopped. Individuals managed to employ creative and flexible forms of resistance through blogging on women's and environmental issues, social media activism, and independent and outside-of-state-control documentary filmmaking, and through everyday practices, or what Asef Bayat calls "nonmovements": acts "that are merged into, indeed are part and parcel of, the *ordinary* practices of everyday life" (2013: 21, original emphasis). As such, "nonmovements assume far more resiliency against repression than the conventional activisms"

(Bayat 2013: 21). The environmentally conscious practices of everyday life since the late 2000s are great instances of such nonmovements. "The growth of vegetarianism and a proliferation of vegetarian restaurants and shops, increased numbers of people who use public transport, shopping in organic food shops and recycling one's garbage are a few examples of the emerging environmentally friendly lifestyles" (Fadaee 2016: 20). Within this context of everyday practices and resistance, the lives of individuals, especially women, as active social agents, have continued to attract documentarians. According to the Documentary and Experimental Film Center (DEFC), the foremost governmental organization supporting documentary filmmaking in Iran, in 2019, "212 portrait documentaries" registered as applicants for participation in the thirteenth Cinema Vérité documentary film festival. Given the registration of a total of "687 films in the festival's secretariat, more than 30% of these works [were] portraits of [various individuals] such as poets, martyrs, veterans of the Iran-Iraq War, figures in cinema, music, sports, and ordinary individuals of the society" (Documentary and Experimental Film Center 2019).

Nowadays, environmental issues, such as air pollution, water scarcity, drought, flooding, soil erosion, and landslides, have become common challenges faced by all Iranians. Yet, "women are indeed the ones most severely affected by climate change and natural disasters, but their vulnerability is not innate; rather it is a result of inequities produced through gendered social roles, discrimination, and poverty" (Gaard 2017: 123). It is in this context that biographical ecofeminist documentaries offer much-needed inspiration, and by centering women activists, they also offer role models who provide audiences with impactful feminist acts that strive to enhance both gender equality and environmental protection. The following section provides close readings of two examples of biographical ecofeminist documentaries made by Iranian women and explores the ways these films contribute to gender and environmental activism.

All My Trees (2015) by Rakhshan Banietemad

All My Trees (2015), written and directed by Rakhshan Banietemad, intimately introduces the viewers to the life and environmental contributions of Mahlagha Mallah (born in 1917), known as the "mother of Iran's environment." The biographical ecofeminist approach frames the film from its opening sequence. Several establishing shots depict Tehran under a cloud of smog while the director's voice-over highlights the city's air pollution crisis. Over the images of the streets and alleys of Tehran, the voice-over continues: "One winter day in 2014, we visit Mahlagha Mallah, a woman nearly a century old ever so firm in her ideals, who feels for the water, soil, and air of her homeland." The title notes then provide a quick introduction to Mallah, including her degree (PhD from Sorbonne University, France), her family, and her founding of a pioneering NGO called the Women's Society for Fighting Environmental Pollution (*Jamiat-e zanan-e mobareze ba aludegi-e mohit-e zist*), which was established in the early 1990s. As such, from the film's opening scenes, the viewers learn that the documentary and the documentarian have environmental concerns, and the film's focus is on a pioneering woman who has tirelessly dedicated her life to address these concerns.

Reflecting on Banietemad's body of works, Fatemeh-Mehr Khansalar writes that since the 1980s, "the environment has been one of her key areas of interest," which is in tandem with "her concern for women and other oppressed groups, marginalized because of their health, poverty, gender, and struggles with addiction. Nature, and also non-humans, are marginalized and silenced entities in our current world, yet Banietemad endeavors to give them a voice and bring their issues to light" (2021: 208). An ecofeminist perspective, both behind the camera—through the director's vision—and in front of the camera—through Mallah's influential presence—serves as a crucial force in framing and discussing the environmental crisis in Iran, exacerbated by politics and official mismanagement.

All My Trees is full of intimate scenes mostly shot in Mallah's home, where she has been living with her family for over sixty years. The large windows of the living room open toward a spacious backyard with trees and a hole, where the trash is composted and shared with others for gardening and plant cultivation. Mallah's environmental activism is thus embedded in everyday practices and merges the private space of the home with public spaces, especially through her NGO's activities. Simin Fadaee argues that Mallah's "main concern over the years has been the environment and the role of women in the life-cycle. Her eco-feminist ideology has made her conclude that any step towards environmentalism should include and address the role of women in society" (2012: 96–7). This is a significant point that is also addressed in the film. For instance, in one scene, Mallah shows the director and the camera the photos of her mother (Khadijah Afzal Vaziri) and her grandmother (Bibi Khanum Astarabadi), both of whom were women's rights activists. A photo of Mallah's mother in a dress she herself designed and made to indicate a woman should wear a topcoat without the veil for her hands to move freely, sparks a memory for Mallah, which she shares: "We were walking in the alley together. Others threw little pebbles at our heads. A stone hit me [near the eye]. I started crying. [My mother] said, 'Don't cry! This is a struggle. Don't you forget that.' You see, this fighting woman suffered so much for the sake of her children to live freely." It is based on this upbringing that for Mallah the fight for the environment is entangled with the fight for women's rights and status. Thus, there should be no surprise that most of Mallah's NGO workers and mentees are women.

Throughout the documentary, the viewers get a glimpse of Mallah's busy days as many come to visit her, update her on the activities of the provincial branches of the NGO, discuss environmental issues and possible actions, and receive environmental guidance. Through conversations and photo albums, the film introduces some of the NGO's activities, such as publishing the magazine *Cry of the Earth* (*Faryad-e zamin*), training teachers, planting trees with the help of school children, and organizing children's march against air pollution. As "the largest environmental group in Iran" and with "many branches throughout the country," the NGO's main focuses, according to Fadaee, have been "consciousness raising and confronting the government with environmental issues" (2012: 97). In addition to these objectives, planting trees has been a major effort by the group to combat deforestation and desertification in the country. In the words of a woman who is visiting Mallah in the film, the NGO's approach has been "pressure from below, bargaining from above. In other words, [Mallah] would write to the ministers and officials as well as take the issue to the masses."

The camera accompanies Mallah as she attends some environmental events as a special guest. At a seminar against air pollution organized by a civil organization, Mallah highlights Iran's lack of proper management and encourages the audience to think about actions that can be taken to protect the country's environment. Throughout the documentary, there is no use of hard data or visual graphs to quantify Iran's environmental crisis. As human rights activist Narges Mohammadi asserts in her speech at the event, "There is no need for any research or gathering of data. It is enough to just look at the city for a moment, or for the body to try a natural process of breathing, to feel the depth of the disaster." In the same vein, Mallah's insights in the film, along with the discussions on her NGO's activities, provide an intimate, yet extensive, introduction to the environmental issues as well as many grassroots efforts that have been undertaken to address them.

To commemorate the national Clean Air Day, Mallah attends an event held at the Milad Tower, the tallest tower in Iran. After planting a tree, Mallah visits a collage of Mount Damavand, the highest mountain in Iran and a significant national symbol, made from painted blue and white toy cars that showcase its snow-capped peak. The collage is a symbolic protest against air pollution that has made this natural beauty and national icon invisible. Satoshi Abe writes about the interconnectedness of nationhood, nostalgia, and Iran's ancient civilization with environmental efforts, suggesting, Damavand "is depicted in the epic *Shahnameh* by Ferdowsi, with which few Iranians are unacquainted. Therefore, Damavand is understood to have symbolic, historical significance to the Iranian nation, and it is in this context that Iranian nature, being reified in Damavand, is juxtaposed with what is interpreted to be a prominent period in Iranian history" (2012: 272). Upon seeing the Damavand collage, Mallah kneels from her wheelchair and kisses the ground, saying, "God, save this homeland!" Throughout the film, Mallah emphasizes her patriotic character and her commitment to serving her country as a drive for her environmental efforts. Moreover, underlining the historical respect of Iranians for the environment, she believes education and consciousness raising can help revive environmentalism among Iranian people. Ultimately, the film succeeds in presenting an intimate portrait of a strong woman and an environmentalist whose life and contributions have inspired many individuals.

The inclusion of the scenes where the filmmaking crew is shown onscreen or directly referenced by Mallah adds a layer of intimacy to the documentary that highlights an intimate collaboration between the filmmaker and her subject—a coming together of two minds with the same priorities. Through these reflexive moments, Banietemad also reminds us that this is a constructed representation of reality aiming to highlight environmental concerns and the contributions of a role model addressing them. The documentary was produced by the Kara Film Studio, an independent professional documentary initiative co-founded by Banietemad and Mojtaba Mirtahmasb, "in which a group of professional Iranian filmmakers expresses their common concerns regarding humanistic, social, and cultural issues via documentary films—simultaneously maintaining their own diverse and distinct vision" (Kara Film Studio, "About"). Reflecting on the film in her director's note, published on the studio's website, Banietemad writes, "Apart from Mahlagha Mallah's role in the history of environmental activities, her exemplary vigor as a woman nearly a century old who continues to bear her social responsibility, is a worthy symbol for the Iranian woman's participation in the realm of the civil society" (Kara Film Studio, "*All My Trees*"). Mallah passed away in November 2021, yet the director's note still resonates as Mallah has provided a rich legacy that will nurture Iranian women and environmentalists for generations to come.

Poets of Life (2017) by Shirin Barghnavard

Poets of Life (2017), written, directed, and edited by Shirin Barghnavard, is part of the Kara Film Studio's Karestan project. Formed in 2015 and in partnership with an NGO, the Entrepreneurship Development Foundation for Women and Youth (*Bonyad-e tosea-ye karafarini-ye zanan va javanan*), Karestan "is a documentary film series on Iranian entrepreneurs. The story of men and women who, both in big and small terms, take risks and change their lives and those of others by creating innovative ideas and values" (Kara Film Studio, "About Karestan"). Some of the major goals of the series are to introduce exemplary role models to Iranians, especially the youth, to document the inspiring lives and significant contributions of these role models, many of whom have remained less known to the public, and to create hope, inspiration, and motivation for individuals to realize and enhance their skills for a better life. The series has so far produced eight documentary films, five of which focus on the lives of Iranian women entrepreneurs: *Jila* (2024), on the life of Jila Kashef; *Touran Khanom* (2018), on the life of Touran Mirhadi; *Mahak: A World She Founded* (2017), on the life of Saideh Ghods; *Poets of Life* (2017), on the life of Shirin Parsi; and *Mother of the Earth* (2017), on the life of Hayedeh Shirzadi. The latter two have environmentally related topics and feature ecofeminist perspectives.

Poets of Life centers on the life and achievements of Shirin Parsi, an acclaimed rice farmer, environmentalist, and social activist, who lives in the village of Shanderman, in the north of Iran. Parsi has dedicated her life to developing sustainable and innovative agricultural methods by producing organic native rice without the use of chemical pesticides and fertilizers. She received a degree in French literature from Paris in the late 1970s and, shortly after, returned to Iran with her husband. As the title of the documentary suggests, love and respect for nature and living in harmony with it can offer a new meaning and appreciation for life, and this theme frames the aesthetic approach of the film. Throughout the film, stunning images of northern Iran's natural beauty are accompanied by a poetic voice-over of Parsi as she reflects on the meaning of life, death, nature, and the environment.

The film opens with establishing shots of Shanderman in the early morning, as Parsi begins her daily tasks: feeding the dogs, releasing the turkeys and hens from their nests, buying fresh bread, and eating breakfast with her family. We then follow Parsi to the farm, where she and her son, oversee the plowing of her rice farms. For the first time, Parsi's voice-over is heard mentioning: "Farming means you plant one seed, you harvest ten. You are not supposed to plant one and harvest 10,000. It's about living sustainably rather than making profit." For Parsi, in fact, sustainability also means negating unjust economic and agricultural practices that treat the land and the environment as solely material resources that could be owned, sold, and exploited for personal gain. Regarding sustainability, Greta Gaard argues that "paradigms omitting or backgrounding discussions of race, class, gender, sexuality, and species effectively ensure that these paradigms will be marked by the 'unmarked' dominant group—white, male, middle class, heterosexual, and human animals. For 'sustainability' to reach its full potential, its advocates will need to recast sustainability in dialogue with an ecofeminist, environmental justice framework" (2017: 9). Shirin Parsi's life and work clearly demonstrate the intersections of sustainability, ecofeminism, and environmental justice as she, in addition to developing and improving sustainable agricultural practices, focuses on the empowerment of women through environmental education and farming opportunities, while simultaneously resisting officials' biases, mismanagement, and economic exploits.

There is a scene at the farm where Parsi shows the Azolla plant to the camera, explaining that the plant was imported by an official from Japan as a food source for cows and sheep. However, when the plant was thrown in the waters of northern Iran, Azolla remained on the water surface, stopping the oxygen from reaching other plants and animals that were beneath it. This issue prevented photosynthesis and negatively impacted aquatic life. As Parsi asserts, "This shows if you disregard a region's ecosystem, and ignore the differences between each country's habitat, then something good could turn into a disaster. We are now facing the Azolla disaster.... Now, the same gentleman is talking about genetic manipulation of rice!" Governmental mismanagement can also be seen in the increased rice imports during Ahmadinejad's administration that saturated the Iranian market, preventing domestic farmers from selling their products. As Parsi mentions, the result was that farmers began selling their lands to make a living. The documentary also offers a brief insight into rapid deforestation in the region in favor of building villas, residential places, and roads. It is within these contexts that Parsi's approach to sustainable farming finds significance.

As part of her environmental and social activism, Parsi organizes a workshop for some of the local women on ways to protect the environment. The group tours some natural lands that seem to be on the verge of destruction due to road building and farm expansion. The workshop continues in a classroom, where Parsi and other educators conduct an activity asking the women to connect various natural elements and species to each other with arrows based on their dependency. And once an educator removes one of the elements, the entire natural cycle gets disturbed. Parsi thus emphasizes to the women: "As humans, we think we own everything... [but] we are [in coexistence with the environment] ... [we are] alongside the trees, alongside the river, alongside the spring." The focus on women's empowerment and knowledge to protect the environment is at the heart of Parsi's environmental and social activism and is highlighted throughout the film.

Parsi is a founding member and the president of the board of directors of a Tehran-based NGO called the National Association of Women Entrepreneurs (*Anjoman-e melli-e zanan-e karafarin*). She hopes to open a branch of the Association in her area in northern Iran to provide environmental school training and local workshops. At an Association meeting with the parliamentary representatives in Tehran, Parsi talks about the obstacles to sustainable farming including food imports (instead of investments in domestic farming and agricultural developments) and gender discrimination. As Parsi points out, "Based on the latest statistics, there are twelve million people doing farming [in Iran]. Half of them are women. But there is no record of their income. A woman's work on the land is never officially recognized. She is at the service of the family without any income." Parsi's criticism regarding gender discrimination in farming thus highlights an urgent need for the acknowledgment and improvement of women's farming labor, to which she has committed herself. Earlier in the film, we meet women farmers working on Parsi's lands, some of whom have been working for her for over a decade and speak highly of her farming practices. On the sweeping images of rice farms with women farmers working, the poetic voice-over of Parsi narrates:

> I am with the hard-working and life-loving women. I always look at their fingertips that have been deformed by water and mud work. And I am with them every day. And I think about their wishes.... In that spread-out nature, with their bent backs, they defy nature's wrath. They defy freezing cold, rain, thunder, and intense heat. And they give new meanings to whatever we see and don't think about it. They are the beautiful poets of life.

Parsi's support for women farmers shows itself in her advocacy for women's labor rights as well as in her own involvement in the farm work as shown in several scenes throughout the film.

Such respect and care for women have been instilled in Parsi by her family since her childhood. In one scene, Parsi depicts some of her family photos and stresses that for her dad, "boys and girls were equal" and that it is because of this respect that she feels "a strong identity as a woman." She has in turn reflected the values and practices of gender equality in her life and professional practices such that even her younger son, Ahmad, who lives in the city of Rasht farther away from the farm, acknowledges that his mother changed his patriarchal views by showcasing that a woman is capable of fighting for her rights and pursuing her goals. Ahmad credits Parsi for his social and environmental concerns, which have motivated him to join an NGO named the Society of Women and Youth Protectors of the Environment (*Jamiat-e zanan va javanan-e hafeze mohit-e zist*). The film succeeds in presenting a poetic portrait of a strong and visionary woman whose environmental and social activism serves as a role model for anyone who cares about environmental protection and women's rights.

All My Trees and *Poets of Life* provide a crucial introduction to the lives and contributions of women who strive to protect the environment and bring about gender equality in order to enhance the well-being and advancement of society.

The works of these women have been driven by two important realizations that can also be found in the vision of women's environmental NGOs in Iran: "first, they are conscious of the historical role of women in environmental conservation. Second, they are aware of the importance of women's empowerment in a society in which women have always been suppressed" (Fadaee 2012: 101). As such, these documentaries perform an activist task by introducing these inspiring women as significant social actors for whom improving environmental protection is intertwined with improving women's status. Here, the documentary medium becomes a powerful tool through which women documentarians intervene in the patriarchal and sociocultural structures to offer groundbreaking representations of women's works and visions. As Stephen Rust and Salma Monani contend, "From an ecocritical perspective, environment is not just the organic world . . .; it is the whole habitat which encircles us, the physical world entangled with the cultural. It is an ecology of connections that we negotiate to make our meanings and our livings. In this habitat, cinema is a form of negotiation" (2013: 1). Within this ecological context, Iranian women's documentaries serve as sites of sociocultural and ecofeminist negotiations while also attesting to the power of documentary as a cinematic form used not only for documentation and representation but also for recognition and advocacy.

Note

1 Examples of biographical documentaries presenting women's lives include Ebrahim Mokhtari's *Mokarrameh, Memories and Dreams* (*Mokarrameh, khaterat va roya-ha*, 1999), Maryam Sepehri's *Thicker than Paint* (*Faratar az rang*, 2014), and Sahar Mosayebi's *Zero to Podium* (*Sefr ta sakoo*, 2017). Examples of environmental documentaries include Mojtaba Mirtahmasb's *The River Still Has Fish* (*Roodkhaneh hanooz mahi darad*, 2002), Mahmoud Rahmani's *My Mother, Oak* (*Madaram baloot*, 2010), and Mohammad Saeed Mohasesi's *Zendehrood, One Special Day* (*Zendehrood, yek rooz-e behkhosoos*, 2013).

8

Que se vayan ellos

Beyond Resilience in Puerto Rican Social Justice Documentary

Zaira Zarza

Subject to legal, political, and commercial restraints as *estado libre asociado*—an unincorporated state—of the United States since 1952, Puerto Rico has endured chronic invisibility, extraordinary inequality, and accelerated gentrification since Hurricane Maria hit the archipelago in 2017. The aftermath of the disaster made the country a perfect fiscal paradise for wealthy foreigners and a laboratory for testing cryptocurrencies (Bowles 2018; Crandall 2019). In addition, a seventy-two-billion-dollar illegal debt had already created unsustainable financial insecurity for the country, leaving its inhabitants in constant uncertainty and vulnerability (Rodríguez Coss 2019; Cortés 2018). These circumstances are evidence of the failure of the nation's economic progress project that began with the implementation of Operation Bootstrap in the late 1940s. A model for "third world" economic development through export-led industrialization driven by Governor Luis Muñoz Marin, this plan aimed to redirect the agrarian Puerto Rican economy toward manufacturing, turning the island into a prosperous industrial region. Providing a tax framework that favored businesses and holders of large amounts of capital, the plan was eventually thwarted due to outside competition, dependency on US corporations, growing unemployment, income inequality, and increased living standards on the island (Santana 1998; Maldonado 2020).

Decades later, Puerto Rico continues to grapple with the legacy of colonialism in the Caribbean context. The new millennium has seen the false promises of development and political autonomy dig a deep hole in Boricuas' everyday lives. In addition, their complex commonwealth status has generated not only political ambiguity, dependency, and disempowerment, but has also laid the foundation for systemic oppression and structural violence. This phenomenon led to socioeconomic policies favoring foreign investment instead of local initiatives by small and medium enterprises on the island. In this sense, when compared to those born and living on the mainland, Puerto Ricans suffer a lack of rights and are considered second-class citizens (Hermilla 1997; Smith 2017). They are, in consequence, left underserved and dependent on US-based administrative decisions.[1] This situation has prompted Boricuas to think and act beyond resilience and against coloniality as they recognize the impact of oppression and neoliberal ideologies on their territory. Political scientists Amelia Cheatham and Diana Roy (2022) note how the country is "a political paradox: part of the United States but distinct from it, enjoying citizenship but lacking full political representation, and infused with its own brand of nationalism despite not being a sovereign state" (par. 1). In particular, "[a]s a U.S. territory, Puerto Rico does not have the authority to control its political economy, limiting the efforts put in place to reduce its vulnerability to natural disasters" (Nihad 2022: 27).

The succession of ecological disasters—Hurricane Maria in 2017, an earthquake in 2020, and Hurricane Fiona in 2022—have contributed to the now popular saying that living in Puerto Rico has become an extreme sport. The benefits of Act 22[2]—now part of Act 60—and the decrease in property values after these events prompted the closing of schools, the displacement of communities, and the privatization of public spaces. Massive emigration ensued (Hinojosa 2018; Alexander et al. 2019). However, Puerto Ricans' primary disaster training has been enduring a decades-long colonial condition.

What place do non-fiction stories take in this context, particularly those by women filmmakers? More specifically, what role do Puerto Ricans, at home and in the diaspora, play in debunking narratives that sell the island as a paradise, fiscal and otherwise? This chapter explores these questions by analyzing how the films *Landfall* (Cecilia Aldarondo, 2020) and *Aquí vive gente* (People Live Here, Bianca Graulau, 2022) highlight the critical role of community organizing in recovery and the constant struggle against injustice, displacement, and crippling illegal debt faced by Puerto Rico. Although distinct in their presentation, these two women-directed documentaries put forth steadfast critiques of the consequences of Puerto Rico's dependence on the United States, a profound love for the country, its enormous potential as an independent nation, and the solidarity values of its people. They succeeded by engaging feminist perspectives in their collaborative filmmaking, ecological preoccupations, and commitment to social justice.

Over the years, feminist documentary studies have explored the representation of women's issues (Lesage 1978), the interdisciplinary aesthetics emerging from the link between multiple feminist and documentary theories (Waldman and Walker 1999), the significance of broader notions of female authorship and agency (Ulfsdotter and Backman Rogers 2018a, 2018b), and the gender non-exclusive perspective of the female gaze (French 2021). In their text "Beyond Story: An Online Community-Based Manifesto," Alex Juhasz and Alisa Lebow recognize the need for communal forms of documentaries as they propose larger conversations about the genre's diversity of formats. As they criticize narrative structures centered on the single story, they analyze how a "dominant mode of cinematic storytelling—developed to serve commercial interests—privileges individuals over collectivities, people over their environments, human will over systemic forces, and in terms of spectatorship, feelings over analysis and passivity over action . . . This individualistic ideology naturalizes bourgeois values and the economic system that supports them" (2018: 2).

I argue that it is in this focus on collectivity and active collaboration that Puerto Rican documentaries by women can be situated within existing scholarship on feminist non-fiction films. Aldarondo's and Graulau's works are illustrative examples of films that not only portray but also become communal responses to the shared trauma caused by ecological and colonial disasters in Puerto Rico.

With funding from the POV showcase of the Public Broadcasting Service (PBS), Cecilia Aldarondo's feature documentary *Landfall* discusses issues of collective trauma and community efforts facing coloniality, climate stressors, and disaster capitalism. The film showcases what happened between the passing of Hurricane Maria and the massive demonstrations against Governor Ricardo Roselló, which ignited the #Rickyrenuncia campaign. These actions resulted in the resignation in 2019 of Roselló and his entire cabinet. On the other hand, using recording artist Bad Bunny's platform for the music video *El apagón* (The Blackout, 2022), the research journalism reportage *Aquí vive gente* by Bianca Graulau explores how Act 22, also known as the Individual Investors Act, causes the displacement of entire communities due to tax exemptions for real estate investors who have become *bona fide* residents, ever since Puerto Rico's Legislative Assembly passed the law in 2012. In a strong critique of exploitative policies on the island, the video—unexpected for both Bad Bunny's fans and Graulau's social media followers—reached over 15 million views on YouTube as of 2024. While these documentaries depict the on-the-ground tactics of local actors addressing social justice issues, they also have the potential to become transnational agents to voice the need for radical change and generate debates on Puerto Rico's current and historical condition.[3]

Critical Approaches to Disaster and Resilience in the Post-Hurricane Maria Era

Local or regional events, such as the 9/11 attacks, the 2004 tsunami in Indonesia, Hurricane Katrina in New Orleans in 2005, Haiti's 2010 earthquake, the Ukraine war, as well as global phenomena like the Covid-19 pandemic, and today's challenges and reconstruction processes in the era of the climate crisis, have all sparked the implementation of and subsequent discussions about disaster capitalism. In her book *The Shock Doctrine* (2007), Canadian journalist Naomi Klein describes this phenomenon as "orchestrated raids on the public sphere in the wake of catastrophic events, combined with the treatment of disasters as exciting market opportunities" (2007: 6). She also analyzes how the free market relies heavily on using shock tactics or the disruptive impact of sudden and unexpected events to exert its power. In direct reference to Puerto Rico in the aftermath of Hurricane Maria, the journalist suggests that

> [t]he real disaster was not the hurricane but the terrible vulnerability imposed by Puerto Rico's colonial relationship to the United States, as well as the forced privatization of health and other services, massive layoffs, huge numbers of school closures; reductions in social rights and in investments for collective well-being; abandonment of social and physical infrastructure; and high levels of government corruption and ineptitude. (Klein 2018: 8)

As portrayed by this chapter's case studies, Puerto Rico became an incubator for disaster capitalism after Hurricane Maria. And while this "battle for paradise" (Klein 2018) made recovery more challenging, disaster—"the storm before the storm"—had already existed there for decades as long-term structural violence. Boricua scholar Yarimar Bonilla calls this condition the "coloniality of disaster," one that compels us to "think of disaster as structure, rather than event" (2020c: 1). She argues "that disaster capitalism needs to be understood as a form of racio-colonial capitalism and that this in turn, requires us to question our understandings of both 'resilience' and 'recovery'" (2020b: 1).

What happens when a permanent state of resilience is the status quo? Is a continuously resilient state the best possible solution for the problems of individuals, communities, or societies? Critiques of the much-debated idea of resilience have been at the forefront of recent discussions in climate change, critical disaster studies, medicine, and cultural studies, among others, as the ability to "build capacity for learning and adaptation" (Folke et al. 2002: 7), "tolerate disturbance without collapsing" (Resilience Alliance 2014: 1), and "'bounce back' or respond positively to adversity" (Maguire and Hagan 2007: 16). Millions of people lose their lives in natural disasters, wars, and other human-caused accidents. When facing events where death is the only possible alternative in the context of a catastrophe, resilience as survival takes on a positive, critical significance. However, survival mode becomes a weapon of colonial power in long-lasting conditions of precarity and dependency. In Puerto Rico's case, resilience meant Boricuas were forced to recover from the catastrophe while trying to survive the precarious state of emergency and resist political mismanagement in a climate of heightened tension and insecurity.

Resilience is also expected from and called upon when communities face long-lasting scenarios of vulnerability, such as Puerto Rico's. Kevon Rhiney talks about the naturalization of disaster as a "necessary precondition to pursuing true resilience" (2020: 2), while Schuller and Maldonado call attention to the "[n]ational and transnational governmental institutions' instrumental use of catastrophe (both so-called "natural" and human-mediated disasters, including post-conflict situations) to promote and empower a range of private, neoliberal capitalist interests" (2016: 62). Resilience then becomes, as Fathimath Nayifa Nihad puts it, "a dangerous concept because it promotes returning to normalcy, on which the resilience discourse is often based, and the 'normalcy' are already dangerous living conditions with a high vulnerability that created the risk (and resilience) in the first place" (2022: 18). For her part, Yarimar

Bonilla asks: "what will these increasingly individualized and privatized forms of resilience and self-reliance produce in a place that was already bracing itself for austerity? At what point does resilience become a form of neoliberal endurance?" (2020a: 5). She goes on to argue that "resilience, it seems, is good for business" (2020a: 9). The Covid-19 crisis also impacted and added to the damage of the state since Puerto Rico's economy relies heavily on tourism. The climate and economic crisis that followed led thousands of Puerto Ricans to leave their home country, hoping for a brighter future on the mainland, leaving behind those most affected and whose homes were already precarious (Sheller 2021). All these reflections point out how Caribbean societies and ecosystems have historically been forced to overcome obstacles and difficulties due to foreign exploitation and local administrative negligence. These conditions become unsustainable in the long term and continue to generate vicious cycles that perpetuate oppression.

As Carmen Gonzalez defines in her analysis of racial capitalism, the disposability of communities affected by climate change, both in their homelands and as migrants, proves a lack of sovereignty and futurity (2021). Facing this panorama, Yarimar Bonilla's vision of post-disaster futures for Puerto Rico raises crucial questions:

> How can we live and act politically in the absence of faith in a better future? How can we develop . . . a kind of hopeful pessimism that can serve to build politically in the face of ruin and the promise of further decay?. . . [H]opeful pessimism opens our eyes to the hard tasks required to transform the here and now . . . [A] "wake of disenchantment," [marks] an era in which the political models of the past have lost their purchase but new political forms, vocabularies, and imaginaries are yet to emerge. (2020a: 157)

Bonilla defines hopeful pessimism in contradistinction to the idea of cruel optimism articulated by Lauren Berlant (2011). While the latter serves to describe the shared loss of faith in the illusions of liberal democracy, prosperity, and accessibility, the former designates the urgent need for collective responses in contexts where the fantasies of modern prosperity were either long dead or stillborn. This consideration indicates how concepts emerging in and developed to analyze the socioeconomic dynamics of privileged regions are not applicable to other locations that do not share the same geopolitical and financial advantages. Cecilia Aldarondo's and Bianca Graulau's films exemplify hopeful pessimism by representing concrete local actions pushing to change the island's existing conditions. They demonstrate how sustained resilience is not the solution to Puerto Rico's problems, nor is radical resistance, since the expulsion of Ricardo Roselló showed people's capacity to mobilize and achieve specific goals, but it did not change the underlying circumstances that generated his corrupt government in the first place. In sum, these women call for accountability toward institutions and governments that detain the civil power to respond to and act upon disaster colonialism.

Two key figures of anti-colonial struggle through their non-fiction work, Aldarondo and Graulau, also inscribe their films on the legacy of feminist documentary tradition. Aldarondo's directorial debut, *Memories of a Penitent Heart* (2016), focuses on a family story similar to those by other women filmmakers, such as Sarah Polley's *Stories We Tell* (2012), Victoria Linares Villegas's *It Runs in the Family* (2022), Mariel Brown's *Unfinished Sentences* (2017), Daniela Abad's *The Smiling Lombana* (2018), and Lourdes Portillo's *The Devil Never Sleeps* (2001).[4] These directors' self-referential documentaries feature family members and the filmmakers themselves via voice-over narration or on-screen presence as they embark on deep excavations and recreations of home video archives. In doing so, they try to reconstruct the memory of loved ones who have died—mothers, uncles, fathers, and grandfathers—through often contrasting testimonies and reminiscences of people who knew them. Even if *Memories* deals with the private story of the director's family, it portrays Puerto Rico as a collective entity that defines power and identity relations. *Landfall* adds to this corpus of films by doing the opposite: expressing the collective trauma through the experience of multiple individuals.

On the other hand, Graulau renews the praxis of reportage in the digital age by conducting in-depth research and broadcasting on open-access platforms. Her TikTok and YouTube videos enrich conversations in the audiovisual public sphere while engaging multiple forms of truthtelling and putting forth values of social justice. In that sense, she proves that non-fiction media narratives can be as valid contributions to public debates from a feminist and activist standpoint as other more conventional forms of documentary film. In doing so, she also deconstructs preconceived ideas of social media platforms as producing mainly superficial and entertaining content and demonstrates the actual possibilities for critical thinking in these networks. From this perspective, Aldarondo's and Graulau's films present the idea of Puerto Rico as an extended family. The reflexive nature of their work conveys the personal and political perspectives of both directors. They construct alternative or counter-histories that address long-standing material and structural concerns, challenging and expanding beyond the convenient discourses of resilience and the radical but ephemeral solutions of resistance.

Vulnerability and Colonial Legacies in *Landfall*

Cecilia Aldarondo's documentary *Landfall* deals with the aftermath of Hurricane Maria in 2017. It spans almost two years, ending in 2019 with the riots that led to the resignation of Governor Ricardo Roselló. The film incarnates what Aldarondo calls "rapid-fire, emergency filmmaking" (IDA Documentary Screening 2021) that, however, does not conform to tales of "disaster porn" narratives (Recuber 2013) prevalent in most international news reporting the events. Instead, it presents the trauma of a category five hurricane, concentrating on community leadership and grassroots organizing. As much as those collective responses imply specific material actions in the context of a crisis, they are also inevitably moved by affect, commitment, and ethics of care.

Diasporic Puerto Rican scholar Larry La Fountain-Stokes calls Aldarondo's films "archipelagoes of pain" (2023) where audiovisual metaphors talk about the loss of dignity and the nostalgia for a country that never has been.[5] Interested in Puerto Rican stories, Aldarondo finished her first documentary after years of unarchiving the hidden life of her migrant gay uncle Miguel Dieppa, who had moved to New York to be an actor and passed away from AIDS in the 1980s.[6] The film's most vital link to *Landfall* is its cultural and spatial conception of Puerto Ricanness. In a monologue, featured in *Memories of a Penitent Heart*, from one of Dieppa's plays, he defines the diagnosis of his singular case of "tropical disease": island fever. For him, "it is a feeling that creeps up on those who have known of wider spaces or long to do so. It's a fear that one's brain will be surrounded by water if one stays here too long." Or as Aldarondo herself describes later in the film, by outlining her country as a schizophrenic place: "small places like Puerto Rico have a special way of making you crazy . . . Everyone wanting to leave. Everyone wishing they'd stayed." She goes on to conclude: "How can you know who you are if the place you are coming from doesn't even know what it is?"

This uncertainty and ambiguity are at the heart of Puerto Rican identity. The idea of being a "nation on the move" (Duany 2000) or a "commuter nation" (Torre and Burgos 1994) also illustrates the regular forced economic migration and subsequent family separations that affect Puerto Ricans on and off the island. This conflict of staying and leaving is key to the story. The production process signified a rich collaboration between a Puerto Rican in the diaspora (the director, Cecilia Aldarondo) and one on the archipelago (associate producer and activist Lale Namerrow). As she recognizes her privilege compared to other Boricuas, who experienced colonialism and the hurricane firsthand, Aldarondo claims that the role of diasporic Puerto Ricans—who only received images of devastation—is to listen and create spaces for people on the archipelago (Aldarondo in Conéctate 2021). At the beginning of the film, Aldarondo talks to her good friend, Lale Namerrow, who marched on the streets of San Juan alongside 350,000 people for the resignation of Ricardo Roselló. Namerrow worked as *Landfall*'s associate producer, and their input was crucial to making sure the film went beyond the nostalgia often produced by distance for those in the diaspora and instead focused on the actual lived experiences of affected communities. The director regrets her absence from the multitudinous protest, while Namerrow describes how they experienced it following the dread of Maria's arrival. Since the film's release occurred amid the pandemic, many screenings took place online. However, this complication—the fate of the documentary was also marked by disaster—allowed the film to have extraordinary outreach, and many exchanges with Aldarondo and Namerrow were recorded and posted on multiple platforms available to extended audiences.[7]

Landfall's anti-colonial stance is evident through various narrative tools. It utilizes archival material as it relates to the progress of Puerto Rico as a thriving society or its promise with assembly lines setting production records. It equates tourism's exploitative practices to the plantation economy, and it presents the complex situation of the island of Vieques—a site of military training exercises since the US occupation in 1941—and the conditions of its inhabitants.

In their documentary, the filmmakers map the island, visiting various communities: Condado, Orocovis, Bartolo, Mayaguez, Rincón, Dorado,

Vieques, and San Juan. In some moments, the film is slow and contemplative, insightful in taking in all the horror a devastating event encapsulates and the solidarity networks that allowed people to survive it. The film critiques the so-called Puerto Rico "of the 21st Century," understood as a fiscal paradise for luxury realtors. *Landfall* follows white investors in conversation with local vulnerable youth, attempting to seduce and manipulate them with the promise of Bitcoin. Owners of multiple venture capital firms, such as Israeli entrepreneur Yaron Brooke, bona fide investor Quinn Eaker, and cryptocurrency magnate Brock Pierce, are key characters in the film's critical approach to vulture capitalism.

The film's characters also include a small community in Bartolo living a form of self-governed socialism, owners of real estate property for tourism in Dorado Beach, and María, a farmer who lovingly tends to her animals and land with her father, trying to develop sustainable agriculture.[8] She talks about how the labor force moved from the countryside to the city during industrialization and how a false idea of development stripped people of their natural knowledge, power, and security and made them dependent on technology and science. While she describes her dreams of buying her land and creating an educational center on her farm, the sun hides completely behind a cloud, leaving the image in shadows. María, the director, and the crew acknowledge this radical, spontaneous change in light on screen, and the filmmakers purposefully left that moment in the final cut, perhaps as a symbol of the "hopeful pessimism" Yarimar Bonilla talks about.

Similarly, Aldarondo joins the efforts of other documentarians, such as José María Cabral (*Plastic Island*, 2019), Natalia Cabral and Oriol Estrada (*Site of Sites*, 2016), and Esther Figueroa (*Caribbean Climate Change: The Take Away Messages*, 2017, and *Climate Change Is a Gender Issue*, 2018), showing an ecological preoccupation with the Caribbean as one of the world's most affected areas by natural disasters and climate change. The film's ecocritical approach is noticeable in the representations of nature and the non-human world, which balance harmoniously throughout what she has called "a place-making film" (IDA Documentary Screening, 2021). At times, cinematographer Pablo Álvarez-Mesa contrasts desolate images of the island after the storm with people's vibrant energy. Other times, the camera lingers softly on the extraordinary beauty of the landscape and its affective sonic and visual power: the sweltering sun, land surrounded by water, waves, caves, trees moved by the wind, rocks, and domesticated farm and wild animals. Some of these can be considered symbols of Puerto Ricanness and islander cultures in the Caribbean.

Multiple collective conversations on politics take place in the film. Hope—or lack thereof—and utopia are the ultimate topics of discussion in these events. During one, a Boricua Afro-Latina and a young Taino woman argue with condescending white men who have come to invest in the island. Rightfully suspicious, they contest these new colonizers' intentions, which are masked under a veil of freedom. Youth also gather around a dinner table to talk about their recovery mode, the urge of not having had the time to process and reflect on what happened and the more than 5,000 people who died because of government inaction. A recurrent statement is that the hurricane survivors made it, thanks to other hurricane survivors, because the country lacked infrastructure and preventive measures to face such an event, and first responders had no contingency plans. The film concludes with Noel Estrada Suárez's 1943 song *En mi Viejo San Juan*. The excitement of the end of the #Rickyrenuncia campaign culminates on a new day when all graffiti is removed, and walls are painted clean as a sad calm after the storm: a reminder that the cause of the country's grave situation remains unchanged.

Against Privatization and Displacement: Social Media Activism in *Aquí vive gente*

Many of *Landfall*'s discussions on dependency and gentrification reappear in the reportage *Aquí vive gente*, by journalist Bianca Graulau in collaboration with Laura Pérez.[9] As a non-fiction narrative style often used in journalistic research, the term "reportage" is distinguished from documentary in terms of, among others, authorial perspectives, temporality, production strategies, and distribution channels. According to François Niney (2009), contrary to the documentary, which is understood as a personal and authorial exploration, the reportage is a matter-of-fact production generally commissioned by a television channel, resulting in an objective report on a subject of social or political immediacy. In this sense, it is perceived as featuring "nobody's point of view" (120). This analysis, however, ignores the activist engagement of independent journalists who work halfway between the immediacy of news coverage or reports and the poetic voice of cinematic non-fiction.

As a piece at the crossroads of reportage and documentary, *Aquí vive gente* conveys the critical potential of activist filmmaking by using social media strategies and platforms to discuss an urgent and contemporary topic while using the documentary's political stance to condemn decades of US colonial imperialism in Puerto Rico.[10] Thus, her work does not align with the narrow definitions of a typical reportage. By using her voice as a narrator and placing herself in front of the camera, Graulau becomes a participant in the story. She demonstrates how there is also subjectivity in journalism where the point of view of the researcher/author is put forward. She also incorporates ethnographic research methods such as interviews, participant observation, and archival analysis. Furthermore, the film is independently produced and created for nontheatrical release on an open-access platform destined for a wide audience. In that regard, *Aquí vive gente* combines two crucial elements to succeed in its alternative distribution method. First, it utilizes an online social media platform known for distributing free content. Then, it takes advantage of a musician's fan base to expand viewership. The team's sensitive eyes and ears explore translocal relations, including city, neighborhood, building, and household efforts against the country's capitalist privatization. They make a point of distinguishing the journalism they practice, which is backed by in-depth research, from much less investigative opinion journalism. Benefiting from the popularity of reggaeton and Bad Bunny's music video *El apagón*, Graulau's work has earned the denomination of *perreodismo*, a portmanteau combining the sensual dance style *perreo* (twerking) and *periodismo* (journalism). Archival footage used in the video features, among others, scenes from the political documentary *Simulacros de liberación* (2021) by Juan Carlos Dávila, an eco-post by Boricua YouTuber Jolsumd, who defends turtles' habitat and beaches as public spaces, and images of *perreo combativo* or militant twerking performances. The latter took place in front of the San Juan Cathedral during the Puerto Rican Summer when feminist and queer collectives led the popular mobilization that overthrew Ricardo Roselló's mandate.

Reggaeton has increasingly become the new protest music in the Caribbean for how it chronicles political tensions and everyday life struggles. In Puerto Rico, the rhythm has been used as a tool for social justice since the 1990s with figures such as Vico C, Tego Calderón, Wisin and Yandel, Daddy Yankee, and the popular band Calle 13. A major cultural phenomenon,

Benito Antonio Martínez Ocasio, also known as Bad Bunny, is one of the most influential Caribbean recording artists of his generation. The Puerto Rican singer, rapper, and songwriter has been a voice for the cause of Puerto Rico's independence throughout his career. He was propelled to the forefront of the international scene through collaborations with renowned artists, such as Cardi B. and J Balvin's *I Like It* (2018), Jennifer López's *Te gusté* (2018), and Drake's *Mía* (2018). His fans appreciate his support of the LGBTQA+ community, which he demonstrates in his lyrics and music videos, such as *Yo perreo sola* (2020) while positioning himself against gender violence in *Solo de mí* (2018) and *Andrea* (2022). He also inspired recent Boricua music and popular culture scholarship. His impact on the Puerto Rican political resistance is taught in a class at Loyola Marymount University, and the Center for Puerto Rican Studies at Hunter College in New York City celebrated a conference titled Thinking with Bad Bunny: The Cultural Politics of Puerto Rico in May 2023.[11]

El apagón transitions into an eighteen-minute reportage showing typical images of popular culture in Puerto Rico: sunny streets, colorful flags, and smiling people playing dominoes, singing plena, dancing bomba, and showcasing the island's African roots. Street protests, militant graffiti art, and local activist initiatives also populate the screen. The music video and reportage balance known imagery and representations of the island and discourses of radical political thinking and social justice action. *El apagón*'s music video includes locals lip-syncing the song, members of the queer community, and people of mixed races of all ages and body types as they praise Puerto Rico for its cultural values and then show discontent with the energy situation in the country. Graulau starts mid-song with a comment on the passing of electricity distribution in Puerto Rico to Luma Energy, a foreign company that has privatized electricity and inflated prices. Toward the end, the music video shows young people dancing to a Bad Bunny live performance and leaving the concert at dawn. A drone then flies over the island, offering exquisite aerial views of its landscape: mountains, rivers, and the Caribbean Sea shore. A female voice sings the lyrics: "I don't want to leave. I don't want to leave. They must go, they must go. This is my beach. This is my sun. This is my land. This is me."[12]

Rhythmic editing emphasizes the urgency of the situation featured in the reportage, which includes interviews with displaced neighbors expressing dissatisfaction with gentrification. In Santurce and Puerta de Tierra, residents feel undermined by the elimination of public housing for expensive Airbnb condos, exacerbating residential segregation. Families are receiving eviction notices requiring them to vacate the premises within thirty days. Maricusa, a Dominican migrant, is one of them. Laura Mía González says these foreign owners hoarding profit have an "invader colonizer's mentality [because] the government has handed them the country on a silver platter." New investors are displacing Puerta de Tierra's community, who are becoming foreigners in their own land—all the more unfair when the neighborhood had been a pillar of residential housing for decades. Brock Pierce also returns as an undesirable character in Puerto Rico's current financial landscape as well as Brian Tenenbaum, an investor who bought a local school for a development project. In the story's behind-the-scenes conversation (Detrás de cámaras 2022), the two journalists corroborate how the list of beneficiaries of Act 22 coincides considerably with the list of donors to the island's government as proof of blatant corruption. Graulau also exposes the massive closing of public schools and the privatization of public spaces such as Dorado Beach by corporate associations like Prisa Group, who are prominent supporters of the political parties in power. A domestic worker, Rosa Rivera Martínez, desires fair access to natural resources for everyone. "It mortifies me—she says—that they treat us as ignorants or criminals." One of the reportage's key moments sees a group of people destroying a pool built in front of a public beach and tearing down a wall that blocked access to it in the municipality of Rincón. As it happens in Aldarondo's *Landfall*, this compilation of voices provides a glimpse of Puerto Ricans' multiple perspectives on disaster capitalism.

While also used as a mechanism of control and mass state surveillance, social networks are, for Graulau, an instrument to create non-fiction narratives on justice struggles. Among other pursuits, she is developing a public transportation cartography of the island to discourage using individualized cars and the subsequent pollution they generate. She also has a YouTube series where she presents a critical history of Puerto Rico and promotes grassroots local initiatives such as turning abandoned lots into vegetable gardens to feed communities after Hurricane Maria. She discusses the damage caused by the clothing industry and encourages recycling and water management while disapproving of pollution and gentrification. She is also vocal about international affairs such as Airbnb's exploitative practices in New Orleans, the legacies of colonization in Hawaii, and tourism as a form of neo-colonialism. The Israel and Palestine conflict is another key focus of her interventions.

Graulau's social media feminism is a fantastic example of how online activism can help political and social justice while inspiring change.[13] She notably demonstrates the revolutionary ways women can use technologies and platforms today to create hybrid art forms in their storytelling, thus resisting conventional narratives and reinventing traditional thinking in journalism and filmmaking. Currently, Graulau utilizes her outlet on social media platforms TikTok and Instagram (@biancagraulau, with almost a million followers and over 25 million likes) to inform citizens and condemn colonialism and how it affects life in her country. Her videos are distributed via TikTok reels and YouTube. They discuss self-governance, minority entrepreneurship, creative industries' autonomy, and grassroots organizing. "TikTok is the reason I believed I could make it as an independent journalist," she says of her virality on the platform. "It's amazing to me that I could start with zero followers, do stories about things that I am passionate about, and find an audience" (Adler 2023: 5).

Conclusion

Landfall and *Aquí vive gente* are urgent, heartfelt love letters to Puerto Rico. While the feature documentary and short journalistic reportage did not have the same production, distribution, and exhibition processes, the feminist activism of these stories combines to bear witness to the consequences of coloniality and the mutual aid, grassroots solidarities, and community organizing implementing strategies to help overcome them. Especially during the post-Covid crisis, they consider how extractive practices disproportionately affect women, people of color, and indigenous communities, leading to displacement and impoverishment. Their critical approaches—one more poetic and cinematic and the other more matter of fact, but both equally forceful—exhibit feelings of uncertainty among the population and different levels of vulnerability facing the experience of disaster, gender dynamics, class divides, and racial capitalism. Both filmmakers display an ecofeminist approach since they understand that "[f]or ecofeminism, striving for new connectivities of care, responsibility and justice, therefore, has to be extended to social and natural realms as they are bound in the same systems of oppression" (Phillips and Rumens 2015: 2).

As demonstrated by the case studies analyzed in this chapter, the place of non-fiction stories, particularly those by women filmmakers, is crucial to understanding Puerto Rico's colonial past and present. Feminist and ecocritical narratives that reject the exoticization of disaster, as well as the conscious use of online media to reach broad audiences, helped in presenting an honest portrait of the island's conditions. Above all, collaboration seemed to be the key to bringing these projects to fruition: between community members at large—including the documentarians in the diaspora and on the archipelago—and between activists and cultural producers across multiple creative industries—journalists, musicians, and filmmakers. Collaboration in this way becomes an act of civic engagement connected to the legacy of feminist documentary filmmaking and digital activism. These films defend the idea that what happened with Hurricane Maria was not only a natural disaster but also a consequence of long-existing colonial status. As devastating as it was, the storm only came to bring light to the oppression of Puerto Rico's crippling debt, corruption, and lack of independence. When resilience is understood as continued survival and becomes the only option for citizens living outside the parameters of dignity and self-determination, striving for it will not provide solutions. The fundamental violation of human rights is a bigger problem. Both documentaries begin and end in the sea and return to it as the ultimate expression of Caribbeanness and more-than-human connections. With their work, these filmmakers strongly critique government neglect and neoliberal economies while sending the world a clear political message about dishonest politicians and exploitative entrepreneurs: "*Que se vayan ellos.*" They must go!

Notes

1 While the country had been a promised land since tax incentives boosted the manufacturing industry, limited self-governance, state mismanagement, the gradual elimination of public sector jobs, benefits reduction, workers' rights, and the massive privatization of the public sphere have marked the country's growing instability. The Puerto Rico Oversight, Management and Economic Stability Act (PROMESA) was created by President Barack Obama in 2016 to perpetuate the

island's dependency and control its unpayable debt via a Fiscal Control Board known as La Junta.
2 For more on the benefits of Act 22, see "Puerto Rico | Sotheby's International Realty" (2018).
3 For more on the realities of racialized filmmakers as those discussed in this chapter, inscribed in the tradition of transnational feminist filmmaking while coming from and working in marginalized contexts, see Lúcia Nagib (2001), Belinda Smaill (2012), and Patricia White (2015).
4 These films reveal controversial untold events through multiple levels of intimacy: from Polley's different versions of her mother's life to Abad's understanding of her *abuelo*'s link to drug trafficking in Colombia, to Brown's reconciliation with her poet dad through creative and affective explorations, to Portillo's investigation of her uncle's death via apparent suicide or covert murder.
5 Other films by Boricua women directors have also addressed this issue. The shorts *After Maria* (2019), a Netflix documentary by Nadia Hallgren, and the fiction story *La capa azul* (The Blue Cape, 2019) by Alejandra López, as well as the feature *Después de María: las dos orillas* (After Maria: The Two Shores, 2018) by Sonia Fritz, also focus on the aftermath of destruction in hurricane-ravaged Puerto Rico.
6 A diasporic tale, the film deals with the selective processes of memory and the conflict between specific interpretations of Christianity and queerness through a tense family-based narrative. But, as the filmmaker explains, the Miguel in her grandmother's scrapbook seemed like the son she wanted to have and not the one she gave birth to. The film is the typical queer diaspora film where the migrant journey becomes the coming-out gay liberation rite of passage for a young man. Ideas of repentance and forgiveness, the suspected queerness of her grandfather, and the ethics of family representation are discussed in the story.
7 See, for example, "Film & Discussion" (2021) and "*Landfall*: Conversation" (2021).
8 The country imports from the mainland 80 percent of the food it consumes, making their diet not only expensive but also abundant in processed foods and lacking in locally grown produce. Therefore, locally grown food initiatives are particularly relevant, and food sovereignty is a recurrent discussion on the archipelago.
9 Paradoxically, the online outreach of both films through Zoom presentations during the pandemic in the case of *Landfall* and on YouTube in the case of *Aquí vive gente* has helped these stories reach more viewers than they would have through traditional distribution.

10 García-Ortega and García-Avilés (2023) analyze innovation in journalistic narrative through new formats in their study of the ephemeral content of Instagram Stories, viral journalism on TikTok, and the adaptation of comics for reportage. The application of these formats and the adaptation to the language and logic of social platforms impact professionals and journalistic practices, challenging the boundaries of traditional journalism. New possibilities are opened for news coverage, there is greater hybridization between information, entertainment, and fiction storytelling techniques, and narratives with a wider emotional impact on the audience are exploited.
11 For more information about Bad Bunny's impact on feminism, gender studies, and decolonial studies, see Damaly Gonzalez (2023).
12 "Yo no me quiero ir de aquí, no me quiero ir de aquí. Que se vayan ellos, que se vayan ellos. Esta es mi playa. Este es mi sol. Esta es mi tierra. Esta soy yo."
13 For more on how social media activism has played a crucial role in civil protests such as the Arab Spring, the Occupy, and the #MeToo and #BlackLivesMatter movements, see Christian Fuchs (2014), Tim Markham (2014), Nikita Carney (2016), and Rosemary Clark-Parsons (2021).

9

The Art of Work Is a Work of Art
Feminist Theater and Live Documentary

Kim Munro

Introduction

This chapter discusses my hybrid theater documentary project, *The Art of Work Is a Work of Art* (hereafter just *The Art of Work*), performed at the Waterside Workers Hall in Port Adelaide in 2023 and redeveloped for the fortieth anniversary of the South Australian queer feminist theater company Vitalstatistix in 2025. The project emerges from an ongoing conversation between myself and the three co-founders of Vitalstatistix. As such, this chapter discusses the first iteration of the project, reflecting on feminist film practices, concepts of utopia and queer temporalities, and archives, as well as the tensions and overlaps between the "live" and the "documented." Drawing on the work of queer theorist Jose Esteban Muñoz, performance and utopian studies, and archival theory, I frame this work as one that employs both documentary and theater strategies to restage various histories of feminism and queerness relevant to the Australian context and beyond.

I write this chapter as part of a creative practice methodology grounded in experimentation, iteration, and reflection, employing what Trinh T. Minh-ha has called a "speaking nearby" (2012). Trinh uses this term to refer to how she approaches the representation of her participants and her refusal to speak "for" them as well as how a film's visuals correlate to the spoken words. Trinh uses this same phrase "speaking nearby" in relation to how she writes about her films: "I *theorize* with my films, not *about* them" (2013: 143). For Trinh, neither the theory nor the writing should illustrate or describe the film; rather, it can serve as a mode of "inquiry, displacement, and expansive enrichment" (2013: 143). This chapter is written mid-way through the project and operationalized as a way of thinking with the project as it further develops.

The Art of Work is about more than the formation and early performance work of Vitalstatistix. Instead, the filmmaking process of working with Ollie Black, Margie Fischer, and Roxxy Bent, as well as the contributing artists, extends to broader questions in my practice. These questions interrogate documentary as a versatile, embodied, and queer space for how we make futures together. *The Art of Work* asks what "documentary" might bring to theater and what "liveness" may offer documentary. Here, theater exists as an ephemeral form and in a state of "becoming," rather than as the fixed object of the documentary film. This chapter also considers questions of how feminist histories can be reanimated and remembered through "non-traditional forms of historiography" (Balsom and Peleg 2016: 16), especially when there is a paucity of archival documentation or when historiography has traditionally been the domain of a patriarchal gaze (Balsom 2022: np). Underpinning this project and this chapter is an investigation of how documentary storytelling and knowledge is shaped through its forms. If, as Juhasz and Lebow argue, politics and form are implicitly entwined (2018), how can new modes of documentary that use live performance challenge socially and culturally constructed ways of thinking as well as ways of interpreting the past? Through exploring such expanded forms of documentary, I make a broader claim for practices that can reimagine activism and utopian ideals and pay homage to radical and queer histories.

Methodology: Creative Practice Research

While much has been written in the past decade about creative practice in an academic context, a great deal of the research has attempted to validate the knowledge gained through practice, whether it contributes back to that creative field or has greater implications for the relationship between theory and practice. Creative practice research is an umbrella term that can describe a number of different approaches. Some of these are methodological, and some are geographically specific. For Candy and Edmonds, "practice-based research is an original investigation undertaken in order to gain new knowledge, partly by means of practice and the outcomes of that practice" (2018: 63). These authors suggest that the artifact is crucial to practice-based researchers, and the gained knowledge is in turn implemented in the finished artifact through a reflective process (2018: 65). Film scholar Susan Kerrigan argues that "Creative practice methodologies are preferred in screen production because they reveal research insights into how audiovisual meaning is made from the perspective of the creator/s of a screen work" (2018: 10). These definitions do not fully describe the relationship between the creative practice and the theories that inform it. The most eloquent descriptions of a creative practice methodology employ equal attention to the materiality of the language. As Ross Gibson writes, "Audio-visual knowledge: how to envisage it, chase it, generate it, grasp it, communicate it, tally its impact and heft? Such knowledge arises, I suggest, when the filmmaker-researcher experiences the immersed, messy routines of creativity oscillating with the distanced analytics of reflective critique and theorisation" (2018: vii). Here, Gibson is less interested in definitions of creative practice research than the generative possibilities of shifting between tacit knowledge and how the practitioner articulates this knowledge within a field of practice (2018). Gibson further suggests that "The creative researcher engages in a cognitive two-step, jinking rapidly back and forth between immersed investigation leading to inchoate understanding, on the one hand, and reflective knowing outside and after the event, on the other hand" (2018: vii).

Like Gibson, Natalie Loveless identifies the importance of "curiosity" within the creative practice research process along with its attendant driving force, "ignorance" (2019: 70). Loveless draws on queer and psychoanalytic theories of "unproductiveness" to argue for a "polydisciplinary" approach to research creation (as it is called in Canada) in order to honor the process of unruly processes and outcomes, rather than merely contributing to established systems (2019: 17). This has resonance with how Trinh approaches her practice, which is also formally experimental. Although Trinh is drawn to certain subjects and questions, entering a film or writing project requires the same sense of openness. What remains constant in her work, she offers, is how the formal techniques of filmmaking can interact with the subject matter throughout the process, resulting in how "a work breathes, moves, pauses, and rests" (Trinh cited in Radhakrishnan 2022: np). It is akin to what filmmaker Jill Daniels refers to as an essayistic approach with her practice of experimentation similar to that of "a *bricolease,* or the 'handywoman'" (2022: 128). In my work, both the theory and the practice are entangled, each being important in how they inter-relate in an iterative process.

Background and the Event

The Art of Work is primarily a project about the three co-founders of the Vitalstatistix theater company in Port Adelaide, or Yertabulti (in the local Aboriginal Kaurna language). In 1984, three lesbian feminists, Ollie, Margie, and Roxxy, all of whom had found their home in Adelaide, set up the theater company. *The Art of Work* excavates the first eight years when the three of them worked together as they wrote, directed, and performed plays; held workshops and music events; championed Indigenous women's music; and fought for a women-only space for theater makers in Adelaide. The original plays were based on issues affecting women at the time, which included body image, sexual harassment, and aging—all of which remain relevant today although gender is not so binary, and feminism has strived to be more intersectional. The three co-founders were supported by a network of collaborators and what they call the *femocrats*, a group of women in power who provided mentorship and advocacy. Before their permanent home at the Waterside Workers Hall in Port Adelaide, Vitalstatistix performed in various theaters around Adelaide and interstate. They would also go on regional tours, sometimes for months at a stretch, entertaining and challenging audiences in community centers, ad hoc pop-up theaters, schools, prisons, and other workplaces such as mines. Performances were preceded by workshops for high-school girls and followed by a discussion of the central issues—with a strong bent toward pedagogy and consciousness-raising.

The Art of Work was performed twice in July 2023 at Vitalstatistix theater at the end of a two-week residency. In the second week, I worked with four artists I had commissioned, all of whom had a history of making work with Vitalstatistix: Emma Beech (theater maker and performer), Sasha Grbich (visual artist), Mish Grigor (performance artist), and Jen Mills (writer). The sixty-minute performance consisted of seventeen short film sequences grouped together in five parts of 4–5 minutes each, and three performances in between. The film sequences incorporated individual interviews; scenes of

Ollie, Margie, and Roxxy unpacking the boxes of archives and reminiscing about their work and adventures; archival photos; VHS recordings of their rehearsals; and excepts from one of the productions, *A Touchy Subject*. The performances devised by the commissioned artists included a table reading of a script that Jen had composed from all the plays written during the eight years, a performance lecture by Mish, and a participatory survey via question cards by Sasha, performed with Emma. The process was part collaboration and in part driven by the individual practices of the artists. Great attention was also paid to the facilitation of the event through the act of hospitality—inspired by the community spaces that many of the performances took place in during the 1980s and early 1990s (Figure 9.1).

As the first iteration of the project, and coming from screen-based practice, I was unsure of how the live elements and the film sequences would sit together. Would the audience's interest be sustained? Was there enough context provided for the interstitial performances? Was there too much talking and not enough movement of bodies within all the dimensions of the theater space? I had approached the commissions with a light touch, giving freedom

Figure 9.1 *The Art of Work Is a Work of Art* directed by Kim Munro. © Kim Munro 2023. All rights reserved.

to each of the artists to interpret the brief with little intervention on my part. Reflecting on the showings from a distance, these questions persist and have prompted me to seek the collaborative input of a theater maker for the next phase of the work.

Feminist Filmmaking and Utopias

The gestation period for *The Art of Work* began more than a year before the event and came out of a friendship with Ollie that began not long after I moved to Adelaide in 2021. Ollie had told me stories, showed me photos, and introduced me to Margie and Roxxy. Seeing the three of them together for the first time, almost forty years after they had first met, felt electrifying. Looking at the photographs and hearing the stories of how these women made work and life together calls forth a specific moment in time when systemic change seemed possible through art. More than once when I was filming, Ollie, Margie, and Roxxy remarked that they thought they would change the world—that it was possible for art, in this case, theater, to change the world by bringing these issues to light and with humor—or to use their tagline, "A lighthearted look at a heavy issue." This was the 1980s, a time of second-wave feminism, of women establishing female-only communities, of the personal-as-political. It is little wonder then that feminism of the 1970s (and early 1980s) was associated with utopian ideals. As Angelika Bammer writes, just as "the utopian dream was being pronounced dead" elsewhere, it was being taken up by feminists who "called for new ways of seeing, thinking, and feeling, new ways of living, loving, and working" and, with that, "new ways of experiencing the body, using language, and defining power" (2015: 2). These new modes of expression can also be seen in the work of feminist filmmakers from this time, such as Chantal Akerman and Barbara Hammer, and later Trinh T. Minh-ha and Lynne Sachs.

Utopian thinking implies an intention, or a process of becoming. Etymologically, from Ancient Greek, utopia means "no place." That is not to say that utopia is impossible, for as Bammer writes, "as soon as we abandon the conventional concept of *a utopia*, we find that *the utopian* is not dead at all, but very much alive in people's longing for a more just and human world" (2015: 4). In her contribution to *The Art of Work*, Mish Grigor centers feminist utopias and collectives in her eight-minute performance lecture, which draws parallels across generations of feminist performance and collective action. Mish, a founding member of experimental performance art collectives POST and APHIDS, lives in Naarm/Melbourne, and her only access to the archives was through a shared Google folder with a few scanned documents and photos. Rather than spending time digging in the archival boxes stored at the theater, which the other artists did to varying ends, Mish wanted to conjure the space of possibility that Vitalstatistix embodies. In some of our conversations during the process, Mish reflected on how much of her time in the collectives was spent discussing how to work together. This had also come up in the interviews I did with each of the three co-founders. I was reminded of Brazilian theater practitioner and political activist Augusto Boal's belief that theater could transform society by transforming the individual. Here, the transformation takes place not only within theater but also through making the work or practicing how to be together.

Acknowledging that "theater is not revolutionary in itself," Boal did believe that it was "a rehearsal for the revolution" (2008: 98). One photo in particular had captured Mish's imagination. The photo showed some of the co-founders and extended network sitting on the steps out front of the Waterside Workers Hall counting the money after a show. This image expressed not the production, but rather the exhilaration of those moments of being together that make a collective. This single photo was the fulcrum of Mish's performance and one that echoed the early days of her own experience in collectives.

Behind the celebrated auteur in documentary filmmaking's canonical history, women have always collaborated around the fringes, doing the organizing, planning, or editing (Zimmermann 1999). What Zimmermann is referring to here is the essential role that these women played as part of the network of production—the roles usually overlooked when histories are told. What looking at feminist practices can show us is that these hierarchies are less apparent. How then to make explicit these networks of women and practices within the work? While this was a consideration when making *The Art of Work* with the co-founders and the artists, what I had overlooked were all the contributors who were less visible—many of whom no longer live in Adelaide and many of whom had passed away. This was also feedback given by one of the audience members with a close connection to the theater and its history. During the interviews and in their shared conversation, Ollie, Margie, and Roxxy would mention the names of different women—co-writers, actors, organizers, set designers, directors, friends, and crew. These women appear in the photographs and the stories as integral members of the expanded collective. Foregrounding this work as a collective project challenges how authorship might look as a shared endeavor in what artist Alex Martinis Roe calls a relational process where individual voices reflect the networks (2018: 15). This is a question of how to represent the non-hierarchical structure through the form—and one I am grappling with as I expand the project moving forward.

While *The Art of Work* is a hybrid documentary-theater project, my background and knowledge are firmly in documentary practice and how it can draw on other disciplines and epistemologies. There are also parallels between documentary film and theater as they intersect with feminism and challenge dominant modes of production. The often-overlooked history of collective filmmaking has been enjoying a recent revival in Australia. This is in part due to an increase in micro-cinemas and local filmmaking groups as well as the 2022 documentary *Senses of Cinema* (John Hughes and Tom Zubrycki), about the filmmaking co-ops of Melbourne, Sydney, and Brisbane, which began in the early 1970s and continued until the mid-1980s in Sydney, at least. This era also saw a number of women's groups dedicated to filmmaking, including the Sydney Women's Film Group, the Feminist Film Workers (1970s–80s), the Melbourne Women's Film Group (established in 1973), Reel Women (1979–83) and the Women's Film Unit (1984 in Sydney and 1984/5 in Melbourne) (French 2003: 13). It is this history of collective filmmaking that *The Art of Work* forms a lineage with while also forging new interdisciplinary possibilities for performing history.

While looking through the archives at Vitalstatistix, I see a woman I recognize. I had met her in a friend's kitchen in Melbourne some years ago. This same friend, an ex-circus worker, introduced me to Ollie when I moved to Adelaide in 2021. The woman in the photo is Robin Laurie, and part of the crossover between film and theater of this time. Laurie, more performer than filmmaker, had made an iconic film with the prominent feminist filmmaker Margot Nash. *We aim to please* is an experimental short that explores female desire and the male gaze through the invention of new cinematic language.

To date, there has been little research on feminist filmmaking in Australia, with one of the few exceptions being the edited collection *Don't Shoot Darling* (1987). This book provides a dedicated space for women filmmakers to tell their own histories rather than being "footnotes to accounts of the exploits of famous men" (1987: np). Prefacing the individual contributions in the book, editors Annette Blonski, Barbara Creed, and Freda Freiberg outline some of the salient features of feminist filmmaking practices in the 1980s, many of which have parallels with what Vitalstatistix were doing with theater: the focus on collaborative practices and role-sharing rather than hierarchical roles; screenings in non-mainstream theaters, women's spaces, and educational institutions; using the films as methods of consciousness-raising and discussions about issues affecting women; and a combination of forms from agitprop and street theater, to critique of mainstream representations of women and melodrama (Blonski, Creed, and Freiberg 1987: np). The authors make the case that the women's movement, combined with the many filmmakers who had also worked in live and experimental theater, had influenced both the subject matter and the filmmaking approaches. This was bolstered in Australia by the establishment of the Experimental Film Fund in 1968 and the allocation of funding toward women's filmmaking in 1975 for International Women's Year, which saw women experimenting with collective modes of production and experimental forms. These films, made by Australian women, were markedly different from the documentaries coming out of the United States and the UK with their focus on consciousness-raising (Blonski, Creed, and Freiberg 1987: np). Within the intersection between the experimental film productions, which often used humor and play, and the more edifying and collectivist intentions of the consciousness-raising films, the women of Vitalstatistix found a form of theater that embraced a multitude of feminist forms.

As noted above, feminist filmmaking often followed two tendencies: those that were formally experimental and aimed to challenge representation (Zimmermann 1999: 73) or those that more closely resembled consciousness-raising meetings and employed realist strategies (Lesage 1978). Such "realist" works, rather than being didactic, have been subject to ongoing scholarly appreciation for their political intent and amplification of marginalized perspectives (Lesage and Warren 2022: 143). In making *The Art of Work*, I find this tension between realist and experimental feminist practices and the parallels with theater to be both challenging and productive. The hybrid project allows both a dedication to the realism and the stories that are so valued by the co-founders, as well as the commissioned components, which are, to a degree, liberated from the same expectations. Sitting alongside the documentary film components, these new performative segments of the project can re-enact methodologies of the times or allow the artists to bring their own practices into view. This goes some way in navigating the complexity of documentary where the need to clearly explicate a story or history is often at odds with a more formally experimental mode of expression.

Queer Temporalities

When I first met Margie, she asked me if I am lesbian or queer. I asked if I could be both, and she said not really. While my politics and theoretical positioning might be queer, I would probably still identify as both, but it could be a matter of my age as fewer young people identify as lesbian than in previous generations. If, as Baker suggests, a queer practice-led methodology should be entangled with one's own subjectivity, then I might ask to what extent the idea of temporalities is at play. Throughout the development of *The Art of Work*, and leading up to the two showings, I kept wondering whether this was a legacy project. This is a question especially pertinent to queer or LGBTQ+ people, even more so if they don't have children, who, as Muñoz reminds us by way of Whitney Houston, "are our future" (2019: 49). Focused on women in their seventies, the project does contain a sense of legacy about what they have created together, as well as what they bequeath to younger generations of feminists and artists, more broadly. Instead of biological ties, these women are rather foremothers or elders in struggle.

The question of legacy is also an ethical one and informs how I set up the space in which I film and how I then sequence the material. The performance of *The Art of Work* begins with a filmed sequence of Ollie, Margie, and Roxxy in the hall opening archive boxes and looking at a photo album from their first paid gig. This forms an immediate connection between the past and the present, as this oscillation between archive and contemporary footage to make "heterogeneous texts" is often the lingua franca of documentary filmmaking (Baron 2007: 14). Throughout the show, the performances and the short films are in constant dialogue with the past, present, and future. As Hjorth, Harris, Jungnickel, and Coombs tell us, time "is always at the heart of performance work and its research activities, particularly the relationship between past, present, and future" (2019: 135). The same could also be said of documentary, with its tendency toward recounting the past or trying to create a sense of present tense while also alluding to the future. Bringing the past into the present, and the future, enables makers, participants, and audiences to engage in the politics of "what if."

Manipulating temporal structures is not new in documentary. However, when telling queer, lesbian, and feminist stories, non-chrononormative structures can help rethink the relationships between these temporalities. They can serve to remind us that time is not ostensibly linear, and the present and future do not always improve on the past. Throughout this project, I have been interested in questions about what practices and methods from the past can be recuperated in order to tell multi-generational stories, something that Martinis Roe argues is essential in creating solidarity through how we relate to those "who came before us and those who come after" (2018: 15)—a kinship born of a politics and practice, rather than through biology. Perhaps these kinds of relationships can help release us from the structure of *chronos,* or at least as a linear and normative mode of temporality, which tends to elide or erase queer stories and subjects.

In her book *Saving Time* (2023), Jenny Odell writes about the twin etymologies of "time," *Chronos* and *Kairos* from Ancient Greek. Where "*Chronos* is the realm of linear time, a steady plodding march of events into the future," *Kairos,* which translates to "crisis," is actually more like "opportune time" (2023: xvii). Odell argues that rather than a comforting knowability, *Chronos* is akin to "dread and nihilism," or perhaps less dramatically, "a form of time that bears down on me, on others, relentlessly" (2023: xviii). In contrast, *Kairos* is a "lifeline, a sliver of the audacity to imagine something different" (2023: xviii). If, as Odell invites us to think, we can embody time more as *Kairos* than as *Chronos,* perhaps we can free ourselves from what Elizabeth Freeman calls *chrononormativity* as the organization of time for "maximum productivity" (2010: 3). And with this, queer subjects can be released from the expectations of time, and the normative milestones such as marriage, reproduction, and childrearing that govern much socialized behavior (2010: 5). In that spirit, *The Art of Work* is also a reflection on aging and temporality that imagines alternative futures through a return to the past. And with this comes the acknowledgment that progress isn't always moving forward; it also means looking back.

Liveness, Performance, and the Feminist Queer Archives

As cultural forms, live performance and documentary film have facets that overlap and diverge, not least around notions of the ephemeral and the fixed. Live performance might make use of pre-recorded audiovisual material, and documentary film might contain performative elements. As I have written elsewhere, live documentary can explicitly perform how knowledge is constructed and at the same time reinvigorate the sense of a collective and a shared experience of being in a space together. However, to date, the potential remains under-explored (Munro 2023: 103). Drawing on Julie Fischer's research around live documentary, Judith Aston explores the nexus between interactive documentary and performance. Here, Aston suggests that a live performance with its inherent ephemerality, manifested through the changing relationship between each audience and performer, functions as an "antidote to the sterility of having everything always on tap" (2017: 223). However, the idea of liveness must also be interrogated in relation to the archive and the notion of "presence." Reading Fischer, the apparent oppositional terms "live" and "documentary" are attributed to disciplinary boundaries rather than any inherent properties of these forms (2014: 9). Sundar Sarukkai asks, then, what is actually being presented through live performance, proposing that it is not the performance but rather the actual physicality of the performer. And rather what is being performed constitutes what can be called an archive (2023: xxii).

Throughout the production phase of *The Art of Work*, I oscillated between trying to understand the archive as a space for possibility, its inherent absences, and its narrative potential. I was drawn to descriptive character notes written in the margins of scripts, which presented as poems. I searched for the missing references to lesbians. And I wondered what stories could be told around each of the snapshots of their tours. On this last point, archival scholar Carolyn Steedman writes, the archive is otherwise dormant, until it is essentially "narrativized."

> The archive is not potentially made up of *everything*, as is human memory; and it is not the fathomless and timeless place in which nothing goes away, that is the unconsciousness. The Archive is made from selected and consciously chosen documentation from the past and also from the made fragmentations that no one intended to preserve and that just ended up there. *And nothing happens to the stuff in the Archive.* It is indexed, and

catalogued, and some of it is not indexed and catalogued, and some of it is lost. (2001: 68)

One of the appeals of the archive is that it presents an experience that is so unlike the many contemporary ways we encounter knowledge. This is something I am reminded of each time I enter the library at the university where I work, which has decommissioned all books except for art catalogs and the odd other. The experience of browsing a library echoes what Bruzzi means when she writes, "it is the deliciously random encounter that characterises the archive which, though methodically assembled, can still surprise" (2020: 17). The intersection of live theater and documentary film can provide opportunities to interrogate how archives are animated. A film about, and with, lesbian archives should not take a conventional form. It must be pieced together with humor and a rag-tag assemblage. Ann Cvetkovich uses Cheryl Dunye's *The Watermelon Woman* alongside the New York-based Lesbian Herstory Archives to highlight the important role that archives have played in lesbian culture, as well as their "innovative and unusual forms of appearance" (2003: 241). In making *The Art of Work*, I also questioned whether there was scope for "unusual forms."

One of my commissioned artists, writer Jen Mills, found joy in a photo album from one of the tours in the mid- to late 1980s, where photos and postcards sat side-by-side, or sometimes just the palimpsest of the photos now gone. In a Fuji film envelope, there was another stack of photographs. Groups of women in various formations had picnics, cooked pancakes, moved chairs, lay on makeshift beds, and played with cats. Reading these images now, there is an intimacy detectable through the women's proximity, their glances, and the way they are dancing together. But it's also the role of the one interpreting these archives to draw that out and make it explicit lest it be eroded and erased. Baron writes that with the advent of New Historicism in the 1980s, historians began to re-evaluate archives "in search of 'evidence' of something very different from what previous historians had sought" (2014: 3). When first approaching the archive, I too looked for the moments of what she calls "eccentric anecdotes and enigmatic fragments" (2014: 3). These came through ephemera such as cut-and-paste collages advertising a dog show and a letter from a regional men's prison where the troupe had performed. After what my archival researcher friend, Martine, had referred to as "the Archive Fever," I turned to a more perambulatory kind of *"cruising"* through the archive—or a way of moving without predetermination, through webs, and in a non-linear fashion (Chambers-Letson, Nyong'o, and Pellegrini 2019: xiii).

The Vitalstatistix archive that I'm using as a source material was collected and collated by the three co-founders of the theater. Martinis Roe emphasizes the importance of this self-archiving, which can capture what she calls the "traces" of everyday practices and politics in action (2018). The filmed conversations also bring the archive into the present tense and, at the same time, animate the past, using the photographs and other documents as memory prompts. I used the method here of photo elicitation, a technique of interviewing participants that can access a deeper part of the brain than through interviews and verbalization (Harper 2002: 13). I should also add here that this was self-generated in a way by Ollie, Roxxy, and Margie when they were deciding what should be in the archives. This process prompted many stories, and they had commented to each other that someone should be filming. The filmed conversations of the three and the archives go some way toward filling the absences that Martinis Roe identifies as inherent in many feminist archives, which she argues often lack information about the social structures and how they operate. She suggests that this is most likely because these structures are constituted of "countless spontaneous daily interactions" (2018: 163) (Figure 9.2).

I had originally imagined that the commissioned artists would restage some of the original work. At the same time, I also wanted the contributors

Figure 9.2 *The Art of Work Is a Work of Art* directed by Kim Munro. © Kim Munro 2023. All rights reserved.

to be guided by "curiosity" and "ignorance," pursuing what they didn't know and what they wanted to find out about. Telling feminist histories is no mere re-telling or filling the gaps left open through patriarchal blind spots. It must also work to change the way history is told, as Balsom argues, "simply populating old structures with new heroines will only reinscribe the marginalization that must be overcome" (2021: np). As the project progressed, and given whom I had commissioned to participate, the interest was more around presences and absences in the archive as well as the politics and methodology of how Ollie, Roxxy, and Margie had originally practiced. Feminist networks, collectivity, audience participation, and hospitality all emerged as themes that drove the project forward. There was also a sense of how these practices might still be relevant, even urgent.

Much of what is contained in the Vitalstatistix archives is documentation of the process of making the work. This includes their research with women about issues affecting them, elicited through the workshops and morning teas they organized. As an archival researcher, one of my commissioned artists, Sasha, had a sharpened view of the possibilities that small glimpses or fragments can afford. What had piqued Sasha's curiosity was a pack of photographs in the archive boxes—all taken of audiences and mostly of high-school students. The audience was an essential part of the early work of Vitalstatistix, which was often pedagogical. Whether with students, miners, or residents of a regional town, Margie and Ollie led a discussion after each performance in order to draw out the themes in the hope that this might lead to deeper awareness and behavioral change.

Rather than a pedagogical relationship, Sasha wanted to invite the audience to be contributors to her segment of *The Art of Work*. With this in mind, she composed twenty-five questions to ask the audience as they entered the theater. While some of these questions related directly to the plays and productions created nearly four decades prior, others were about more contemporary issues, such as the climate crisis and our relationship to non-human species. Sasha had also recorded underwater sounds of the Port River, a significant feature of the local area. The subtle sounds of water currents and cracking shrimp were played over a speaker as the audience answered the questions and replayed as she and Emma took to the stage at the end of the performance to read them out in a call-and-response. These moments, Dolan describes, are "small but profound" ways "In which performance calls the attention of the audience in a way that lifts everyone slightly above the present, into a hopeful feeling of what the world might be like if every moment of our lives were as emotionally voluminous, generous, aesthetically striking, and intersubjectively intense" (2005: 5). This work, bookending the evening, performs brief moments of utopianism, which might be the best we can hope for.

Conclusion

This chapter sketches out some reflections on making the first iteration of *The Art of Work Is a Work of Art* and articulates the intersections between creative practice, queer and feminist theory, archival research, documentary film, and live theater. I have positioned this work as a documentary, while also drawing on the practices of spontaneity, collectivity, and utopianism that theater can afford. The process of making *The Art of Work* has provided an opportunity to think about how to make a work in a way that pays homage to collective actions and forgotten histories. Where Trinh argues against the production of a "new object of study, or a new product to consume," *The Art of Work* aspires to what she calls "new ways of seeing, perceiving, and living in the world" (Radhakrishnan 2022: np).

As an iterative project, *The Art of Work* is still in process. Employing hybrid and intersectional practices that foreground how people make work as they make life together reminds us that "beyond this 'now' of material oppression and unequal power relations lives a future that might be different" (Dolan 2005: 7). Through reflecting on the development of this work as part of a network of creators and histories, the chapter has aimed to elucidate some of the tensions and opportunities at the intersections of documentary film, theater, and queer and feminist archives.

Part IV

Documentary Voice and Feminist Perspectives

10

"Are We on the Same Page Here?"[1]

Moving Beyond "Us" and "Them" in *nîpawistamâsowin: We Will Stand Up* and *Kímmapiiyipitssini: The Meaning of Empathy*

Gail Vanstone

In her essay "Strategic Anti-Essentialism/Decolonizing Decolonization," Nandita Sharma argues that if we aim to escape "the unevenness of the Columbian exchange" that refuses to see putative groups of natives and migrants (settlers) as coexisting in a shared field of colonial and now postcolonial power, we must bring both groups into the "*same field of analysis*" (2015: 167) to break this dualism and find a new way forward. She is, of course, referring to Sylvia Wynter's vision of a new "species-inclusive" account of humanness, a "new world view" that moves beyond the binaries of colonizer/colonized or perpetrator/victim marked by atrocities and accomplishments of the planetary five-centuries-long event of "1492" toward a transformation that, while accounting for the complicated relationalities, opens a way to "help transmute how 'we' relate to—and therefore narrate—what it means to be human, with/in our habitats" (Kaiser and Thiele 2017: 412).

In Canada, a group of Indigenous filmmakers, the majority of them women, are advancing this approach through their documentary film production, a remarkable body of work that deserves greater attention. As Māori filmmaker Barry Barclay, renowned for giving his people a voice, reckoned, it is as though "invader Cinemas" have overridden their voices, marooning them in their ancestral home, an island within a modern "nation-state" (2003: 9). This, despite the fact that twenty-first-century Indigenous feminist cinema enjoys a global presence. While these films received critical acclaim at the time of their release, the corpus as a whole merits greater examination as an emerging and urgent body of work. Significantly, the stories these women raise through film offer radical pathways to the kinds of transformational relationalities that align with Wynter's vision.

This paper draws attention to two of these filmmakers, Tasha Hubbard (Cree, Peepeekisis First Nation, Treaty 4) and Elle-Máijá Tailfeathers (Blackfoot, Sami, Kainai First Nation, Treaty 7), who, I argue, draw on the qualities of Fourth Cinema to project and convey urgent Indigenous knowledge. Hubbard's *nîpawistamâsowin: We Will Stand Up* (2019) and Tailfeathers's *Kímmapiiyipitssini: The Meaning of Empathy* (2021) interrogate pressing issues of Indigenous experience in Canada that call for deep analysis and radical change. Both filmmakers speak in a feminist register, braiding together a series of overlapping narratives, mapping out a prescient new worldview of inordinate promise. Difficult, complex territory to navigate, yet territory that summons all, shifting from "them and us" to "we" for an attentive hearing. This territory is set out in the form of braided narratives, a conceptual model that captures the complexity and depth of each film, discerned through filmic imagery and Indigenous storytelling in "conversation" with each other. The filmic structure emerging conflates notions of "land" and "body" into a powerful maternal narrative, inviting sustained contemplation. Approaching the films from this stance encourages spectators to reflect on the complicated tapestry of each film where the filmmakers "plait together different narrative threads, distinct in terms of both narrator and story, to grapple with both the poignant fissures that fracture the most intimate attachments between individuals and the chasm that historical violences carve between social groups" (Bancroft 2018: 262).

When Barrie Barclay coined the phrase "Fourth Cinema" in 2001 to invoke the political dimensions of Indigenous cinema, he said, "Indigenous eyes would find their *ancient core values reworked with vitality and richness* and that the non-Indigenous would be encouraged to see *through a more accurate pair of glasses*" (2003: 6, my emphasis). The Fourth Cinema Barclay proposed does not privilege the creation of new cinematic language as a given. Rather, it seeks to *rework* cinematic language—to the point of proposing the expression of Indigeneity within the norms of First, Second, and Third cinemas, as both *nîpawistamâsowin* and *Kímmapiiyipitssini* do.

Fourth Cinema becomes an umbrella term expansive enough to embrace these examples of Indigenous cinema in the international arena, yet one that still reflects "the specifics of individual cultural formations and iterations" (Murray 2008: 2). Hubbard's *nîpawistamâsowin: We Will Stand Up* (2019) interrogates the real and dangerous nature of racism inflicted on First Nations through the justice system, and Tailfeather's *Kímmapiiyipitssini: The Meaning of Empathy* (2021) counters the opioid crisis in First Nations communities with harm reduction strategies. Both fulfill Barclay's proposition with skill, offering wisdom for both Indigenous and non-Indigenous peoples through overlapping narratives and silent filmic evidence working in concert to convey their stories.

Underlying this investigation is an opportunity to broach a culturally sensitive question, namely, how can non-Indigenous, particularly westernized audiences "come to understand" the significance of what they are seeing in the spirit of Wynter's "new world view," a vital undertaking if we are to enter into Sharma's "*same field of analysis*" following a path to mutual truth and reconciliation. If we seek this "new world view," we must ask: How can we (the non-Indigenous) become better attuned to the voices and visuals of these filmmakers? How might we better attend to the teachings embedded in, in this case, feminist Indigenous documentaries, to engage in a process of decolonization, a necessary step to seeing through Barclay's more accurate set of glasses?

For Barclay, Indigenous films possess an "interiority"—a radical spirituality expressed both in attitude and in practice—and a way the Indigenous people see and situate themselves in the world that public intellectual and writer Thomas King (Cherokee/Greek/German) calls "Indianess."[2] In King's lexicon, Indianess is "a sensibility running counter to or lying behind normative western cultural modes [and] acts as a decentering, destabilising and decolonising force" (Vanstone, Winston 2019: 234), a way of being-in-the-world often denied to the global community of First Peoples. For Neal McLeod, who writes on Indigenous poetics, it is "the embodiment of Indigenous consciousness" (2014: 4), Barclay's radical "visual counter point that focuses on transformation and change, [effectively moving] Indigenous knowledge to centre stage" (2003: 6). The imbricated structure and substance of both *nîpawistamâsowin* and *Kímmapiiyipitssini* deliver this through the inimitable voices of their filmmakers.

Hubbard's and Tailfeathers's films launch from a Fourth World perspective engaging Indigenous storywork as methodology. "Storywork," a term coined by Jo-ann Archibald (Sto:lo), speaks to the ability of a story to take on its own life and "become the teacher . . . effectively educat[ing] the heart, mind, body, and spirit . . . with the power to help with emotional healing and wellness" (2008: ix–x). For Leanne Betasamosake Simpson, stories are the fabric of daily life and foundational practice for the Indigenous, "The practice of telling stories is the practice of generating a diversity of meanings. It is a practice of deep relationality, not a looking at, but a looking with or a looking through or a *thinking through together*" (2021: 6). Further, this stance is an opening to a dialogue where, according to Kim Anderson (Cree Métis), Canada Research Chair in storying Indigenous relational futures, "Indigenous feminist thought can help re-create a world that validates life in all its forms" precisely because it issues from an Indigenous perspective (2010: 82). Within this framework, the film-based stories of Hubbard and Tailfeathers constitute resonant instruction, at their root, a form of "decolonizing research" necessary for both Indigenous and "settler"[3] audiences, in particular because they offer vital material for scrutinizing the workings of white colonial mentality alongside Indianess.

This opportunity for examination is important since Barclay's concept of Fourth Cinema is built on the notion of the Fourth World, a global community of Indigenous nations, named thus by Grand Chief George Manuel (Secwepemc, BC) in the 1970s. Wanting to distinguish between the decolonization of the third world and the decolonization of Indigenous peoples who had lost their freedom and way of life under "colonial masters," Manuel claimed, "We are a fourth world, a forgotten world, the world of aboriginal peoples locked into . . . states but without an adequate voice or say in the decisions that affect our lives" (1974: 6). His belief in the right of self-determination for Indigenous peoples is the territory where Hubbard and Tailfeathers ground their work, mobilizing film as a vehicle for asserting survivance and sovereignty.

Colonization: The Canadian Context

nîpawistamâsowin: We Will Stand Up and *Kímmapiiyipitssini: The Meaning of Empathy* offer stories best understood in the light of a Canadian version of colonization, marked by a longstanding troubled relationship between

Indigenous peoples, settlers, and governing bodies in Canada. Colonization here follows an all-too-familiar trajectory. From the fifteenth century onward, explorers mapped out territory in the "New World," claiming it for their patrons, European Crowns.[4] Justifications were derived from Doctrines of Discovery and *Terra Nullius*[5] as offering legal underpinning for Crown land titles; land understood as empty, inviting settlement. In the nineteenth century, the British Crown would negotiate a series of treaties with First Nations to regulate land management with its immigration policies, with Indigenous peoples forced to move to government-specified reservations, their movements tightly controlled by Indian Agents, representatives of the Crown. Presented as "nation to nation" agreements, such treaty formulations, in reality, served Crown interests.

Simultaneously, the Canadian government passed the Indian Act and instituted a nationwide network of government-sponsored Residential Schools, religious boarding schools designed to assimilate Indigenous children, eradicating their "Indianess" utterly. Attendance was mandatory. As Duncan Campbell Scott, deputy superintendent of the Federal Department of Indian Affairs (1913–32)[6] (in)famously claimed, "Our objective is to continue until there is not a single Indian in Canada that has not been absorbed into the body politic.[7] Abuse (physical, psychological, and sexual) was rampant, resulting in innumerable cases of intergenerational trauma still plaguing survivors and their children today. More recently, the previously undetected graves at former residential school sites surfacing today bear witness to undocumented (hidden) student deaths, another ugly secret of Canadian colonization.

In the mid-1980s, survivors of the Residential School system brought a series of class action suits against the government, seeking compensation for the damage they had suffered and causing the government to establish a Royal Commission on Aboriginal Peoples (1991). The abuses in the Residential School system, a key finding, led to the Indian Residential School Settlement Agreement (2006). An important condition of the agreement was the establishment of a Truth and Reconciliation Commission (TRC) to hear survivor and community leader testimonies[8] to determine the impact of colonization in Canada. Chief Justice of Canada's Supreme Court Beverley McLaughlin would refer to Canada's treatment of its aboriginal people as "attempted cultural genocide"[9]. Non-Indigenous Canadians were confronted with the stark reality of a brutal history that they (for many, unwittingly) shared. When the final TRC report was published in 2015, it issued ninety-four Calls to Action, calling on federal, provincial, and territorial governments to ameliorate conditions for Indigenous peoples in their jurisdictions[10], beginning a long process of education and action. It is against this backdrop that *nîpawistamâsowin* and *Kímmapiiyipitssini* are set.

nîpawistamâsowin: We Will Stand Up

Hubbard brings authoritative heft to her filmmaking practice as a filmmaker, as an Indigenous intersectional feminist,[11] and as a professor in the Faculty of Native Studies at the University of Alberta.[12] While her primary band affiliation is with the Peepeekisis (Cree) First Nation, Treaty 4, she also claims a connection with Thunderchild First Nation, Treaty 6, effectively spanning territory in the provinces of Alberta, Saskatchewan, and part of Manitoba. When *nîpawistamâsowin: We Will Stand Up* was released in 2019, it won Best Canadian Feature Documentary at Hot Docs Canadian International Documentary Festival (2019), the Canadian Screen Award for Best Feature Length Documentary at the Canadian Screen Awards 2020, the Colin Low Award for Best Canadian Documentary at the 2019 DOXA Documentary Film Festival, the Golden Sheaf Award for Best Multicultural (Over 30 Minutes) at the 2020 Yorkton Film Festival[13] in Saskatchewan, and the 2019 Discovery Award from the Director's Guild of Canada. Today, the film is accessible within Canada on the website of the National Film Board of Canada in both English and Cree language versions.

nîpawistamâsowin: We Will Stand Up (2019) takes as its starting point the 2016 death of Colten Boushie, a young Cree man in rural Saskatchewan. It details his family's quest for justice, drawing parallels between their quest and the troubled history of anti-Indigenous racism in western Canada against the backdrop of the 2015 Truth and Reconciliation Commission Report[14] to address the structured racism at the heart of Canada's legal system. And, in the telling, Hubbard delivers a complex and urgent argument through her film that affirms Indigenous sovereignty and survivance (Baker 2005: 111) and calls for Indigenous alternatives to "the destructive logics of the settler colonial state" (Simpson 2017: 50). Hubbard braids her narrative strategically, conjoining past history with the present, bringing her audience, Indigenous spectators, and "settlers" alike, into a deliberation of justice, ethics, and reverence for the land, here, the Saskatchewan prairies.

Through her and her team's camera work and the choice to narrate the film in her own voice, Hubbard examines the territory from within a Fourth World feminist perspective, which launches from the title, *nîpawistamâsowin* (we stand up for others), issuing from the authority of women, the figure of the mother in particular, bound up in "their unique contributions in the lifegiving process" (Anderson 2010: 82). Underlying this positionality and connected with women's responsibility to take care of the earth is the Indigenous belief in the primacy of "earth" for its generative life-giving structure, as Hubbard notes in the opening moments of her film. For Joyce Green (English, Ktunaxa, and Cree-Scots Métis), "the nearly universal connection to land, to territory, through relationships framed as sacred responsibility is a fundamental of Indigenous culture" (2017: 20). Reclaiming feminist subjectivity, then, entails "taking a look at our history and understanding how Indigenous women traditionally had authority in all areas of society—political, social, economic, and spiritual . . . authority dismantled by colonisation [and] its imposition of Western values [resulting in] a loss of balance in Indigenous families, communities, and nations" (Anderson 2016: xxiv). Throughout the film, a constellation of "mother" narratives, interspersed with images of the land, asserts maternal subjectivity and invokes reverence for the land as originating maternal force, signal tenets of Indigenous knowledge.

Hubbard's undertaking reclaims the maternal voice and resituates it in a position of authority, *nîpawistamâsowin,* invoking a chorus of women's voices braided together in its narrative structure. Here, empowered motherhood becomes sovereignty, with motherhood as both practice and ideology, "the source of Indigenous female authority in the family and a way of seeking authority in national Aboriginal politics" (Anderson 2010: 83). Underlying and driving this stance is an Indigenous feminist consciousness that works toward "resisting oppression, reclaiming Indigenous tradition and culture, incorporating traditional Indigenous beliefs into our modern lives, and acting on responsibilities inherent in our new-found identities" (Anderson 2010: 85).

From an intersectional feminist standpoint, Hubbard relates the historical context hovering behind Colten's death and the community's failure to secure justice in the subsequent trial of the shooter, Gerald Stanley. Her technique centers the voices of those experiencing overlapping, concurrent forms of oppression, allowing the audience to understand the depths of the inequalities and the complexities of relationships among those involved. To capture these complexities, Hubbard braids a number of narrative threads strategically in the film, bringing her audience, Indigenous spectators, and "settlers" alike into a deliberation of justice. For Corinne Bancroft, the braided narrative offers the storyteller "a set of strategies that help train readers [spectators] to hold multiple, often incommensurate, subjectivities in our minds simultaneously, pushing us to embrace new channels of responsibility that recognize many subjects" (2018: 263). The tragedy of Colten's shooting and his family's exhaustive quest for justice form the film's core, bookended by Hubbard's own story.

Hubbard's film establishes an unwavering focus on the land and calls viewers to consider land as sacred—life-sustaining and vital for human survival. From the opening sequence, Hubbard boldly aligns herself with the earth as the camera pans over a sweeping expanse of prairie to a chorus of birds and cicadas. She is leading an expedition onto the land. A fencepost and barbed wire fencing loom in the foreground, bounding the natural landscape, but are no barrier to the filmmaker. Hubbard's first act is to step onto the land, prying open the barbed wire barrier, allowing her son and nephew, who are accompanying her, to enter the expanse beyond. Hubbard's voice is heard off-screen, subtitled in Cree, "Put the backpack over first. Okay, I'll hold it, you crawl through." Stepping down on one strand of barbed wire and raising the one above it with her hand, she creates a space for the boys to pass through. "Okay, you're in! Good job!" A moment later, Hubbard joins them, pointing to a strip of land in the distance, "When I was little this whole area was natural, now someone is cultivating it," colonization explained. A moment later, the boys are silhouetted against the sky. "Do you ever want to go back, like, how it was . . . before the settlers?" Quannah asks his cousin. "Not sure," Oskiya replies, tacitly acknowledging inherent ambiguities in the "now." An aerial view of the land, with superimposed surveyor grid lines denoting farm properties, dissolves into the natural landscape, a graphic reminder of colonial "ownership."

In this act of aligning with the prairie, home to the Indigenous from "time immemorial" as she says, Hubbard launches her deliberation, examining the colliding ideologies of land, all life-generating for the Indigenous but an opportunity for the accumulation of wealth for the colonizer, manifested in the contours of "the white regimes of power that historically and continuously impact Indigenous peoples in Canada" (Posca 2023: 72). *nîpawistamâsowin*'s stance, then, invokes Manuel's teaching that for the Indigenous this means holding a common attachment to and reverence for the land. "Our Mother Earth should not be speculated, bought, sold, mortgaged, claimed by one state, surrendered or counter-claimed by another" (1974: 6), countering the settler narrative (Figure 10.1).

Hubbard's voice-over narration witnesses Indigenous history and presents her as the subject of her own story, another strand in the braid. A "Sixties scoop"[15] baby, Hubbard was adopted by a white family who would help her find her birth parents to ground her Indigenous identity. Now, intimately aware of the complicated history of the Canadian prairies and the reality that Indigenous people are often faced with racism, Hubbard determines to teach her son and his cousin that this is their territory, their identity: "I try to make things different for my son so that he grows up knowing all his relations across the prairies—our motto—we belong here, even if people try to make us think we don't." Hubbard has taught the boys not to accept racism and not to internalize it. When news of the August 2016 death of Colton Boushie, shot by a white rancher on whose property Boushie and three of his friends had driven onto, reaches Hubbard, she is stunned. Operating by the Cree

Figure 10.1 Two Indigenous boys walking on Saskatchewan prairie. *nîpawistamâsowin: We Will Stand Up* by Tasha Hubbard. © Tasha Hubbard 2019. Reproduced with the permission of Tasha Hubbard. All rights reserved.

belief that children belong to themselves, not their parents, but that family is responsible for keeping them safe, Hubbard had always taught the boys to look after themselves. Colten's death is a stark truth that teaching is not protection enough.

If Hubbard's story bookends the film, Colten Boushie's death, the subsequent flawed trial of his killer, and the family's quest for justice take central focus. Debbie Baptiste, Colten's mother, emerges as a primary figure of maternal authority and witness to the trial. Her filmed testimony and subsequent quest for justice stand as a powerful rebuke in the face of her enforced silence at the trial itself.[16] Through Baptiste's testimony, the audience receives a tender portrait of the twenty-two-year-old, enumerated in a collection of family photographs bearing witness to an inquisitive little boy and promising young man loved by his family and valued in his community.

Speaking directly into the camera, Baptiste condemns the way her son's life was taken: "He (Stanley) could have shot the gun in the air," but, no, [he thought] "they're on my land and . . . without considering a life . . . goes up behind my son and shoots him in the head." We also learn that when the RCMP[17] came to deliver the news of her son's death, they surrounded and searched her house, asking Baptiste if she had been drinking, *although she had done nothing wrong*. In this witnessing, Baptiste's voice joins the chorus of voices reclaiming Indigenous women's voices muffled by colonization and, likewise, revealing the contours of racist police practice.

The Indigenous community is disbelieving when the RCMP issues a press release that, astonishingly, shifts attention from the shooting to the Indigenous youth who entered the property and were suspected of theft, Colten's shooting the result. The following day Gerald Stanley is charged with second-degree murder. Public reaction is swift and racist. The film, using computer screen captures, documents a number of messages drawn from the barrage of social media posts from the settler community (Facebook pages, one account, "Farmers and Firearms" alongside individual posts from settlers in towns and cities). Every message contains anti-Indigenous racist language, coded through vulgar stereotypes, the series of screen captures evidence of the sinister fabric of cyber racism.

Sherene Razack, a distinguished critical race scholar, observes that what is immediately apparent here is the predominance of a settler narrative rooted in stereotype. For her, such social media posts suggest that the Indigenous subject "is considered to have brought their death upon themselves." In this case, the stereotype paints Indians as known thieves [even though there is no evidence that Colten attempted theft of any sort]; therefore, the stereotype kills the Indian, rather than "the violence of the state through colonisation . . . or active brutality" (Razack 2015:113).

Subsequent farm community town halls to discuss rural crime, filmed by Hubbard's crew, add another strand to the narrative braid. Testimony, this time by (white) settler farmers, reveals the degree to which stereotypes fuel an ironclad racist prairie script, lurking under a belief that "Indigenous people stand in the way of settler colonialism, contesting settler entitlement to the land and throwing into question settler legitimacy as the original and rightful owners" (Razack 2015: 7).

At the trial, since the use of film in court is prohibited, Hubbard uses court drawings to augment her crew's filmed footage outside the court (at one point, Hubbard, camera in hand, appears on screen). Proceedings bear witness to a host of procedural irregularities: the car (the shooting site) containing Colten's body left out in a rainstorm for twenty-four hours, destroying valuable evidence; a blood spatter expert who never visits the scene, instead drawing her conclusions from photos taken by investigators; potential Indigenous jurors dismissed; an all-white jury selected; potential Indigenous jury members rejected outright by the Stanley team; expert testimony discounted, hearsay testimony accepted.

Building her argument, Hubbard incorporates her very first film, a six-minute graphic film,[18] into *nîpawistamâsowin* in an illuminating "film within a film" structure. Her graphic film "tells history," detailing the historical events leading up to the signing of Treaty 6 that resonate eerily with key elements surrounding Colten's death and the ensuing trial. Artist renderings from the Stanley trial reveal a number of chilling parallels (police brutality, legal proceedings tipped in favor of the settler, deadly consequences for standing up for one's community), echoing the historical narrative. When Stanley is found "not guilty," the Indigenous community is disbelieving, as Chief Danny Starchief says on camera, "Justice crumbled today."

nîpawistamâsowin follows the family's protracted quest for justice from the Red Pheasant Reserve to the provincial Saskatchewan government, then on to Ottawa, seat of the federal government, and finally to a United Nations global forum in New York. When the family resolves to petition the Saskatchewan government, calling for an overhaul of the justice system, Jade Tootoosis Colten's cousin, encouraged by her *Kookum* (grandmother), emerges as a spokesperson.

Hubbard, who travels with the delegation filming their meetings, traces Tootoosis's coming to voice, another strand in the film's maternal braid. The delegation brings a petition for justice to Saskatchewan's premier, then to Ottawa to meet with Canada's prime minister and all major political parties. On camera, politicians display goodwill, but no promise of action results.

Back home, the delegation decides to take its message to the United Nations Permanent Forum on Indigenous Issues (UNPFII)[19] and chooses Jade as the spokesperson. Tootoosis presents their case. Viewers see her speaking directly into the camera; beside her, Debbie Boushie sits holding up a photo of Colton, and Hubbard stands at the back of the chamber. Tootoosis calls on the Special Rapporteur on the Rights of Indigenous Peoples to undertake a study of systemic racism in the Canadian judicial and legislative systems and recommend that Canada establish a Royal Commission on the Elimination of Racism in the Canadian Judicial and Legal System, as other Indigenous people in the court flood the aisles behind her in support (Figure 10.2).

The film ends with a sequence that invites reflection and contemplation: Hubbard is filmed braiding her son's hair; in a cutaway shot, we see Quannah and his cousin walking toward a prairie field where horses run free. The image dissolves into a graphic depiction of Colten Boushie standing with the horses, smiling back at the boys. The sequence as a whole invites viewers to consider the generations-spanning impact of colonization against the backdrop of this particular moment.

Hubbard lays out the provocation, *nîpawistamâsowin* offers the path, encouraging audiences to probe history and consider what "we" might do now.

Kímmapiiyipitssini: The Meaning of Empathy (2021)

Two years after the premiere of *nîpawistamâsowin: We Will Stand Up*, Elle-Máijá Tailfeathers's *Kímmapiiyipitssini: The Meaning of Empathy* (2021) followed in its footsteps, likewise winning the 2022 Ted Rogers Best Feature Length Documentary Canadian Screen Award, the Colin Low Award for Canadian Documentary (2021), then the Rogers Audience

Figure 10.2 Jade Tootoosis testifies at the UN Forum. *nîpawistamâsowin: We Will Stand Up* by Tasha Hubbard. © Tasha Hubbard 2019. Reproduced with the permission of Tasha Hubbard. All rights reserved.

Award for Canadian Feature Documentary at the Hot Docs Canadian International Documentary Festival in Toronto (2021), and the Audience Choice Award—Canadian Documentary Feature at the 2021 CIFF Calgary International Film Festival, Canada, and Trailblazer Award, Reelworld Film Festival (2021). *Kímmapiiyipitssini: The Meaning of Empathy* sets out an intimate and deeply personal portrait of Tailfeathers's home community, Kainai First Nation, and their collective struggle with an opioid overdose crisis. A co-production between Seen Through Women Productions and the National Film Board of Canada,[20] the film is available in Canada on the NFB website.

Tailfeathers is both a gifted actor and director, appearing in Jeff Barnaby's *Blood Quantum* (2019) and Danis Goulet's *Night Raiders* (2019). She co-directed *The Body Remembers When the World Broke Open* (2019) with Kathleen Hepburn and played a lead role in the film. As the director of *Kímmapiiyipitssini: The Meaning of Empathy* (2021), she won Emerging Filmmaker at the Hot Docs Canadian International Film Festival (2021).

When the opioid crisis[21] hit her community in 2015, Tailfeathers was disturbed by mainstream (non-Indigenous) narratives circulating in popular media, fueling hackneyed stereotypes of the "drunken Indian." They framed the crisis from a "trauma porn perspective," dwelling on stories of sorrow and grief, utterly (and erroneously) overlooking the valuable work being done by the community, a narrative Tailfeathers rejected outright: "The same sort of imagery was used over and over again, shots captured on a long lens from faraway on boarded up houses that nobody lives in, or of people that were taken without their consent. It was really problematic and didn't represent the community that I know and love" (Boutsalis 2021: 30).

Tailfeathers felt that as a filmmaker, she had a responsibility to document what was happening, particularly when so many in her community were working tirelessly to combat the crisis (Pacheo, online). Using film as a medium, Tailfeathers was determined to craft a truer and more personalized study of her community, highlighting their generative approach to grappling with the opioid crisis. Witnessing the widespread grief the crisis triggered, touching her own family with the death of her cousin, sealed Tailfeathers's resolve. Over the next five years, she would gather evidence, filming and interviewing her community members and engaging in community action to build a radically different, carefully braided narrative. The result is a loving, multi-layered portrait, carefully drawn, combining and sharing the collective knowledge of all those involved, gesturing to a better, more self-determined future.

For Tailfeathers, making the documentary was a masterclass in learning how to work ethically in her community. Her first year was spent in development, research, and relationship building, and when she was ready to begin filming, Tailfeathers ensured that her small (non-Indigenous) camera crew completed a two-day mandatory cultural competency training to instill an appreciation for Blackfoot worldviews and protocols. Participants had a say over how they appeared in the film, and when Tailfeathers showed them a rough cut, no one asked for changes. The result is a singular portrait of sustained resistance and survivance. *Kímmapiiyipitssini* offers viewers a significant body of carefully nuanced evidence to examine the very human contours of "what it's like living with substance use disorder [and] what it's like to work on the front line" (Boutsalis 2021: 30).

The fabric of Tailfeathers's storywork in *Kímmapiiyipitssini* shares key qualities with *nîpawistamâsowin*, although their subject matter is quite distinct.

Like *nîpawistamâsowin*, *Kímmapiiyipitssini* is an example of film as activism. Both films reverence the land and maternal authority, borne out amply in their structures. As the dramatic trajectory of each film builds, the camera cuts again and again to magnificent landscapes, establishing land as home *and* land as identity. Both directors are much in evidence through their films. Hubbard, often with camera in hand, films, assembles vital evidence, and Tailfeathers, an indefatigable force, researches and interviews subjects, assisting her mother in community education and advocacy, her crew engaged in filming.

The opening moments of *Kímmapiiyipitssini* establish Tailfeather's indisputable connection to her ancestral lands. An open stretch of prairie fills the screen, a buffalo calf grazing on an open stretch of prairie land, mother close by. The scene is one of tenderness and tranquility. A woman's voice can be heard, softly laughing, "Are you dreaming? Have you got your mamma's face (the calf and its mother gaze into the camera)? Do you hear your mamma's voice (the calf runs to its mother)?" Moments later the screen reveals a glorious landscape of breathtaking proportions, foothills, and mountains, Tailfeathers narrating in voice-over. We learn that this is Kainai territory, her reserve spanning 1,400 square kilometers, the largest in Canada. We learn that the Kainai (Blood) First Nation is one of four nations in the Blackfoot Confederacy (Figure 10.3).

For film scholar Dorothy Christian (Secwepemc and Syilx Nations), land, story, and cultural protocols are inseparable—felt, but difficult to articulate.

Figure 10.3 Buffalo calf and mother on Kainai territory. *Kímmapiiyipitssini: The Meaning of Empathy* by Elle-Máijá Tailfeathers. © Elle-Máijá Tailfeathers 2021. Reproduced with the permission of Elle-Máijá Tailfeathers. All rights reserved.

Explaining, Christian references a conversation with renowned author and knowledge keeper Maria Campbell (Métis), "[T]he land doesn't speak out loud ... the environment doesn't speak out loud. It talks to you in other kinds of ways. And that's what's important . . . so there's a whole other language that sometimes isn't spoken that you have between you and the connection to the land" (Christian 2019: 45). Threaded through the film at strategic moments, viewers witness Kainai territory, filmed in every season. And, often, as a community member sets out their story, the camera cuts away from the individual to capture the landscape, a visual cue that this person is Blackfoot and an integral part of this land.

Kímmapiiyipitssini, like *nîpawistamâsowin*, presents the mother as an exemplar of Indigenous sovereignty. More than ever, she is a contemporary figure of female authority on whose teachings Indigenous peoples depend as "part of the political discourse related to healing and rebuilding" (Anderson 2010: 86). In this case, the mother is Dr. Esther Tailfeathers in league with her daughter in a powerful mother–daughter team. As an activist *and* filmmaker, Elle-Máijá records testimony from her community. Her mother is one of the few medical professionals in the area and assumes the role of community leader and knowledge keeper, dispensing treatment, education, and care, offering life-generating encouragement and healing. Early in the film, Esther details the magnitude of the crisis, telling her daughter that hundreds of lives have been lost to drug abuse, "a good part of a generation of people, most of them in their twenties and thirties—children, brothers, sisters, aunts, and uncles—orphaning kids . . . so we've lost a lot of power in our community." The voice-over continues, the screen filled with images of young people at a festival, perhaps a powwow, celebrating, having fun, survivors, left in the wake of the crisis. With the arrival of fentanyl, the urgency of the crisis pushes the community to seek radically different solutions. Eyes turn to models of harm reduction strategies, arising out of activism and community collaborations in Vancouver, British Columbia, likewise reeling from the crisis.

The power of this film is multi-layered, apparent in its braided narrative structure. On one hand, *Kímmapiiyipitssini* functions as instruction, setting out a methodology on how to identify and instigate a range of workable harm reduction strategies when total abstinence is not effective. The film crew follows Esther and Elle-Máijá and their delegation to Vancouver, where Esther has arranged a visit to the Portland Hotel Society[22] and Insite, Vancouver's legal supervised injection site. Viewers learn about their programs as those coping with addiction demonstrate how treatment can work. The group learns about how the ethical exchange program works at the Community Managed Alcohol Program Coop, which produces homemade beer and wine. Someone in the group sniffs an open bottle, confirming with laughter that it *is* beer. The Coop exchanges its brews in limited amounts for bottles of rubbing alcohol and solvent thinner consumed by individuals struggling with severe alcohol disorder. The Kainai delegation is interested in the Supportive Recovery Program with psychosocial and clinical support, thinking that access to opioid replacement therapies and trained health care workers could save lives at home. They visit the Needle Deposit, known for reducing the number of bloodborne infections, and the Needle Exchange, which collects discarded needles and syringes, promoting safer drug-use habits. The camera crew follows a Spikes on Bikes team as they hunt for discarded drug paraphernalia and homeless drug users holed up in hard-to-reach spaces—alleyways, side streets, parking garages. Team members are armed with clean needles and naloxone kits, ready to call for backup for drug users in distress. Later, back in Kainai, the community discusses possible implementation, weighing skepticism with hope (Figure 10.4).

Like Hubbard, Tailfeathers uses a braided narrative to tell her community's stories—those with substance use disorders, first responders, medical professionals, and local community leaders, all battling an epidemic—

Figure 10.4 Blood community members training with Naloxone kits. *Kímmapiiyipitssini: The Meaning of Empathy* by Elle-Máijá Tailfeathers. © Elle-Máijá Tailfeathers 2021. Reproduced with the permission of Elle-Máijá Tailfeathers. All rights reserved.

not of their making—pursuing these more life-affirming harm reduction strategies as a better way. The strategy of braiding individual stories together encourages a species of humanizing. These are stories to be considered singly and as a whole, inviting the viewer to appreciate their particularities and their interconnectedness. For a visual storyteller like Tailfeathers, this relationality is expressed through a generative giving back to the community precisely through her visual narrative.

The interconnected structure of *Kímmapiiyipitssini* reveals a deeply rooted Indigenous congruency that is, in fact, the film's gift of hope. As Emerance Baker has argued, "loving Indianness is survivance." In her words, "the making and telling of our stories teach us to do more than react to and survive in this world: they bring us ways to heal ourselves, our families, and our communities" (Baker 2005: 111). We witness the working of "loving Indianness" in operation through each individual story. Tailfeathers's strategy is clear. These are community members with names, people with responsibilities, aspirations, and plans for the future. They may have inherited burdens they do not deserve, but they are willing to combat them actively to overcome their problems. The camera introduces us to George and Leah, homeless, waiting for treatment. We learn of their romance, George's gift at beading, "My friend taught me in jail," he tells Tailfeathers, Leah's children, fourteen and seven years (likely in foster care), and their decision to enter into supervised substance reduction treatment. Through their experiences, it becomes clear that existing health care protocols, as they are, are almost impossible to navigate. Esther,[23] a respected public figure advocating for change, is filmed in the process of persuading a politician that the reserve needs its own detox center so that individuals can go directly from detox into treatment, ensuring greater success. Footage shifts to an office in the local Fire Department. A uniformed Roxi White Quills tells Elle-Máijá that Blood pride has been trampled by colonization. Looking at her white colleague across the table, she says, "We want our non-Indigenous employees to understand why we are like this . . . that intergenerational trauma is real." This is a particularly significant strand in the braid since Roxi is asking settlers to examine and consider the fabric of colonization from an Indigenous perspective.

The camera crew films several appointments in Esther's office. Lori, another maternal figure, clean for several months and in treatment, looks after her own and her deceased sister's children. She and her friend Mel discuss the criticism they get for using Suboxone to wean themselves off fentanyl. "They don't understand that it works, that it's really helping," they say of family members, illustrating the community "hesitation" that those advocating total abstinence express against harm reduction strategies. Mariah, Lori's daughter, newly using, with aspirations of becoming a nurse, and her boyfriend Shea, two years on fentanyl and wanting to become a wind turbine technician, meet with Esther and go into treatment. Later, the pair appear on screen preparing to write qualifying entrance exams at Red Crow, the local high school, a positive gesture to recovery and future accomplishments. Infusing all of these stories, filmed lovingly by Tailfeather's crew, is an ethic of care—detailing the unremitting efforts on Esther's part to diagnose, treat, educate, advocate, and the tireless effort by her daughter to compile film evidence.

Kímmapiiyipitssini ends on a note of hope, bringing its elements together. In its closing moments, Esther sits in her office, examining a new baby, offering advice and encouragement to the mother, off-screen, who has successfully faced down her drug use. We hear a woman's soft laughter, words identical to those in the first moments of the film—"Are you dreaming? Have you got your mamma's face? Do you hear your mamma's voice?"—lilting like a lullaby. It is Esther's voice, the maternal force, a powerful strand of the braid, there from the beginning. She says goodbye to her patient, and looks around smiling, "Okay, have to get back to work," she says, the camera tracing her progress down the hall and through the door as, presumably, she returns to another aspect of her practice, nurturing, engendering survivance.

What, then, do these films offer audiences, the Indigenous, and those wishing to see through a more accurate pair of glasses? Corinne Bancroft sees the braided narrative as a strategy that encourages "readers [or viewers] to hold multiple, often incommensurate, subjectivities in our minds simultaneously ... to pose questions about the possibility of human attachment in the shadow of our violent histories" (2018: 263). The spaces between narrative threads become apertures through which we can apprehend that which we cannot usually see, an intersubjective field linking people through a web of everyday attachments as we witness in the Kainai and Red Pheasant communities. While Bancroft's theorizing is designed for fiction, her concept lends itself effectively to film, as *nîpawistamâsowin* and *Kímmapiiyipitssini* reveal. In both films, "the space between narrative threads, the twining together of distinct stories, pushes readers [viewers] to face the way history still bleeds into the present and challenges us to develop a type of responsibility that is attentive to different and possible incommensurate human experiences" (2018: 265). Is it possible that this technique allows the filmmakers to create productive tensions with the power to push us to new modes of recognition,[24] in what Barclay calls a reworking of cinematic language from a Fourth Cinema perspective?

Author and critic Lee Maracle (Salish/Cree, Sto:lo Nation) has often said that story is a kind of instruction, a teaching. Story is central to the oral traditions of Indigenous learning because the story invites the listener in, to participate in the meaning-making. While the Indigenous narrative may contain some of the same elements of the European stories, Maracle claims the nature of Native storytelling is different and radically distinct:

> The difference is that the reader [viewer] is as much a part of the story as the teller. Most of our stories don't have orthodox "conclusions"; that is left to the listeners who we trust will draw useful lessons from the story. . . . The listeners are drawn into the dilemma and are expected . . . to actively work themselves out of it. (1990: 11)

Notice, Maracle calls the story a "teaching." In both *Kímmapiiyipitssini: The Meaning of Empathy* and *nîpawistamâsowin: We Will Stand Up*, we encounter the interwoven/braided stories of mothers caring for their children and the land, the quintessential maternal entity, sustaining those who live on her, entwined with a difficult story of historical and contemporary colonization. We all live in a world of these consequences. Maracle would suggest that we need to attend closely to the stories Hubbard and Tailfeathers are telling and ponder their storywork long after screening the films so that we might digest and use the wisdom offered to help understand and address related dilemmas and to help us navigate situations wherever we might find ourselves.

As we have seen, both Hubbard and Tailfeathers speak from a Fourth World perspective, drawing on the authority of the feminist maternal in Indigenous culture and aligning themselves closely with the land as a life-engendering entity. Do these two films encourage us to examine the degree to which it might be desirable to establish the critical value of Fourth Cinema to the twenty-first century critical filmmaking agenda? I would like to suggest that such a debate would be especially valuable in light of the urgency of current environmental concerns (of immediate mortal importance to Indigenous communities globally) as well as raising critical questions about the related management of land and the contested ground around substance abuse and its treatment.

With this agenda, I think about how the non-Indigenous scholar might approach such a discussion. Sylvia Wynter's question arises, "Are we on the same page here? . . . struggling to move beyond the knee-jerk limits of the *Us and Them*" (Wynter and McKittrick 2015: 49). A starting point is to listen to the prescient voices of these two Indigenous filmmakers, sounding through their documentaries. Their films are sterling examples of visual "storywork" embodying contemporary knowledge production, which for elder Jo-Ann Archibald is a genre of decolonizing methodology[25] with the power to rectify the damage of colonization. After all, "the braided narrative may be a central genre that helps contemporary [audiences] to imagine a globalized interconnectedness." In this way these films might train viewers in a different sort of ethics, one that demands a historically and politically conscious responsibility (Bancroft 2018: 270, 278). Significantly, the stories Hubbard and Tailfeathers tell offer radical pathways to the kinds of transformational relationalities that align with Wynter's vision, extending valuable knowledge to Indigenous and settler eyes, nudging us toward the promise of Wynter's "view"—*if* we would "see" them.

Notes

1 Wynter, Sylvia and Katherine McKittrick (2015), "Unparalleled Catastrophe for Our Species? Or, to Give Humanness a Different Future: Conversations." In *Sylvia Wynter: On Being Human as Praxis*, Katherine McKittrick (ed.). Durham and London: Duke University Press, 49.

2 This term is coined by Thomas King (2014) in *The Inconvenient Indian: A Curious Account of Native People in North America*, Doubleday Canada.

3 The term "settler" functions as an imperfect umbrella term to classify the non-Indigenous, who migrate(d) and settle(d) in Canada.

4 In 1497, John Cabot would claim territory now called Newfoundland for the British Crown; Jacques Cartier, exploring the Gulf of Saint Lawrence in 1534, claimed it and what is known as Montreal today in the name of the King of France.

5 Pope Nicholas V issued a papal bull in the mid-1450s authorizing Christian kings to enslave people and seize their lands and goods in any non-Christian

territory. *Terra Nullius* suggests that the land is unoccupied, belonging to no one, whereas European explorers were met, often, within minutes of setting foot on North American land (Manuel and Derrickson 2017: 189).

6 https://www.thecanadianencyclopedia.ca/en/article/duncan-campbell-scott, accessed October 10, 2023.

7 Scott's controversial statement is drawn from Alanis Obomsawin's 2014 documentary *Trick or Treaty?*

8 The TRC would record over 7,000 testimonies between 2009 and 2015, detailing a devastating history of abuse and neglect.

9 Sean Fine "Chief Justice says Canada attempted 'cultural genocide' on aboriginals." Globe and Mail, May 28, 2015 https://www.theglobeandmail.com/news/national/chief-justice-says-canada-attempted-cultural-genocide-onaboriginals/article24688854/, accessed October 10, 2023.

10 https://irshdc.ubc.ca/learn/the-indian-residential-school-settlement-agreement, accessed October 10, 2023.

11 According to Kimberlé Crenshaw's 1989 definition, intersectional feminism is "a prism for seeing the way in which various forms of inequity often operate together and exacerbate each other." https://www.law.columbia.edu/news/archive/kimberle-crenshaw-intersectionality-more-two-decades-later, accessed September 6, 2023.

12 https://gwst1501.wordpress.com/2020/03/23/dr-tasha-hubbard/, accessed July 17, 2023.

13 https://en.wikipedia.org/wiki/Tasha_Hubbard#cite_note-YorktonThisWeek-2020-13, accessed August 10, 2023.

14 https://www2.gov.bc.ca/assets/gov/british-columbians-our-governments/indigenous-people/aboriginal-peoplesdocuments/calls_to_action_english2.pdf, accessed August 12, 2023.

15 The term *Sixties Scoop* was coined by Patrick Johnston, author of the 1983 report *Native Children and the Child Welfare System*. It refers to the mass removal of Aboriginal children from their families into the child welfare system, in most cases without the consent of their families or bands. https://indigenousfoundations.arts.ubc.ca/sixties_scoop/, accessed May 26, 2023.

16 Since the case is *Regina v. Stanley*, the Boushie family has no official standing.

17 The Royal Canadian Mounted Police (RCMP) is the official police force in the province of Saskatchewan with a mandate to prevent, investigate, and maintain order involving federal, provincial, and municipal laws. https://www.rcmp-grc.gc.ca/en/sk/about-division, accessed September 30, 2023.

18 "Canadians have been breaking their promises to Indigenous people" is narrated by Hubbard and outlines the troubled history of Treaty 6, which reveals a

government strategy of starvation to gain compliance from Indigenous tribes and trials and hangings without legal representation when they resisted. https://saskintercultural.org/cultural_resources/tasha-hubbard-treaty-six/, accessed June 10, 2023.

19 The UNPFII is a high-level advisory board to the UN's Economic and Social Council. According to its mandate, it provides expert advice on Indigenous issues related to economic and social development, culture, the environment, education, health, and human rights. https://www.un.org/development/desa/indigenouspeoples/aboutus/permanent-forum-on-indigenous-issues.html, accessed September 30, 2023.

20 As an agency of the Government of Canada, the NFB is Canada's public film and digital media producer and distributor, maintaining a national and international presence: https://www.nfb.ca.

21 The opioid crisis, a worldwide phenomenon of epidemic proportions, has affected every region in Canada, with the heaviest concentration of overdose cases in the provinces of Alberta and British Columbia. The crisis stems from the introduction of street drugs cut with fentanyl (100 times stronger than morphine) and carfentanil (100 times stronger than fentanyl). Medical studies estimate a total of 38,514 apparent opioid toxicity deaths in Canada between 2016 and 2023. https://health-infobase.canada.ca/substance-related-harms/opioids-stimulants, accessed October 23, 2023.

22 PHS is a Canadian nonprofit society located in a former local downtown hotel converted to housing for the homeless by the Downtown Eastside Residents Association.

23 Tailfeathers served as medical lead in Alberta Health Services' Indigenous Wellness Core until her resignation in June 2023 in reaction to political meddling with the appointments process, her departure deemed a significant loss by experts in the field. https://calgary.ctvnews.ca/medical-lead-walks-away-from-indigenous-wellness-core-afterhinshaw-s-job-offer-is-revoked-1.6452419, accessed January 13, 2024.

24 I owe a debt of thanks to Donna Cowan, former NFB Community Audience Development officer, for sparking ideas that led to this article and for alerting me to the success of these two documentaries in the public forum, encouraging me to think about how they might achieve tangible change: "The Audience Development team works with groups across the country who want to organize a screening of an NFB film. Although requests came from everywhere, we try to focus on sectors that could elicit the most impact. For WWSU, the legal organizations and policymakers were targeted; for EMS film, it was the medical

sector (post-secondary schools, Alberta Health Services, CAMH) and the harm reduction social nonprofit agencies (both within cities and also on reserves) that were most interested. These two films were our top two most booked Indigenous-made films during my tenure" (Donna Cowan, personal email November 6, 2023).

25 Christian, Dorothy Archibald (2019). "Indigenous visual storywork for Indigenous film aesthetics." *Decolonizing Research: Indigenous Storywork as Methodology.* Zed Books, London. 49.

11

Making Documentary Media

Approaches to the Deep Image

Aparna Sharma and Priya Sen

Sharp disparities, deep contradictions, living histories, and rapid change—these are the forces that face a media-maker working in India today. Documentary filmmakers in India work to historicize and interpret the contests between a range of intersecting forces including culture, caste, gender, language, region, and religion—all with a view to intervene in and shape public discourse. As the forces and realities operating in society unfold and morph precipitously, filmmakers are compelled to ask questions about the standpoint, scope, and approach for making documentary media.

India can be understood as a media-infested landscape where "big media" backed by either the state or large corporate enterprises pervade. Against this backdrop, media that are smaller in scale and that target specific audiences work to counter hegemonic narratives, images, and discourses. Documentary media belong to the category of small media, where they sit alongside other forms such as independent and regional film, community radio, and video, to name a few. The multiplicity of forms is reflective of competing agendas for media-making. Some media promote glittering and propagandist images. Others seek to demystify and argue out the issues in society. Still others adopt a messy approach, aiming to interpret and complicate the terms of discourse in the public sphere. The media landscape can appear both charged and energizing, exhausting and depleting. Within this wider context, documentary films have assumed a productive instability through which they confront and argue with the neat and stable institutionalized images and discourses circulating in society.

Working across different regions of India, we—Priya Sen and Aparna Sharma—have in our media practice been drawn to examining social environments and the experiences of communities inhabiting them. Sen works in non-fiction media to explore urban lives and experiences. Sharma makes ethnographically informed and experimental documentaries sited primarily in India's northeastern region. With different approaches to practice, we situate cameras amid collectives and communities—be they those that share sociocultural ties or those that come about through urgencies that bring people together, such as political protests or epidemics. Placing ourselves with cameras in these contexts, we explore and learn about peoples' experiences and memories, embodied actions, and the ways by which they make sense of their environments and the histories that have come to shape their worlds. In our work, an impulse to explore takes precedence, and this is distinct from media that communicates preconstituted, highly defined, and targeted messages, such as documentaries promoting political agendas, a form that has assumed currency in contemporary India's contested political sphere.

Our political positions and commitments inform our work, though politics do not make up the primary areas of our practice-led inquiries. When we think of the political, we are considering how through practice we might ask questions and make sense of social realities, ideas of cohesion and difference, avenues for voice and rehearsed routes to silence—all of which can be seen operating in the rapidly evolving formation that is contemporary India. As filmmakers, we have come of age in a society that continues to make strides following the liberalization of the economy in the 1990s. Escalating market forces have been unleashed, and those have in turn spiraled disparities and strife. Whole apparatuses, often masculinist and muscular, are now in place that normativize majoritarianism, cultural homogenization, and the vilification if not outright annihilation of alterities in being, thought, and practice. We share a commitment to comprehend and intervene, in any measure, into such realities that are before and around us, that touch us and those about us.

The impulse to explore articulates itself into what we term as a practice of the deep image. The deep image is not a static or stable formation; it is a practice of making that is geared to opening and understanding social environments and how people navigate them at given points in time, in history. The deep image is an emergent method of work, and it is not geared toward offering conclusive readings about sociocultural phenomena and realities. The practice of the deep image rests on the understanding that the environments people inhabit are not inert or neutral. They are charged with forces—explicit or implicit, forceful or subtle—that intersect with and shape people's lives and memories. We are interested in examining how such forces get enacted and how people make sense of them. In Sharma's work, the focus on cultural heritage and material culture practices becomes a means to examine and contest the summary understandings of the northeastern region as one that is removed from and discordant with the Indian mainland.[1] In Sen's work, the deep image is a practice of engaging with immediacies and urgencies—political and environmental—with a view to witness and make sense of their workings in the fabric of everyday life in the city of Delhi.[2] In these works, our aim is to emplace the viewer in positions from where they may *sense* and derive meanings, interpretations, and connections that complicate and enrich their understandings.

In defining the deep image, we are not referencing a specific aesthetic but a kind of practice, an approach to making that is geared toward deepening understanding of the environments and the times we live in and the connected realities that make up people's lived experiences. For this, the deep image emphasizes a filmmaker's presence in the world and their pursuit of meaning by being themselves immersed in sociocultural phenomena alongside others.

Priya Sen and Aparna Sharma met at the 65th Flaherty Seminar in the United States in 2019 where Sen was exhibiting some of her films. Sen and Sharma got into discussions about the scope and limitations of making documentary work in India today. This essay and the following interviews are an articulation of some of the discussions we have had about our approaches and methods as media-makers. Our individual voices, how we have come to media, our methods, how we understand and articulate what we do, as well as the contexts in which our works circulate are markedly distinct. On account of these distinctions, we have adopted an interview format in this chapter. Each one of us viewed select films made by both of us and then posed interview questions to one another to bring out how we both think about the deep image in our different yet connected ways. The reader will note the distinctions in our practice as well as in our voices. These distinctions are vital to the practice of the deep image that we do not see as a singular and stable method or aesthetic. The deep image must be read as one among other ways of *framing* and understanding our media practices. Our aim in proposing and discussing the concept of the deep image is to offer ways by which the realities around us can be approached and comprehended without necessarily being mastered or closed down in response to any limited lines of reasoning.

Priya Sen

AS: I am keen to know your thoughts on the form of your films. Related to that, would you share some aspects of your methodology for developing your films?

PS: For me form is a question I have for every work. Thinking about form is a way of submitting to the unknown and finding some anchoring within that. Very early I started to play with form as such, unaware of its hold, wanting it to hold and not necessarily knowing how to make that happen. I came into an understanding of form as intuitive more than predetermined. I will speak through the last two films I have made.

In my most recent two films: *No Stranger At All* (2022, henceforth NSAA) and *Faasla* (2021) (a collaboration between Nicolas Grandi and myself)—the formal decisions are more articulated, front and center of the works. *NSAA* is composed of material that I filmed at a time that was quite charged. It started in the winter of 2019 with protests in Delhi around a discriminatory citizenship law and the violent ways in which the State responded to the protests against it. The collective rage and exuberance of three months of protest was followed by a complete withdrawal of life due to the Covid-19 pandemic. For the next two years I wrote and recorded visual media notes that felt like a search along the edges of disquiet and premonition pertaining to the situation that was unfolding before all of us. My visual notes were in fragments and commanded some intensities. *NSAA* was composed through these notes that are incomplete, nearly fictive and based on tenuous associations. The film is like the timeline of a city at a specific moment in time, a kind of angle in history. It is held together by a shadowy protagonist who is wandering perilously.

Faasla, which preceded this work, was a series of video letters that my collaborator Nicolas Grandi (based in Buenos Aires) and I (based in Delhi) composed to each other during the initial months of the pandemic. This was a way of responding to one another and perhaps creating a structure

Figure 11.1 *Faasla,* directed by Priya Sen. © Priya Sen. 2021. All rights reserved.

for the anticipation of a response. The form that work took followed from this impulse. It was an epistolary exchange composed through video and text, responding in succession to each other. We wanted to access a certain continuity through the disruption and loss of a known universe (Figure 11.1).

In terms of how I see my relationship to practice, I might call it "embodied" and something that I have spent time with. It is mostly solo but within collective energies. It comes from unsettled notions of narrative and untethered practices of gathering and presence. It is a way of moving with the camera and of being still with it. My practice with filming has deepened over the years, yet I still find it to be new.

AS: As a filmmaker, what areas are you interested to work on?

PS: I have never thought in terms of topics or themes. My films usually come from the ways in which I attempt to engage with certain urgencies that may or may not have anything to do with how topical they are. The diversity in my films might come from wanting to be in multiple spaces, sometimes simultaneously. There are questions at the heart of this work that have to do with the practice and how it might respond to the wildly fluctuating realities or non-realities (a manner of speaking/realms of material/of fantasy and so on) of this time.

This time, this city, this chaos, this person, these people, these unequal claims, this alternate reality, this closing . . .

If I had to broadly speak of what motivates me right now to make films, I would perhaps state the above. I am also interested in the ways in which I have been changed by filming, by making films. The process has almost inevitably made me access parts of self and the world and considerations thereof of their nonbinary-ness and interrelatedness. I am motivated by the historicity of these ideas within moving image practices. I have also been motivated by ideas of the non-personal unconscious that we might be able to bring to the fore through practices such as filmmaking. By this I mean certain affective resonances that make it possible for image/sound work to translate across viewing cultures and geographies outside of identity tropes.

At a time when state censorship and the criminalization of dissent in this country are reaching a crescendo; in this time of social media feeds, Instagram reels, and an entirely new ecosystem of "content" being produced—which is exciting because it feels close to egalitarian—I can sense a shift in the ways in which I might be thinking of this kind of work. It is not something I have a language for as yet, and it lies within an amorphous feeling of dread, urgency, loss, but also hope. I am not yet able to articulate it. It feels different from an earlier practice—one of manners of presence, of "subject positions," of asking certain questions of the filming self. For example in *Yeh Freedom Life*, 2019, in which I was alongside and close to the protagonists of the film, in their worlds, manouvering the social realities they were facing while making filming decisions led to a certain form of film and filming. I filmed over fifteen months in Ambedkar Nagar, a dense, working-class neighbourhood in Delhi, with women who were in relationships with other women and tried to keep up with their tumultuous and erratic loves. The filming style was both observational as well as interactive—the relationship between the filmmaker and the people in the film became part of the filming process. I have since moved from Delhi for work, for a fellowship, and I am interested to see how this moment will inform formal choices and ways of being. As of now it is difficult to know.

I have always found my ground in a sense of place. I have made almost all my films in Delhi (even though I have filmed in many more places). It is in Delhi that I have found my voice tenuously and through different sites, through many life phases as well as phases of the city's relationship with power. A sense of connectedness to place has allowed me to situate myself. Since and after the pandemic though, there has been a sense of uprooting, if I can call it that. I am curious to see how this will change my relationship to filming. I might add that filming for me is an embodied practice of moving quite literally through the world, and I am curious to see how the loss of connection to place might change it.

AS: What do you mean by urgency? Could you list some urgencies for the reader to get a better sense of what you are working with?

PS: By urgencies I mean this time we are in; the continuous, clear, and present danger of this time itself in India. My most recent film, *NSAA* was filmed over two years starting in December 2019 at the protests in Shaheenbagh in Delhi, around a citizenship bill discriminating against Muslims in India. I started filming as did thousands of others, unable to do much else and looking to keep a record. Shaheenbagh was where these protests began, started by the older women of the neighborhood, in response to police violence against students at the Jamia Millia Islamia University a few days earlier. These protests took over the city in a wave of resistance and euphoria, only to be silenced by the pandemic a few months later. The suddenness of the shift was profound. Through the next many months of uncertainty, I filmed the protests as they moved online, as public life was suspended, as our days and nights started to merge. About the film that I made, I wrote, later:

> Over the last two years in Delhi (and sometimes in Calcutta), during and after the anti-CAA protests, and during and after the pandemic lockdowns, I wrote, filmed and recorded, as days and nights turned from collective rage and exuberance to withdrawal and solitude. The search was along the edges of disquiet and premonition, in fragments and intensities, through wandering and not-staying. Perhaps down pathways made from adjacent knots of desire, seeking solace, seeking life. This video/essay has been composed from those notes, recordings, slivers of prayers, non-intended sound, stranger-love, lamentations and extreme longing, in a city that absorbs, mirrors, tears apart, and simultaneously allays both remorse and euphoria.

"Urgencies" also extends to and does not always suggest a present moment and a certain temporal logic. Delhi, where I have lived, is a medieval city where time collapses and expands through layers of history, through the workings of power, and through constantly shifting built geographies. The term "urgencies" is then akin to time travel where every moment is connected to every other moment. It is to be within such folds and fields of time that I am possibly speaking about. What is equally "urgent" is the form this might take. *NSAA* is about a certain affect that I hope is translated, made from incomplete, fragmented "fictions" about a city at a certain time. Fragments and intensities that do not add up to a singular narrative or story, rather that allude to the ways in which a shift is felt or barely perceived, that moment which to me is full of possibility. Perhaps these are synonymous with what I broadly term "urgencies."

AS: How did you come to filmmaking?

PS: I was at the Mass Communication Research Centre, Jamia Millia Islamia in Delhi for my MA in the mid-90s, and for the first time I watched films outside of mainstream cinema. (This was before the internet, and at a time when TV was very exciting.) I remember watching *The Times of Harvey Milk* the 1984 documentary by Robert Epstein, and *I've Heard The Mermaids Singing* and *When Night Is Falling* by Patricia Rozema—and being utterly speechless with revelation!

I had never watched queer cinema before and was very newly queer myself, but had no language for it other than being in love. This was the time when we watched Anand Patwardhan's films including *Ram Ke Naam* (1992) and *Father, Son and Holy War* (1994). It was post-1992 when the Babri Masjid, a sixteenth-century mosque in Ayodhya, had been destroyed by mobs during a political rally by Hindu nationalist groups, a precursor to the moment we are in right now in India. We watched films in our film appreciation course from cinema's canons and histories. I felt my world opening up. Simultaneously we had to work on our projects and from the very start I sensed something internal, something subversive that had to do with these new loves I had discovered, something that felt like a secret.

After completing my studies at Jamia, I worked in a TV production house on a travel show for Star TV, called *The Great Escape* for a year. I loved it, it was exhilarating. But I knew that cinema was where my heart lay, and I applied to study for an MFA in the US. I was at Temple University, Philadelphia, from 1999. At Temple we learned about personal film, avant-garde film movements, cinema verité, and we watched films in museums, independent theatres, in New York City and in class. We were surrounded by film in a way that felt like a parallel universe.

I remember, though, being quite resistant to a certain expectation of making films about a South Asian or Indian identity. I was more interested in ideas of "place," of a certain alienation I was beginning to sense in "place." I was drawn to an amorphous un-belonging, as it were, not wanting to be pinned down by a discourse around identity. I was into a wayward and undetermined exploration with this medium that I had started to make my own. Through film school, I worked with black and white reversal film that I filmed on a Bolex camera. I filmed on my own, took chances with light readings, did not use a tripod, and held my breath every time the film came back after processing. I fell deeper in love with the medium, and I slowly started to acknowledge the person/the self/the stranger who was filming. I roamed around Philadelphia, took black and white photos with my Nikon N2 camera of neighborhoods—some crumbling and abandoned, others gentrified and affluent in an adjoining block. I photographed railway bridges, highways, graffiti, the river . . . I did not know how to film people, and I did not try. All I knew was that the city emerged around me: in light and shade, in crowds and emptiness, in homesickness and a certain freedom I felt from home itself.

When I made my thesis film in Delhi at the shrine of Nizamuddin Auliya, I switched to video, to trying to film with people, to situate myself somewhere, to follow my love for mystical poetry through Qawwali, but also to be entirely new, entirely unknown, and to see where that led me. My first documentary, *The Knower of Secrets*, 2004, also my thesis film for my MFA, now rests in PADMA, short for Public Access Digital Media Archive, as a timeline that can be publicly annotated. To me it's a perfect home.

AS: Why do you work with documentary materials—images and sounds? What does this allow you to do that perhaps a fictional image may not?

PS: I am interested in a certain construction and production of images and sound as a manner of gleaning from the world that has the impulse of documentary rather than fiction. I am also interested in ways each can take on the other, that is, fiction and documentary—where the two meet, where they coalesce, and can perhaps become indistinguishable. I have never considered

Figure 11.2 *NSAA* directed by Priya Sen. © Priya Sen. 2022. All rights reserved.

myself to be a documentary filmmaker, but someone who works in/with nonfiction registers.

My films have mostly been seen as "experimental documentary" even though I have been quite ambivalent of such categories. What I have understood better is that they "work" in different ways in different viewing cultures (Figure 11.2).

I often use footage that I have gathered over the years, across formats, as "found footage" in my films. The texture and materiality of the medium, its glitches, grain, and dropouts, become part of the image as much as any other element. I work against the tyranny of new formats and constantly updating equipment. Though this is often seen as low production value!

Documentary materials in my practice function in a few different ways formally: I like to see this material as eclectic and shapeshifting, sometimes bound by its own "realness" and sometimes more open, sometimes as fiction. I see this work and the material as a way of being in and maneuvering how we are to consider living in an increasingly violent world. My ways of filming are too wayward to fit into the considerations and control of fictional setups, but I do use documentary material as fiction, which is not very unusual. Documentary material perhaps allows me not to constantly have a frame. I find this to be a relief.

AS: In your work you seem interested to complicate binarisms whether they be of "self" and "other," "self" and "world" . . . How might we think about this as a way of devising the deep image?

PS: I do not set out to complicate binarisms! I do not, in fact, think in terms of binarisms or as phenomena being so linearly and literally pitted against each other, or on a scale in which it is possible to measure one against the other, or on a spectrum of comparison. At least that is not my entry point nor my motivation to work in the ways I do. "Self" and "other" are extensions of each other, a bit like form and content, and it is how I approach filming—to ask different questions of subject positions but to not diminish a certain inherent power dynamic. If binaries get complicated, that is an effect. I would like to think of "self" and "world" but again not as separations to be analyzed outside of each other. My attempt is for the form to be able to move beyond such separations. I have been told that my films feel very intimate, as say in *Yeh Freedom Life* in which there is a relationship with the protagonists of the film or with the neighborhoods they live in. I was recently told that *NSAA* also feels extremely intimate, and that in a sense, to reverse the phrase "the personal is political," in this work "the political is personal."

I usually film, edit, and sound design my films. The practice lies in all three modes. In that sense I see myself as a soloist and moving image artist rather than "filmmaker" because of the implicit demarcation of roles in the latter. If there is a word that I might use, it is "transience"—as a mode/manner/a way of being in the midst of constant flux. Hence it is not binaries then that become the logic with which I proceed, but something more ephemeral. *Faasla* that contains video letters between Nicolas Grandi and myself is constructed from within a certain obvious precarity and uncertainty—a formal translation of the ephemerality to which I am referring.

I think political work can be expanded through language outside of an activist mode. Politics is a framework for what I do, so there is no question of it being apolitical. And like all complex politics, there isn't a singular reasoning but possibly a kaleidoscopic view. When I think back on my process with films, I realize this is how I work through ideas. It is not about arriving at a truth or resolution or a distant plane where the answers are there for the taking. It is about the uneven, unresolved, circuitous paths that one takes in order to get to a place, only to realize that the views are different from there and the roads have disappeared. The horizon itself shifts with each arrival as it were. This to me is indicative of a certain depth that one travels with each work— the "deep image, the deep horizon" and the endlessness of how we enter into them. Once it is entered, there is a breadth (and depth) of territory, of ground, that has to be covered. The "deep image" implies these multiple registers and positions that the work then develops around. Whether this is an exploration of relationships within urban frames (*Yeh Freedom Life*), or an exploration of a time in a city reeling under a new political imagination (*NSAA*), there is an immersive quality to it that perhaps allows for subjectivities to keep shifting and language to keep expanding. I see this as a way to speak of the "deep image" as an aspect of my practice and process.

AS: How do you see yourself evolving as a filmmaker?

PS: My practice with film has always felt like an extension of how I move through this world—it is embodied, intimate, and restless. I perhaps understand it better now, recognize its impulses, and have more language for it. I have moved into a place of camaraderie with my film practice—it accompanies, speaks, and thinks alongside me. I am less anxious about the uncertainties within which I work—be it around funding concerns, formal ideas, or the expectations of an audience. The search, the seeking, the questions around presence, and how to navigate the opacities and silences that surround us in our social/communal, political, and private worlds, is where this practice has come to be. The fragmentation and violence of this moment is the frame itself.

I am deeply drawn to an accompanying scholarship—to text and archival material, to reading and annotating. This has deepened over the years and filming is part of this immersive process. Currently I am a fellow at the Radcliffe Institute and Film Study Centre at Harvard.

This has allowed me time, space, intellectual and creative resources to think through this work.

Aparna Sharma

PS: How did you start working in Assam, and what might your relationship to place be?

AS: My interest to work in Assam goes back to my years as an undergraduate student of Journalism at the University of Delhi. At that time Assam was regularly featured in the news on account of the insurgency there. I was interested in learning more about what was going on in that region and, I also had a question as to whether insurgency was the only way by which we could understand the region and its situation. I wanted to know what everyday life looks and feels like in a place that is witness to such extreme and sustained forms of violence. I had undertaken an undergraduate research project that involved a comparative analysis of news from Assam that got reported in the national (Delhi-based), regional (Kolkata-based), and local newspapers (Assamese). My project's findings were that news about insurgency in Assam was very relevant, but it was too negative and limited in its approach to understanding the Assamese people and their concerns. The voices of the Assamese were often absent from much reportage.

I am not from Assam. I have worked in that region in some or the other capacity for nearly two decades, and I understand myself principally as an outsider. I am aware that in fields such as Anthropology, the position of the outsider is perceived as limited, even extractive given the histories of colonialism. In the context of Assam, the insider–outsider position gets mobilized in very charged ways on account of the complex histories of colonialism and migration from other parts of the Indian subcontinent to this region. In my work in Assam, I am driven to understanding complex and competing histories and experiences—quite a few of which get obscured, suppressed, or simply censored from the broader frameworks of say the "nation" or "terrorism," especially when these larger categories are constructed along very narrow and restricted lines of engagement.

Speaking about my relationship to place, in the case of Assam it has been processual. Over a decade ago when I actively started working in Assam, I was a newcomer who provoked curiosity and even some suspicion. I had contacts within the Gauhati University who assisted me in my work, and over the years I have regularly returned to Assam, undertaken a range of assignments and shared my work with the local communities. Sharing my work has led to awareness and dialogues about what I do in the region. I have guest-lectured and conducted workshops at the universities there and, on occasions my work has been highlighted in the local exhibition spaces and media too. With time I have developed sustained connections with people who live and work in Assam. All this is to say that sustained work and presence in the region have contributed to replacing a perception of myself less as a neutral or disinterested outsider, and this in turn has helped me deepen my sense of connection with Assam.

PS: How does this inform the shooting and editing choices and the construction of voice or narrative?

AS: My work in Assam started with a very felt need to understand the culture and history of that state. I have completed two feature-length films in Assam: *Kamakha: Through Prayerful Eyes* (2012) and *Mihin Sutta, Mihin Jibon* (English title: *The Women Weavers of Assam,* 2019). My films have focused on communities of artisans and crafts-persons, the crafts they practice, and their livelihoods. I am interested to depict people in active terms; so you will see them doing work, making things, and talking about the work they do. The people I have featured in my films have very evolved relationships with what they make. I am interested to learn about the histories of their crafts, the place that those crafts occupy in their lives, and how they see their work relating to the cultures of Assam. When I am filming it is important to create an environment in which people can express the multiple dimensions of their work so that their livelihoods are not seen in any reductive or limited terms (Figure 11.3).

When I made *Kamakha* I was focusing on artists who live in the vicinity of the Kamakhya temple, which is an ancient site of fertility worship. I documented the visual and material artifacts artists make inspired by the Kamakhya temple.

Figure 11.3 *Kamakha,* directed by Aparna Sharma. © Aparna Sharma. 2012. All rights reserved.

In *Mihin Sutta, Mihin Jibon* I focussed on an institution, the Tezpur District Mahila Samiti (TDMS), where women from socio-economically challenged backgrounds are trained and supported to earn a livelihood weaving Assamese textiles. In my cinematography, which I do myself, I aim to depict people making artifacts in the sites or the worlds that they inhabit. By worlds I mean the social and cultural environments in which people live and work. I make it a point to shoot processes of making in such a way that the viewer sees the wider environment or context in which those processes are performed. The spaces in which people work are not merely backdrops for their activities, and therefore, they should not be blurred or out of focus. For this I often use a wide-angle camera lens as it gives a wider field of view in which people do not seem extracted from their worlds. When I edit, I try to provide the viewer a sense of where and how what they are seeing has taken place. I pay attention to details such as the rhythms of work, sounds of activities, as well as the overall atmosphere, lighting, and the mood that it creates in a place and, peoples' embodied movements and behaviors while they work.

As for voice and narrative in film, I am committed to editing a film as close to the order in which it has been shot. I feel this helps bring out how a filmmaker's relationship with people and places develops over time. Here I am influenced by observational cinema that emphasizes depicting proceedings in the order in which they unfold before the camera.

Often, a documentary is thought to be a platform that gives voice to those who do not have access to the means of representation. I feel this is a very narrow way of understanding voice in a documentary. To me, multiple elements come together and make the distinct voice of a documentary film: the materials and people that a film focuses on, the environment in which it is set, the approach to cinematography and editing, and a filmmaker's presence. What a filmmaker is hoping for, and which even people included in a film come to share in, is building some sense of coherence and meaning in relation to what is depicted.

PS: How did you come to work in long form, and can you speak more about the ways in which you shape narrative through being around the people in your films?

AS: I am interested to observe how people embody and perform the knowledge of making the materials that they do and, to bring out the relationship between what they make and the environments that they inhabit. One thing I do in my work is to learn making the things that I am documenting in a film. When I made *Mihin Sutta, Mihin Jibon,* I learned to weave. In *Kamakha: Through Prayerful Eyes,* I had documented a painter making abstract paintings inspired by Goddess Kamakhya. I tried to learn his technique of painting. Learning to make what I am documenting helps me to better know and understand the processes I am documenting—the labor they involve and the steps they are made up of. Such an understanding helps me relate more deeply with what I am documenting, and I don't feel removed or distant from the things around me when I am with a camera.

Further, the processes I document often mean many things to different people: they are a source of livelihood, they are artistic and aesthetic, and they often have personal associations attached to them such as memories, dreams, and even whole communities' shared aspirations. For example, when I made *Mihin Sutta, Mihin Jibon,* every weaver told me that she had learned to weave from her mother or elder sister. The weavers also expressed their sense of cultural pride and memories of lost loved ones from whom they had learned to weave. They often spoke of the challenges they face as crafts-persons in contemporary times. There are multiple and very lived dimensions to the processes I document. Bringing out these dimensions on screen requires a sustained presence and pace in the documentation process as well as the film itself.

So I feel that long form comes about because of the materials with which I am working.

PS: What is your relationship with poetic registers?

AS: I have always admired poetic documentaries, and I find that watching poetic documentaries is more engaging and pleasurable than, say, watching an expository documentary. All documentaries educate and inform the viewer, but poetic forms of documentary, I find, give the viewer more room for experience and interpretation. This is something I am interested in both as a film viewer and maker.

One of the films that has had a deep impact on me since I first watched it as a student in film school is Dziga Vertov's *The Man with the Movie Camera* (1929) and, I remain inspired that a woman, Elizaveta Svilova, edited that masterful film whose meanings are so embedded in its montages. I learned a lot from Vertov and the Soviet masters about how an image provokes affect and how the editing of images, down to their very duration and sequencing, can produce meaning. I have also learned a lot from filmmakers of the Indian parallel cinema, such as Mrinal Sen and Kumar Shahani. Shahani's *Bhavantarana* that focuses on the classical dance form of Odissi is to me a very powerful experiment depicting how a modern medium such as cinema converses with a "classical" form that has been shaped by very complex histories of the Indian subcontinent. I also draw inspiration from observational cinema, particularly the work of filmmakers such as David MacDougall and, more recently, Wang Bing, who adopts a loosely observational style. Observational cinema's emphasis that the structure of a film should not be external to it, but rather it should come from the order of proceedings as seen on camera, commands a kind of poetic quality that I have found very productive to work with while filming.

I don't approach the poetic forms in terms of their techniques. I strive to document materials as closely and in as much detail as I can, and then I study my materials (over a long period of time, sometimes a few years even) to find ways to use them that do not limit or close down their meanings or possibilities. Sometimes this means using long-duration shots in sequences. On other occasions, this requires revealing things in the film at a very measured pace. My point here is that there isn't "a" way of working with filmed materials. What I feel I often need is space to document things with a sense of curiosity as well as respect toward what one is witnessing through the viewfinder. It is my hope that these sentiments transfer to the viewer, at least in some ways.

PS: How does the "deep image" describe your work? Is it a mode of image-making, is it inherent in practice, is it an effect of viewing?

AS: I started to think about the "deep image" from the time of my doctoral work in the UK, 2003–7. I had undertaken a practice-based PhD in which I made a film that looked at the cultural life of a Gujarati community living in South Wales. My interest from that time has been in thinking how documentary might depict cultures as living and processual, not fixed. It is crucial for me that the material cultures and heritage that my films depict are shown as *living*, being shaped and formed by community members, a culture's active practitioners. Often the practices on which my films focus are considered traditional, and somehow implicit in the understanding of something being "traditional" is that it does not change; it is fixed. But as Raymond Williams points out, all cultures have two aspects, that is, what is known and followed, what members of a culture are "trained to" and, what is new and created through observation and questioning, "the new observations and meanings, which are offered and tested" (1989: 4). To me it is the latter, the creative side of things that is most interesting because it is here that one can see how a culture's day-to-day values and activities are interpreted, questioned, and advanced by those who practice them. In *Mihin Sutta, Mihin Jibon,* I included interviews in which some of the weavers shared how they occasionally create new designs that are inspired by their environments. These designs are not necessarily considered as "traditional," but they reflect how the weavers are experimenting and creating new forms through their practice (Figure 11.4).

A further dimension of reflecting things in process has to do with suggesting to the viewer how a documentarist's relationship to the people and things that they document is also a living and evolving one. I am influenced here by ethnographic filmmaker David MacDougall's concept of "deep reflexivity."

Figure 11.4 *Mihin Sutta, Mihin Jibon,* directed by Aparna Sharma. © Aparna Sharma. 2019. All rights reserved.

According to MacDougall, a filmmaker's position is dynamic, constantly evolving in relation to what they are documenting. He states that "The fieldworker [here filmmaker] often works in a way that is exploratory and intuitive. This is a dynamic process" (1998: 89). While undertaking documentation, I am very aware of my position in multiple ways, say as an outsider, my identified gender, socio-economic background, etc. At the same time, as my documentation process advances, the connections between myself and the people, practices, and places I am documenting deepen and open new lines of meaning in the film that I hope enrich the viewer's experience. As an example, in *Mihin Sutta, Mihin Jibon*, I developed a two-phase documentation schedule, eight months apart. I filmed the moments of meeting the weavers after a gap of eight months and included their reactions to me and my own thoughts on returning to them after a gap in a voice-over for the film. My return to the weavers brought out a sense of our being connected in some ways, and this was almost like a new layer introduced into our shared worlds. To me, including references to how a filmmaker's relationship with the people and places they are documenting evolves through time adds a subtle and deeper layer of meaning to the film. I don't think that this can be the primary focus of a film; it can only be suggested.

For me, the deep image is a mode of practice that provokes and allows a viewer to read more than a single or determined meaning in what they see; it allows them to absorb, to make connections with and interpretations about what they see. I suppose another way of saying this is that the deep image offers space to a viewer to engage with the material without feeling any compulsion toward *reading it right* or *getting the point,* as it were. As a filmmaker, this to me only comes about when documentation is done with an eye toward detail so that the things we see on screen can be understood as living and evolving through time. I feel a filmmaker has to explore and develop a mode, a method of work that is founded on a dynamic and respectful connection between them and those who they document. The deep image is therefore a practice that reflects things in process, as living, and it builds on cinematic reflexivity, that is, knowing and sensing the method by which a work has been made without that being the singular focus of the work. In sum, I feel the deep image is geared to suggest the complexities of the realities people face without resolving or reducing those complexities into any kind of limited registers or even aesthetic techniques.

PS: What might the role of time be in the construction of the deep image?

AS: The deep image in my films comes from sustained and long-term collaboration with people. Time is needed to research and build rapports with people so that the process of documentation is a mutually creative and meaningful one. Another related way that I think about the deep image is in terms of slowness, an image that is built on details and which slows things down. In many ways, I am working against fast-paced, rushed, even superficial modes of audio-visual communication such as those on social media or even popular news media that tend to reduce and oversimplify the meanings of things. In the process the image somehow loses a life of its own. I think documenting things in detail and with consideration toward how they evolve over time allows viewers to access spaces and meanings toward which they may have previously had very limited exposure, and this can be very enriching.

Moving image media such as films are time-based. In the process of shooting and editing, one thinks quite a lot about time: the duration of shots when they are shot, the duration of shots when they are edited, and the sense of duration of the film as a whole. There is also another consideration about time that comes up in my work. I often think about where a film is sited and how the flow of time is experienced in that place. Does time in a place feel rushed or stretched? Is there a slowness in the flow of time that is pleasing, or does it feel testing or demanding? Several factors are at play here: seasons, times of day, the histories experienced in those places, the nature of peoples' activities, peoples' own dispositions, and how those shape the experience of time. This thinking about time cannot be reduced to a filmic technique one uses while shooting or cutting a film. It is a kind of awareness that one carries within oneself that then informs cinematography and later editing.

PS: How have you seen yourself evolve as a filmmaker? Do you sense shifts in your film practice over the years?

AS: Besides documentary, I have an interest in experimental work, and most recently, I made a short film using photographic stills shot on my phone, *Still Light* (2021), 3 mins. Being an experimental film, I was following my own thinking on how light impacts our perception of place. (I developed this during a period of quarantine during the pandemic.) It was a refreshing experience to work on this film because it is not long-form and I was working all alone. I share this because I feel as a maker it has been most energizing for me when I have made disparate kinds of work and challenged myself to do things toward which I am not immediately drawn.

Notes

1 *Kamakha: Through Prayerful Eyes* (2012), [Film] Dir. Aparna Sharma, India: Distributed by Berkeley Media LLC. Available at https://search.alexanderstreet.com/view/work/bibliographic_entity%7Cvideo_work%7C3227773; *Mihin Sutta, Mihin Jibon* (*The Women Weavers of Assam*, 2019), [Film] Dir. Aparna Sharma, India, distributed by the Royal Anthropological Institute of Great Britain and Ireland. Available at kanopy.com; Sharma, Aparna. 2021. *Still Light*. In, *Sightlines Journal*. Issue 5: 2023. Australian Screen Production Education and Research Association. Available at https://www.aspera.org.au/still-light

2 *Yeh Freedom Life* (2019), [Film] Dir. Priya Sen, India; *Faasla* (2021), [Film] Dir. Priya Sen, India; *No Stranger At All* (2022), [Film] Dir. Priya Sen, India, distributed by Arsenal Institute for Film and Video Art, Berlin.

12

Feminism as Documentary Method

A Conversation

Irene Lusztig, Hannah Jayanti, Noorafshan Mirza, Rosa-Johan Uddoh, and Andrea Luka Zimmerman

Introduction

The conversational chapter that follows emerges from a multi-day gathering of five artist-filmmakers—two of us based in the United States and three based in the UK—in New York City, during the summer of 2023. Using a collective dialogue framework and a shared co-writing and co-editing process, our goal was to explore expansive ideas around feminism as a method in our respective documentary practices. Our gathering aspired to articulate capacious ways of understanding feminist documentary-making that are not necessarily tied to traditionally "feminist" or gendered subject matter. In the introduction to their edited collection *Feminism and Documentary*, Diane Waldman and Janet Walker call for a wide-ranging approach to documentary scholarship that can "bring feminist approaches and concerns to bear on works usually exempt from them" (1999: 6). Yet, on the practice/filmmaking side, we've observed a persistent and frustrating conflation of the idea of "feminist filmmaking" with work that centers women as subjects. Sensing a narrowing of the documentary industry in terms of what forms, processes, and approaches are supported, we hoped to arrive, together, at a set of ideas that might untether content from form, process, and politics, through a commitment to feminist approaches.

By design, the heterogeneous range of creative practices represented in our group pushes against normative boundaries of "documentary." We work variously inside of and in opposition to the documentary industry, on screens, in galleries, and in community spaces and with performance, social practice, public art, archives, collage, multi-screen installation, activist organizing, curation, teaching, football coaching, and sewing (to name just a few of our many ways of working).

Beginning with time spent sharing our work and getting to know each other's practices (several of us were meeting for the first time through this project), our gathering also foregrounded spaciousness and hospitality as methods. Over three days, we shared meals, images, experiences, rest, and space as we traversed a wide-ranging terrain of topics. With this conversation-essay, we hope to put forward ideas of a feminist documentary method invested in listening, vulnerability, power-sharing, encounter, failure, community process, co-creation, screening spaces as gathering/conversation sites that disrupt or exceed the framework of creative capitalism, and new approaches to form and visual language.

Practice

Irene: My first film *Reconstruction* (Lusztig 2001) began with a set of questions about historical absence and what would it feel like to try to encounter or get to know my grandmother, who died when I was three, through a filmmaking process. I moved to Romania, where my parents are from, and immersed myself in an everyday practice of being in a place, meeting people, and spending time in archives. I developed a deep listening practice, and that's something that I've carried into other projects. I think a lot about what can happen when you bring something out of an archive and invite people out in the world to be in conversation with something from the past. What does it mean to make a space where a conversation across time can happen? What does it mean for a filmmaker to be a facilitator?

I've just finished a film (*Richland*, 2023) that's very different from my previous body of work that focuses on women. It's a film made in a nuclear community, where I'm thinking about land and the history of nuclear weapons and American militarism and spending time in politically conservative American communities. I've been thinking about how I can use methods that I've developed in feminist film contexts, where I'm making work with and about women. Can I still make a generous listening space in a community where I feel a lot of ideological difference? What does it mean to work with a feminist methodology and framework, but not on a project that's about gender?

Rosa: I started to make artwork in the first place because I was interested in foregrounding an idea of radical self-love inspired by the writing of Audre Lorde, particularly her essay "The Uses of the Erotic" (Lorde 1984: 53–9), and centering that as a project in my life. That's my essential guiding principle in my practice, and I work through performance, multi-media installation, writing, and, of course, film. Inspired by Black feminist practice and writing and cultural studies, I'm particularly interested in the effects of popular culture on Black self-formation.

I think that, often, race might be about copying or resembling someone you've seen on TV. While this is something I'd experienced as a child myself, this really hit home when making my film *Practice Makes Perfect* (Brown & Uddoh 2021) in a school in Southend-on-Sea, in Essex, and I saw how these thirteen-year-olds started to naturally mimic and parody what they consumed on TV and social media as soon as we (my co-director, Louis Brown, and I) gave them a camcorder to operate themselves, and some freedom. They broke out of this role they'd been playing (perhaps for me?!) up until then as "school children" and became these cutting and playful cultural critics. For me, performance, TV, and film can be identity-altering, life-altering mediums, if we encourage active, playful, and creative engagement with the screen. We hear a lot nowadays about the "importance" of "representation," but how does representation actually feel in our bodies? Does it feel good? How can it feel good?

Hannah: For the last ten years, I've been practicing place-based filmmaking. My last feature film, *Truth or Consequences* (Jayanti 2021), was a speculative documentary set in a small town in New Mexico, and for ten years I've been working on a multi-media documentary project called *Topography*[1] (Jayanti and Porter, forthcoming), which is set in and around public lands within the United States. When I started this body of work, I was looking for ways to make documentaries that weren't sensational or defined by character arcs. I had an experience as a kid of watching documentary films and feeling like they were so far from my lived experience. They seemed fixated on exceptional people, and so much of the narrative was crafted around catalytic moments. I felt like I wasn't seeing stories that made sense of the messier or smaller parts of my life. I wanted to know what it would be like to bring value to those moments where I could say, "that's a meaningful life." As much as I can draw a causal line in my work, that was the generation for me.

Making place-based films is an approach I stumbled on that opened up a different kind of documentary filmmaking for me. When you start thinking in terms of place, it's a very different orientation. It can hold the very small, it can hold things that seem unrelated, it can hold different ways of organizing meaning. There's a possibility of thinking about interdependence over individuality and elevating marginalized histories over the dominant narratives that are really, really strong. And, through that, it can also potentially create different futures. In mainstream media culture, documentary is thought of as a thing that documents the past, but it could just as easily be talked about as something that creates because it becomes the way that we understand our world.

Noor: I've always worked on very long research-based projects, submerged in the process. Going deep feels like it is a metaphor, but it's also a desire to have been a free diver. You've got no oxygen tanks, but you just train to go deeper and deeper and deeper. The final work could be performance, object making, or film and video. On occasion, it can be works that aren't documented—they're happenings, they're gatherings—well before I even had a language for socially engaged art practice. Underneath all the different works that I've made, the baseline theme has to do with addressing inequality and structural violence. How to speak to, without reproducing the violence.

Between 2007 and 2016, I worked on an iterative, collaborative project called the Museum of Non-Participation,[2] a "museum without walls" inspired by experiences moving between London and Karachi, initially launched in a space behind a barber shop in Bethnal Green. The project included interventions, newspapers, wall chalking, reading groups, language exchange, performance lectures, audio works, walks, political theater, and speech acts. The "museum" served as a creative, conceptual institution where we, as artists, delved into our complicity within neoliberal power systems and structures, and into the intricate dynamics of resistance. Reflecting on the Museum of Non-Participation project, I was consistently negotiating with structures of power in order to create autonomy in spaces where that was not present. I have always been intrigued by leveraging art spaces and their boundaries. Despite their inherent rigidity, they offer potential for opening up. Where are the edges? What are the rules? What occurs when we widen access beyond the usual boundaries?

Andrea: I resonate a lot with these approaches of trying to find a language for who we are, where we are, and how we make a world with each other, in a really fluid and different way. I think all of our work does that. My first filmmaking collective was called Vision Machine,[3] and we explored how we can use filmmaking as an obstinate tool, re-visioning mainstream expressions into a form able to counter its tropes, using filmmaking as a practice of self-re-imagining. We had a free film school in a community hall in East London and made films together, which led to a way of working that could address structural violence not as an abstract event, but integral to the formation of self.

We are often seen as we are represented and even become how we are seen to be—say, the way in which films depict a working-class person or an unhoused person—and this is so deeply problematic. My work is a counter-memory to this way of history-making. For me, formally, that means that I work in hybrid and layered forms of filmmaking. My work is deeply informed by years of thinking about public housing, decentered violence, and marginalized, and often rebellious, communities. The world that I'm drawn to is incomplete. It's full of contrary thoughts, feelings; it's slippery, it's messy. That's an important space for me, always challenging who gets to define that imagining and what gets valued within the culture. Not to forget to strive to make a space for those that are less able to participate in it and to make space inside of oneself for what one does not know, and may never know, is really crucial. My work is focused on what could be—it is about vernacular beauty, refusal, insertion, spaciousness.

Form, Content, Process

Noor: How do you navigate or negotiate form and content? Is that something that's always oscillating?

Rosa: Whenever I make a work, it starts with research. I'll get really deep into the research and then I decide what medium is appropriate to tell the story or to ask the question that I want to ask. I have this idea that if I can find a medium that works, that will convey some of the meaning on a level that is felt more bodily, or more abstractly, or in the mood. That's meant that, in my artistic practice so far, often I've learned new mediums from scratch. That's how I came to film, and I've got a bit stuck on film, because the content that I've started to make is about the representation of Black people *in* popular media and film.

Noor: I started off unconsciously making very white male structural films. With a Super 8 camera. I was remaking *Zorn's Lemma* (Frampton 1970) without knowing it. My long-term collaborator, Brad Butler, and I began with non-fiction filmmaking and gradually embraced storytelling. Our projects evolved to be increasingly fictional, transitioning from experimental, avant-garde materialist cinema to our latest work—a fully immersive installation feature film for the gallery displayed across five screens. There is a collection of works that started with *Hold Your Ground*

(Butler and Mirza 2013), which is about choreographing nonverbal performative works for the camera, a form of storytelling through the body. Out of one work comes the seeds for another.

Irene: Process generates form: when you don't know what a project is going to be until it's finished and in the world, the form is constantly being made through encounters, through thinking, through research. I can't see those things as separable.

Hannah: In my experience, the way that you're talking, Irene, about a process-based emergent form—the idea that you would listen, collaborate, gather material, and then edit a structure that would continue that practice of listening and collaborating—is not very legible in the documentary industry.

Part of what I have been practicing is going into spaces without a set idea of what I am looking for, without knowing what I hope to find. And then being wary of whenever I start to think that I know something. I don't know if anyone else has this experience, but when I think I know what the person is like, or what they're going to say, or what the film might be, it's very subtle, but I start to ask more leading questions and to leave slightly less room for the other person. I was filming in the Badlands of South Dakota, and my friend Richard would take me out on walks. We'd search for which plants were in bloom while he shared his deep knowledge of their medicinal qualities. Off camera, he had told me that he was a child when they bombed the reservation where he grew up, and, on this particular walk, I had it in the back of my head. We went up to this overlook, and it was very beautiful, and I thought, "Oh, now's my moment. I can ask him about the bombing." I put my camera on him. I think in some really embarrassing way, I go, "Oh, hey, by the way, remember that thing you told me? What was it like to be bombed?" And the dynamic changed. Richard is really loving and, I believe, considers me a friend, so he went along with it, but his posture got more rigid, and he became formal and less comfortable. And I realized, "Oh, ten minutes ago we were filming plants; and now I am a non-Indigenous person, a person from New York, pointing a camera at this person and asking about violence, and he's telling it to me, and we're acting out these roles."

I believe moments like those come from a kind of embedded conditioning, an understanding of what "story" is, what capturing means, or what you "need" for the edit. I feel grateful that I'm sensitive to these moments and notice when they are happening. But it reminds me that it takes something to center an ethical and political practice. It takes a constant reorienting.

The world is not pulling for that, the edicts of "good documentary" are not pulling for that, our egos are not pulling for that; so much is not pulling for that way of being in the world.

Rosa: You know, I'm so glad you shared this moment because it is really illustrative of the difficulty with documentary.

Andrea: Maybe one nice way would be if we go around and everyone just summarizes how you approach working with people. Is process more important than outcome?

When I make a documentary, it's a life practice for me. I think I'm a very odd person—I feel odd in the world. It's not just class, I've always felt awkward. I never fit in anywhere very easily. I was either too this or that, so I just never understood who I am, properly. And now I've come to know that this is an asset when I work with people. Because it allows me to be sensitive to their energy. People can express themselves in their own way, and that's usually way better than if I would have edited it how I imagined it to be.

In my documentaries, participants get to see footage twice before the film is released—first only material filmed with them, and then what I am editing, in context. This usually means that people are not afraid to bring themselves to the conversation, as they have a chance to see it, and even ask me to put scenes back in that I thought might be too vulnerable, like showing someone in crisis or difficulty. I'm seeking narratives that are imperfect.

Hannah: I've been thinking about sharing. I used to make films where I was this really good listener, where I didn't share very much, and I thought that generosity looked like absorption. And I've really been learning that generosity is reciprocity.

One of the "good practices" of documentaries is if someone tells you something, you wait so that you can edit without your voice. Like in an interviewing class, I think that's what you're taught, right? If someone says something, especially if it's emotional, you are supposed to pause. But that breaks relation completely. If I really think reciprocity is generosity, I need to talk at a moment that might screw up my edit. If someone shares something vulnerable, I need to be willing to share something vulnerable back, and I need to be willing to consider putting that on camera.

Rosa: I find that really moving, what you said. Recently, I've started to try and form relationships in my life with people around me, with family, with a new partner in a different way. I was in a codependent relationship previously for many years and I didn't realize because I didn't understand— and what you said really hit this on the head—"generosity." I didn't understand that generosity wasn't about de-centering myself, wasn't about making all of the space for someone else. I think actively not doing that, instead trying to relate to people in a *truly* generous way, in a loving way, takes real bravery because it means I have to constantly reveal myself. I hadn't really thought about how this more intimate practice carries into relationships with labor and work but listening to you, I think it absolutely does. Terms like "generosity" and "reciprocity" sometimes get thrown about in "feminist" filmmaking. But they exist in the wider context of unequal power and labor structures. The quality of the relationships we build in film are not going to be exempt from the abusive or loving relationship dynamics we have in our everyday lives with family, lovers, friends, et cetera; in fact, they are directly related.

Noor: My practice centers working collaboratively and collectively. The way I work with people usually starts from within a duo and expands to an ensemble way of co-creating. One film work, for example, *The Scar* (Butler and Mirza 2018), took five years to produce and has had many iterations along the way: workshops, devising, co-authoring scenes with participants and collaborators, filming and editing, reflecting and re-shooting, working across different cities and multiple languages, slippages in translation—what is said, unsaid, and unsayable. The filmic process itself defines and co-creates a temporary community. My work is literally about kinship and, in some ways, surrogacy for family. Working with people is a place of belonging, a place of home and of community building. Because my experiences within my family and home were challenging and sometimes harmful, I have been on a healing journey. This journey has taught me that I can redefine what family and home mean to me, creating a space that is nurturing, forgiving, and healthy.

Irene: I think the ways that we're taught to present ourselves as kind and generous, these ways of being in the world that are listening-centered and relational—they do often live very close to trauma. I definitely learned how to be a listener in a particular way from spending a lot of my childhood holding family trauma. From my childhood, I learned that I have a great capacity to stand next to someone's trauma and be with it. I think that has formed the way that I am in the world and the kind of filmmaker that I am. I also think that's very gendered: a lot of us have learned ways of holding things that are hard—like being good listeners—in ways that are self-effacing.

Hannah: I want to acknowledge everyone for sharing. I really appreciate whatever it took to share. In line with this conversation, one of the questions I often get asked after my films is, "How did you get them to open up to you?"

[*laughter*]

Andrea: I think we all get that!

Hannah: I think about what do I wish they would ask me?

Irene: There's something about "how did you get someone to do this?" that's such an extractive framework. I make work to be in community with people. It's not like you're "getting" someone to do something, but that they're actually giving you so much. The question could be about what was transformed in you.

Hannah: Or—how were you being in the world such that you ended up in a conversation like that with someone you clearly love? I feel like there are other organizations of questions that would create spaces for someone else, maybe someone in the audience, where they could think, "Oh, I could do my version of that." They want to know how I did that, but it's like, what do you want to do? What are you longing for? What are you trying to make in the world?

Lineage

Irene: I'm curious to hear from each of us what are the ways that we think about our lineage—what we're in conversation with from the past. And, also, how we relate to the idea of mentorship—and how those two things talk to each other.

One thing that's been really nice about this group is that we're a few different ages and in different places in terms of how long we've been working. This idea of intergenerational dialogue and learning is such a foundational and powerful part of the feminist framework for my work. But, also, so much of that lineage is hidden and hard to find and something I really needed to work to look for—like self-educating about the tradition of the 1970's collective feminist documentary filmmaking in the United States that has really influenced my work.[4]

What does it mean to encounter people and communities that came before? I'm wondering how that kind of time travel and intergenerational thinking works for you.

Rosa: In my performance practice—which is what I started off doing before I was even making films—I tried to embody famous characters or people that I saw as a way of understanding them, what we get from their representation and the limits of representational politics in general. There were a lot of different people that I performed as a version of, like Moira Stuart,[5] or more recently Una Marson,[6] the Jamaican producer and activist who worked for a brief, but influential time in the UK in the 1930s, and Venus and Serena Williams.[7] All of these characters weren't within "Art," but were genuinely role models in my life who, in a roundabout way, got me to being a filmmaker. I guess I didn't really know any Black performance artists, some influences were performers from popular culture—fields where Black performance has historically been encouraged, like sport and music. Later, I came across people like Adrian Piper and I was like, "Oh, my goodness." [*laughs*] And Lorraine O'Grady, and lots of Black performance artists that were working in New York around that time.[8] But even though I now know a lot more of my foremothers in the artistic sphere, non-Art" performers are still formative to my practice because they are adept at engaging a mass audience on critical issues, and that's something I want to learn.

Noor: Such a brilliant question. I was listening and time-traveling at the same time. Growing up in a village in England, I didn't know about race, I didn't know about class, I didn't know about gender, yet I was subjected to all of those intersectional identities. My first role model was Poly Styrene, the first Black British woman of Punk. I was young when Punk was having its moment in England. I'd already been labeled "badness." I'd already been "a disruption." I didn't fit—worse than didn't fit. I left home at eleven and I was running the streets at 12, 13. With Punk, you could rip up your clothes. So, I made my own clothes and then I became this . . . feared but revered within the community, badass punk. Music became my initial home and form of community.

It took me until I was twenty-five. When I got to art school, and I was trying to again express this mixed identity, I was just shamed for that by the tutors. I then went down this track of white, male abstract painters. It took me ages to find my own lineages. It took me ages to find women artists. It took me ages to find women of color artists. I'm still trying to find South Asian artists.

Hannah: My father is a documentary filmmaker, and my mother is a visual anthropologist. I grew up with documentary filmmakers of that generation, who are now in their sixties and seventies,[9] which showed me that one could make films, which is a rare privilege. And yet, I never saw it as a path for me, and I considered myself to be totally unartistic. It wasn't until my mid-twenties that I started considering myself someone who could make things. And then I started realizing the influence those filmmakers had on me—female verité cinematographers who would bring their kid to shoots, directors who would stay at our house and talk vibrantly into the night, filmmakers like my father who felt truly alive while editing. I had those models, which I know most people don't. But somehow, even with that, finding my own expression and artistic lineages felt like such a tough and long journey. I found inspiration in works that gave me license to experiment or a sense of possibility. Like live jazz, which formally felt so extraordinary—this extreme skill that was built improvisationally in community. Also, formally challenging literature like László Krasznahorkai, where form matches content. Then, films like *Daguerréotypes* by Agnès

Varda (1975), which seemed so small and simple, but somehow held a whole existential world.

I've also been thinking about how I'm mentoring twelve filmmakers right now (in a lab). For people who are working in formally challenging ways, or ways that center process, what would it look like to be somebody who gives them license? Who says, "so much of the world is going to tell you that that's not a way of working, but you should center that!"

Andrea: It is also about access. When I grew up there was so much violence and never enough food, never nothing. And yet, in my tower block, on public television, I saw *Stalker* (Tarkovsky 1979) when I was thirteen, and the Viennese Action Group literally back to back with each other. So, a guy with a carcass running around, blood everywhere, performing. And I was like, "Oh, my God, that's my world!" I was like, "That's what I want. That's what I want."

It's been such a rebellious journey. On the one hand, it was scary and unstable, on the other hand, full of wonder. I could drive a car at thirteen or I had friends who just could get anything one would want. Things were possible in some way, in the edge world. On my council estate, we had a caretaker who took me to queer performance bars. I could perform versions of me that were unbounded. It made something possible.

I was very drawn to the insistence of the poetic in political, worldbuilding filmmaking that came from what is called Third Cinema.[10] This filmmaking insisted that you can only have political revolution if you also have poetry and philosophy. The exclusion of this is a particular Western idea that denies difference, class, racialized, and gendered realities.

I want to say: I love cinema. I love what it can do. It is like poetry. We can say something that touches us even if we don't yet have the language to speak it. I believe in these kinds of constellations where people make spaces for each other. So, for me, the lineage is to make spaciousness, regardless of everything that is trying to make that impossible.

Some people don't make it. I know people who died because they couldn't make that; they couldn't survive in the hardship of the world. It's not just what came before; it's also what we do now and what we invigorate.

Rosa: I really appreciate what you've said about people who didn't make it and weren't able to do it. A lot of our conversations this week have been quite heavy, talking about our trauma and our emotional stuff. I think that's because it is really life and death. We see people in our communities who haven't been able to make that space and they've suffered for it. That makes me realize it's a really important skill to have—to be able to express yourself and make space for yourself against all the odds and all the things that tell us that it's silly or indulgent or not valuable.

Noor: Back to "poetry is not a luxury" (Lorde 1984). It's not a luxury! You can say, "Oh, art's not a life and death situation," but actually it is. In that life and death is mental health, isn't it?

The Cracks

Andrea: All of us are trying to work regardless of the structures that exist. And we all have documentary practices or art practices that have tenderness or gentleness. We either can say, okay, do we situate ourselves against these horrible extractive practices? Or do we propose another way through the things that we do?

Noor: As you were speaking, what came into my mind is, where are the cracks in which you can exist in order to do the rehearsals and the modeling?

Irene: The classroom is that space for me—a space where we can model things with people who are younger and still in a formation process.

Noor: Small groups?

Irene: I believe in that. That was the whole consciousness-raising model[11]— you talk to your neighbor, you make a group, you describe your life, and through a listening and sharing practice, you collectively identify deep structural problems, and then you can build out from there. It starts in a really small-scale space.

The whole history of feminism is a history of systematic erasure, generation after generation. It has always been a feminist project to recuperate, rediscover, or lift up again. I think the documentary industry does exactly the same thing—whenever I work with younger filmmakers who say, "I want to do a weird thing," there's such a rich and deep history of that exact weird thing that's just been erased.

Rosa: I think it makes you feel ashamed as well. I feel shame when I feel like I should have known. [*laughs*] But obviously it is a structural concerted effort funded by millions and millions of pounds to stop people who are just starting to make work from knowing about what has come before.

Nothing that I know about, nothing that I make my work about I have been taught. And I have been to "good" schools. And maybe it's good that it hasn't been taught, because if it had been taught, how would they have taught it? Then, perhaps, I would think I knew and not look for it myself. Whereas, the way that I've come to know about Black history and feminist organizing is because I've been in a space where I've had a traumatic experience, and so I need to find something else.

Hannah: For me, it becomes like a hunger, a desperate need to find out about other ways of working. I wonder if it somehow was brought into more codified knowledge systems, whether it would occur less as a vital need to find other models or to find the discourses that you're actually a part of.

Noor: My journey has largely been one of self-education. I was thrown out of school for asking questions because I was a disruptive body. I was the brown working-class girl in a rural white community that could not be curious, that could not be smart, that could not be inspiring. Despite attending two reputable educational experiences spanning five years, it's taken me two decades of hands-on practice to unlearn and transcend the formal education I received.

Rosa: I wasn't a student that long ago, so that's a really big thing, still, in my mind when I teach. . . . Thinking about the reasons why I found attendance difficult, which were to do with chronic anxiety, and feeling like I couldn't leave the room that I was in because I was being looked at. And I *was* being looked at, because I was the only Black person there, I was the only person from Croydon there, I was queer.

Now, I think about that, and I'm thinking about this shame, and really noticing the efforts that I put in to turn up to places. I notice myself still being in an educational environment, now as a lecturer, and thinking about the force of my labor. That really helps me, because then I think, what's shameful about that? To be here and to continue to try and live in this system, it's kind of amazing.

Noor: So much about the structures are about forced assimilation. We need to talk about class in these institutions! Race and class. I went to the Royal College of Art in the mid-'90s. There were three of us—three working-class people of color. And you check in with each other, but for me, it wasn't safe. It just wasn't safe to bring your full self. When you talked about that, it really resonated with me. I just feel like I'm still so masked. I question, is my niceness and my kindness, is it actually part of my alignment with my spirit, or is that a survival strategy?

Rosa: Recognizing that labor, I think, is the first step. That's why consciousness-raising groups work. That's how I found myself going to Sisters Uncut (a UK-based activist group fighting against domestic and state violence)[12]—going to those meetings, attending that every week on a Wednesday afternoon like it was church. It was so much effort, and it cost money to travel, but if you keep turning up, then you notice all these behaviors—the searching, the passionate fighting, the careful organizing, or even, at certain moments, the sitting still and being a "good girl"— become more of a choice. Because, without that, you think it's just "you."

But perhaps it's not "you," but they're specific behaviors or methodologies you've adapted to survive, or even thrive.

Now, being an exhibiting artist and a teacher, it's so easy in the flux of life and practice and the difficulties of that, to feel like you *are* the institution. People tokenize me all the time. It happens constantly. It's really difficult to actually say, no, I am not that, "I am not your negro."[13] [*laughs*] I'm engaging for my own reasons. And people do say, "If you don't like it, leave." But I'm like, "To where?" Let's say I did just see art as a job, and I wasn't getting spiritual nourishment from it. Let's say I was like, "Yes, you know what? This career isn't working for me," and I just left. Where would you go that you would necessarily be paid well and looked after? There is no industry that is not exploitative.

Noor: I think I've always been an artist because I have no choice. I've tried so many times to not be an artist. I'm in a place where . . . the CV is impressive, but it has rarely paid the rent. Over the years I've had three commercial galleries, but that never paid the rent. And I just don't know if I can continue to produce art when my labor is not fully acknowledged.

This question around feminist practice and sustainability—economic sustainability, spiritual sustainability, a place of belonging. . . . For me, art was always the place of belonging, but then I realized I was in an abusive relationship. The last five years I've been divesting from spaces of harm. I'm in a very, very real moment of like, what kind of future can I have as a practice? Because I just think the infrastructure is still so precarious and I don't want to be so precarious in another decade, another fifteen years when I'm seventy.

Hannah: As you were talking, I was thinking that I recently started a PhD program, and it was really hard to start for me. New York is where I very intentionally built community, and so I felt like I was leaving that, and leaving a career trajectory that I still believed was linear. I was still taken with the metrics of the documentary industry. I don't know if I believed in them, but I was really like, "Oh, those are the metrics." You do the things, you get the accolades, you get the—and that's how you build a thing in this world. It's been interesting, because now a bunch of my friends are having an experience similar to the one that you're talking about, about having done the things, gotten the external signifiers, and it still being deeply precarious.

Rosa: I see that, too.

Andrea: I think much of this also has to do with how notions of inclusivity and sustainability are shaped by institutions, often populated by people who may not share a knowing of what can be severe precarious circumstances. I think institutions will actually only be credible if they have people around the table with very different lived experiences figuring it out together. There's no other way. I really don't believe that an institution can otherwise not be harmful in some way. The solidarity is academic, not lived. And risk—within gender and ability justice or anti-racist frameworks—risk is not shared.

Rosa: I think that's really it, what you said about risk. That sense that you're taking a real personal risk to do something worthwhile is underlying a lot of our practices. But when that personal risk isn't there, that's when the work produced or the process gets really strange. You'll be working with people you thought were also risking it, you thought you were "in it together," but then suddenly you realize . . ."Oh, no." [*laughter*] I've assumed a shared level of urgency that isn't really there.

Irene: I don't know if you already know Jill Godmilow's *Kill the Documentary as We Know It* (2022) provocation.[14] Her critique of the "liberal" documentary is around the way that it creates a sense of closure where you can think, "Now I can put this problem away because the film has done this work of moving to resolution." It creates this passive, middle-class audience, making assumptions about which bodies are in the room and generating closure and completion at the end, so that you can feel like you've had an encounter with this difficult thing, and it's now over.

Hannah: I also think there are a lot of narrative structures that do that by making it clear that the person on the screen is really different and separate from you. You learn their bounds, you learn their demographics, you learn their class, you learn their biographies, and so you can very easily be like, "I get to witness somebody having an experience, and it's different than mine. I get to learn about the world through it." It creates no implication. I think about spaciousness in the moving image, where you have to start to grapple with your own relationship to capitalism, or your own relationship to extractive practices, or your own relationship to judging other people. It doesn't close it for you.

Making Space

Andrea: We can't live outside of these structures, but I work at the edge of these structures. How do we even make these spaces?

I feel like we have the right to screw with power. And I don't say that lightly because I know it affects people in many different ways and violence is real and extreme. But I also think that messing with power is a very creative thing. I believe art is for everybody because art is healing. It's to express, to dream, to make new futures, and also to mess with power. It's all of these different things for me.

Noor: When I was running no.w.here (1998–2018), an artist worker's collective that programmed workshops, screenings, exhibitions, and other events,[15] yes, I worked hard and long hours, but I was drawing down resources because I knew there was power in being able to draw down resources for the many and being able to hold that, and then be able to really leverage it. I'm all about how to create infrastructure. How do I actually create infrastructure where we're not atomized or individuated? What I've done all my life is build community because that's what's held me as well.

I was a member of the Precarious Workers Brigade[16] for ten years. It ended up becoming a feminist collective, only because all the men dropped out because all the boring day-to-day organizing wasn't glamorous. By default, it became a feminist organizing space. We kept turning up for each other every week. Long deep friendships were built through organizing. We were all artists, all cultural workers. But it was never about what we were making as artists; it was always about transforming the working conditions under which we were in.

You can rehearse change, and you can model change in one space because that gives you the space to do that. Then you apply that in the space that you can't model. Then you just keep pushing. It became this motto which was "practice legislates." Your practice legislates; your practice redefines a new boundary. It was intersectional as well, across different struggles.

I think the training I've taken from this life, as an artist, is that I do feel that I could literally be plopped anywhere in any situation, and I would survive. I would make community, I would find food, I would co-create something, I would build. That is priceless and, at the same time, so undervalued. Artists should have a presence in every facet of society.

Andrea: Would it be worth just doing another round, thinking about when we, as makers of space, felt held and truly happy?

Hannah: I think the moment that I felt the closest to my practice was while making *Truth or Consequences* (Jayanti 2021). I thought that I was making a film, and then I realized that the film was just one part of a larger project. It's what enabled me to start thinking that you could work expansively. My partner, Alexander Porter, and I did all this work around articulating what the commitments of the project were. We discovered that the core commitment was listening. We were like, "Oh, if the commitment of this project is listening, then we need to see if we're listening in every area." This goes back to the form and content question. For us, it can't just be that we're listening to some people on camera. The entire project has to be about the act, the full act of listening.

The film was based in this town in New Mexico, and so we had tons of calls with people in the town. And we said, "What do you wish that a film like this could do?" Then we spent the next year and a half co-creating a free public arts and film festival with them. The invitation of the festival was, if you want to do something, tell us, and we'll find you a space. There was no curatorial hierarchy. Everyone got to make whatever they want. It was a magical week.[17] That was one of the moments where I was like, "Oh, *this* is the project." I hold that as a beacon—I make work so that it could potentially facilitate things like that.

Andrea: *Estate, a Reverie* (Zimmerman 2015) was made over seven years in the public housing estate where I also lived. Before *Estate*, we made *i am here*,[18] where we replaced the windows of boarded-up flats with photographs of faces of those still living there, and those recently pushed out. This project meant I had to talk to everybody in my housing estate, and we all got to know each other. We managed to use one of the empty flats for neighbors to get their photographs taken. Then, people brought their other neighbors, and food, and people started hanging out, and this community social space emerged. We ended up having this flat for almost four years. And I ran a cinema in there. I wanted to have a shared language with my neighbors in order to make *Estate*—we discussed film language, tropes, cliches: *Nostalgia for the Light* (Guzmán 2010), John Smith films—he came and donated his time for free. Sally Potter came, and donated her time too.

We're talking about a studio flat in a council estate, which was probably the size of the room we're sitting in here—it's tiny. We often had like forty-five people, literally, we were like sardines. And it was free. Half of the seats were reserved for people from the estate, and then they could bring friends, or word of mouth meant there were lots of people who would come. There was always free food. It was so generative.

Rosa: Just recently, I went to the Huntington Library. I went to see the Octavia Butler Collection. She has all these folders in there where they kept all her writing and motivational notes that she's written to herself. This one, for instance: "I want a large 2,500 to 3,000 square foot house with three bedrooms, living room, dining room, and a library that I will also use as an office. I want my library that's about 30 X 40—a big room that I can have library-type shelves."[19] What an amazing dream! [*laughs*] There are just piles and piles of these notes that she's written to herself, all slightly different manifestations and slightly different goals, but above all, the strength of *this* goal, being a best-selling author, written over and over again. I just thought it was really interesting to see someone's practice of maintaining creativity. I don't think it's necessarily about, "Oh, I'm going to manifest a large amount of money." I think it's about, as I think she writes somewhere else, cultivating strength of character. And when I was in the library, I was thinking—this is my happy space. Being somewhere that I've chosen to go for my own needs.

Noor: Reflecting on all of it, the last twenty-five years of practice is being in praxis, in production. It's been so thriving. I just think there are too many projects to name, too many. Like no.w.here in itself, it was a madness project. We literally inherited all the equipment—it was in pieces. We had to put it back together. But there's nothing but the most incredible, joyous, pleasurable memories of so many things that happened in that space. So many screenings, so much production, so many incidental drop-ins, conversations, bits of tea, laughter, banter. It was just . . .

Andrea: It was amazing.

Irene: Sometimes the classroom feels like a space of thriving for me. Not always, but it can. And, like Rosa, being in an archive can feel like that for me too . . . a space of meeting things that are alive and from the past that maybe no one's looked at in a long time, but I can recognize kinship with things from a long time ago. I've definitely had experiences filming with just one other person where something transformative happens and we're in a really emotional moment together where something significant has shifted through the interaction we've just had.

Rosa: Hannah, you said earlier on that you had this moment where you realized you still thought that your career would be linear and that if you did all the right things, you were going to get this and that track. You spoke about the moment when you realized it wasn't that, and that the accolades and the CV weren't going to look after you. I have a lot of that because I'm thirty. I've been making work for a shorter amount of time, and I think there is still a bit in me that is like, "Oh, there's a track and I have to be on it," but I think just listening to you, it actually makes me really excited to be falling off the track.

Andrea: The risk of making *with*, including making mistakes along the way, and allowing for the generosity of learning with each other, is so precious. However, this is not shared in the larger cultural framework. Often feminist film practices are in relationship to, say, patriarchy, or other kinds of dominant film forms. We don't even engage with those conversations in that way. It seems crucial to intergenerationally understand and share how we can keep surviving intact. How can you bring your whole self into the space, where you also work, so we don't have to compromise who we are in order to be able to make films?

Notes

1 *Topography* is an ongoing, multi-format documentary project, directed by Hannah Jayanti and Alexander Porter that is set in and around America's public lands. Through films, live-edited performances, installations, and community collaborations, the project unearths historical conflicts that have shaped the US landscape while exploring paths to environmental justice and ecological restoration.
2 See https://mirza-butler.work/projects-i-texts
3 Vision Machine Film Project (1999–2010) was a collective co-founded by Christine Cynn, Joshua Oppenheimer, Michael Uwemedimo, and Andrea Luka Zimmerman. Works developed though Vision Machine include *Erase and Forget* (Zimmerman, 2017), *The Look of Silence* (Oppenheimer, 2014), and *The Act of Killing* (Oppenheimer, 2012).
4 Including films like California Newsreel's collectively produced *The Woman's Film* (1971), Julia Reichert's and Jim Klein's *Growing Up Female* (1971), Geri Ashur and Peter Barton's *Janie's Janie* (1971), and Joyce Chopra and Claudia Weill's *Joyce at 34* (1972), among others.
5 Moira Stuart is a Black British broadcaster who presented news for the BBC for thirty-four years, from 1981 to 2007, always serving an impartial manner and iconic outfits and hair. The performance Rosa is talking about, influenced by Moira Stuart, is *Performing Whitness*, directed by Rosa-Johan Uddoh (London, 2019), a single-channel film.
6 Una Marson was a Jamaican broadcaster, writer and activist, and the first Black broadcaster at the BBC, working there from 1941 to 1945. The artwork Rosa is talking about is "Una's Voice" in Rosa's book *Practice Makes Perfect*, ed. Lizzie Homersham & Gavin Everall (London: Book Works and Focal Point Gallery, 2022).
7 See Rosa-Johan Uddoh, "The Serve" in *Practice Makes Perfect*, ed. Lizzie Homersham & Gavin Everall (London: Book Works and Focal Point Gallery, 2022).
8 Including performance works such as Adrian Piper's *Mythic Being* (1973) and Lorraine O'Grady's *Mlle Bourgeoise Noire* (1980–3), among others.
9 Such as Vikram Jayanti, Deirdre Evans-Pritchard, Joan Churchill, and Les Blank, among many others.
10 A movement of political and poetic cinema, as opposed to a neo-liberal, imperial cinema based on passive and consumptive entertainment (which is

11 Developed by radical feminists in the late 1960s and popularized widely during the 1970s, consciousness raising (C-R) groups were a critical political organizing tool in which women met regularly in small, local groups to share personal experiences and collectively move toward recognizing patriarchal and sexist structures in society. For further historical context, see Pamela Allen's *Free Space: A Perspective on the Small Group in Women's Liberation* (Times Change Press, New York City, NY, 1970) and Carol Hanisch's germinal 1969 essay "The Personal Is Political," archived on Hanisch's website http://www.carolhanisch.org/CHwritings/PIP.html

12 Sisters Uncut is a feminist group taking direct action for domestic violence services. It is made up of women and gender-variant people who live under the threat of domestic violence, who fight alongside all those who experience domestic, sexual, gendered, and state violence in their daily lives. See "Feministo," Sisters Uncut, accessed October 26, 2023, https://www.sistersuncut.org/feministo/

13 See the documentary based on James Baldwin's unpublished writing, *I Am Not Your Negro*, directed by Raoul Peck (USA: Magnolia Pictures, 2016), film.

14 In "Kill the Documentary as We Know It," her 2002 essay published in *Film/Video Journal* (Vol. 54, No. 2/3), filmmaker Jill Godmillow argues against what she calls "pornography of the real," which she defines as "documentary's exploitation of 'real life situations' to produce that titillation of difference which middle-class audiences seem to need and enjoy . . . that encourages them to unconsciously accept, in the movie theater, in the dark, when no one is watching, the secret sentiment best characterized by the phrase, 'Thank God that's not me,' while also encouraging them to peek at the devastated, the distorted, the dispossessed and the daringly, dramatically different."

15 From 1998 to 2018, Noor Afshan Mirza and Brad Butler were co-directors of the artist film lab no.w.here, through which they ran hundreds of workshops and film screenings. no.w.here re-invigorated the analogue film equipment formerly from London Filmmakers Co-operative and The Lux Centre, re-establishing and making available 16mm and super 8 equipment, training, processing, and film techniques in a building in Bethnal Green. In 2018, no.w.here was handed to a younger generation who are running a POC workers co-operative: not/nowhere.

16 Active between 2010 and 2018, the Precarious Workers Brigade was a UK-based group of precarious workers in culture and education. https://precariousworkersbrigade.tumblr.com/about

17 *Meteoric* is a free and public arts festival in Truth or Consequences, New Mexico, with film screenings, workshops, art installations, performances, facilitated conversations, public forums, and collective meals. https://meteoric.world.
18 *i am here* (2009–14) was a large-scale public art project installed on the facade of the Haggerston Estate, East London by artists Andrea Zimmerman, Lasse Johansson and Tristan Fennell. See more at https://www.fugitiveimages.org.uk/projects/i-am-here/.
19 Unpublished personal notes, Octavia E. Butler Correspondence and Photographs, The Huntington Library, San Marino, California.

References

Introduction

Balsom, E. and H. Peleg (2022), *Feminist Worldmaking and the Moving Image*, Cambridge: MIT Press.

Connell, R. (2015), "Meeting at the Edge of Fear: Theory on a World Scale," *Feminist Theory*, 16(1): 49–66.

French, L. (2021), *The Female Gaze in Documentary Film: An International Perspective*, Cham: Palgrave Macmillan.

Nagib, L. (2020), *Realist Cinema as World Cinema*, Amsterdam: Amsterdam University Press.

Ulfsdotter, B. and A. B. Rogers (2018), "Introduction," in B. Ulfsdotter and A. B. Rogers (eds.), *Female Authorship and the Documentary Image: Theory, Practice and Aesthetics*, 1–6. Edinburgh: Edinburgh University Press.

Ulfsdotter, B. and A. B. Rogers, eds. (2018), *Female Agency and Documentary Strategies: Subjectivities, Identity and Activism*, Edinburgh: Edinburgh University Press.

Van de Peer, S. (2017), *Negotiating Dissidence: The Pioneering Women of Arab Documentary*, Edinburgh: Edinburgh University Press.

Walker, J. and D. Waldman (1999), "Introduction," in J. Walker and D. Waldman (eds.), *Feminism and Documentary*, 1–36. Minneapolis: University of Minnesota Press.

Warren, S. (2019), *Subject to Reality: Women and Documentary*, Urbana: University of Illinois Press.

White, P. (2015), *Women's Cinema, World Cinema: Projecting Contemporary Feminisms*. Durham: Duke University Press.

Women Make Movies. (2021), "Voices of Afghan Women Collection Available to Watch for Free," 27 August. Available online: https://www.wmm.com/voice-of-afghan-women-collectionavailable-to-watch-for-free/ (accessed February 8, 2024).

Chapter 1

Balsom E. and H. Peleg (2022), *Feminist Worldmaking and the Moving Image*, Cambridge, MA: MIT Press.

Benamou C. and B. Matías (2013), "Remembering 'Punto de Vista: Latina' in Two Voices," *Camera Obscura*, 28(1 (82)): 135–45.

Coffman E. and E. Stein (2018), "New Day Films: Collective Aesthetics and the Collection," in B. Ulfsdotter, and A. Backman Rogers (eds.), *Female Authorship and the Documentary Image*, 22–39. Edinburgh: Edinburgh University Press.

Conference of Feminist Film and Video Organizations Working Group. (1975), "An Ongoing Manifesto," Collection of Ariel Dougherty, Schlesinger Archive, Radcliffe Institute for Advanced Study, Harvard University.

Evans, B. (2016), "Rising Up: A Memoir of the London Women's Film Group," *Feminist Media Histories*, 2(2): 107–21.

Fabian, R. (2018), "Reconsidering the Work of Claire Johnston," *Feminist Media Histories*, 4(3): 244–73.

Freude (1979), "Notes on Distribution," *Camera Obscura* 1-2(3-1): 151–156.

Kohn, E. (2023), "How to Survive the Documentary Apocalypse by Staying Small and Strange," *Indiewire*, April 2, 2023. https://www.indiewire.com/features/general/32-sounds-interview-samgreen-1234833498/

Lesage, J. (1990), "The Political Aesthetics of the Feminist Documentary Film," in P. Erens (ed.), *Issues in Feminist Film Criticism*, 222–37. Bloomington: Indiana University Press.

Mohanty, C. T. (1984), "Under Western Eyes: Feminist Scholarship and Colonial Discourses," *Boundary 2*, 12/13: 333–58.

Nichols, B. (1991), *Representing Reality: Issues and Concepts in Documentary*, Bloomington, Indiana: Indiana University Press.

Ramirez Soto, E. (2022), "'Why Didn't You Write to Me? On Friendship, Exile, and Transnational Collaboration," in E. Balsom and H. Peleg (eds.), *Feminist Worldmaking and the Moving Image*, 267–87. Cambridge, MA: MIT Press.

Rich, B. R. (2013), "The Confidence Game," in "In Practice: Women Make Movies at 40," *Camera Obscura*, 82(28.2): 157–65.

Samer, R. (2022), *Lesbian Potentiality and Feminist Media in the 1970s*, Durham: Duke University Press.

Seguí, I. (2022), "Between Nearness and Incommensurability: Andean Women's Documentaries in the 1980s," in E. Balsom and H. Peleg (eds.), *Feminist Worldmaking and the Moving Image*, 91–113, Cambridge, MA: MIT Press.

Shohat, E. (1996), "Post-Third-Worldist Culture: Gender, Nation, and the Cinema," in Jacqui Alexander and Chandra Mohanty (eds.), *Feminist Genealogies, Colonial Legacies, Democratic Futures*, 183–209. London: Routledge.

Warren, S. and J. Lesage (2022), "It was there all along": An Intergenerational Dialogue About Feminist, Realism and Documentary," in Erika Balsom and Hila Peleg (eds.), *Feminist Worldmaking and the Moving Image*, 141–64. Cambridge, MA: MIT Press.

White, P. (2006), "Cinema Solidarity: The Documentary Practice of Kim Longinotto," *Cinema Journal* 46(1): 120–8.

Zimmerman, D. (2017), "Film as Activism and Transformative Praxis: Women Make Movies," in Kristin Lené Hole and Dijana Jelača, E. Ann Kaplan, and Patrice Petro (eds.), *The Routledge Companion to Cinema and Gender*, 189–98. Milton Park, Abingdon, Oxon; Routledge.

Chapter 2

Balsom, E. and H. Peleg (2022), *Feminist Worldmaking and the Moving Image*, Cambridge and London: The MIT Press.

Bisschoff, L. and S. Van de Peer (2020), *Women in African Cinema*, New York: Routledge.

Castro, T. (2022), "The Many Feminist Histories of Documentary," in E. Balsom and H. Peleg (eds.), *Feminist Worldmaking and the Moving Image*, 41–62. Cambridge and London: The MIT Press.

Dahr, J., dir. (2017), *Thank You for the Rain* (film).

Diang'a, R. (2016), "Message Films in Africa: A Look into the Past," *Cogent Arts & Humanities*, 3(1): 1–12.

Diang'a, R. (2017), "Themes in Kenyan Cinema: Seasons and Reasons," *Cogent Arts & Humanities*, 4(1): 1–11.

Docubox. (2023), "Summary of Docubox Achievements from 2013-2023," internal document.

Dovey, L. (forthcoming 2025), "Towards People-oriented Approaches in Film and Screen Studies," in B. Karam and B. Mutsvairo (eds.), *Handbook of Cinema in the Global South*, Bristol: Intellect.

Dovey, L. (2023a), "Intermediality in Academia: Creative Research through Film," *Arts,* 12(4). https://www.mdpi.com/2076-0752/12/4/169

Dovey, L. (2023b), *Out of the Box: The Screen Worlds of Judy Kibinge* (film).

Dovey, L. (2023c), *From One Woman to Another: The Screen Worlds of Bongiwe Selane* (film).

Dovey, L. (2020), "On Teaching and Being Taught: Reflections on Decolonising Pedagogy," *PARSE*, 11: 1–26.

Dovey, L. (2015), *Curating Africa in the Age of Film Festivals*, New York: Palgrave.

Dovey, L., A. Agina, and M. W. Thomas, eds. (forthcoming 2025), *Contemporary African Screen Worlds*, Durham: Duke University Press.

Dovey, L., J. McNamara, and F. Olivieri (2013), "'From, by, for' – Nairobi's Slum Film Festival, Film Festival Studies, and the Practices of Development," *Jump Cut*, 55. https://www.ejumpcut.org/archive/jc55.2013/DoveySFFNairobi/index.html

Ellerson, B. (2020), "Fifty Years of Women's Engagement at FESPACO," *Black Camera*, 12(1): 246–54.
Ellerson, B. (2016), "Teaching African Women in Cinema: Part Two," *Black Camera*, 7(2): 217–33.
Ellerson, B. (2015), "Teaching African Women in Cinema: Part One," *Black Camera*, 7(1): 251–61.
Ellerson, B. (2002), *Sisters of the Screen: African Women in the Cinema* (film).
Ellerson, B. (2000), *Sisters of the Screen: Women of Africa on Film, Video and Television*. Trenton, NJ: Africa World Press.
Gerima, H. (2021), "Where Are the African Women Filmmakers?" *Black Camera*, 12(2): 168–75.
Hennefeld, M. and L. Horak (2024), "Editors' Introduction: Why We Curate Feminist Film Archives," *Feminist Media Histories*, 10(2-3): 1–9.
Heredia, S. J. Jacques, S. Keller, and B. Loayza (2022), "First Person Feminine: A Discussion," in Balsom and H. Peleg (eds.), *Feminist Worldmaking and the Moving Image*, 399–413. Cambridge: The MIT Press.
Hjort, M. (2019), "In Defense of Human Rights Filmmaking: A Response to the Skeptics, Based on Kenyan Examples," in M. Hjort and E. Jorholt (eds.), *African Cinema and Human Rights*, 103–24. Bloomington: Indiana University Press.
Kibinge, J., dir. (forthcoming), *Goat* (film).
Kibinge, J., dir. (2015), *Scarred: Anatomy of a Massacre* (film).
Kibinge, J., dir. (2013), *Something Necessary* (film).
Kibinge, J., dir. (2009), *Killer Necklace* (film).
Kibinge, J., dir. (2008), *Coming of Age* (film).
Kibinge, J., dir. (2004), *Project Daddy* (film).
Kibinge, J., dir. (2002), *Dangerous Affair* (film).
Kibinge, J. and J. Akomfrah, dirs (2010), *Headlines in History* (film).
Kinyanjui, W., dir. (1994), *Battle of the Sacred Tree* (film).
Lekow, M. and C. King, dirs (2019), *The Letter* (film).
Lesage, J. and S. Warren (2022), "'It was there all along': An Intergenerational Dialogue About Feminism, Realism, and Documentary," in E. Balsom and H. Peleg (eds.), *Feminist Worldmaking and the Moving Image*, 141–57. Cambridge: The MIT Press.
Levin, N. and P. Shongwe, dirs (2023), *Reverie* (film).
Mango, C. (2023), *The Presence of Women in the Kenyan Film Industry: Applying Postcolonial African Feminist Theory*, PhD thesis, University of Glasgow.
McNamara, J. (2016), *The Culturalization of Development in Nairobi: A Practice-based Approach Toward Understanding Kenya's Urban Audiovisual Media Environment*, PhD thesis, SOAS University of London.

Minh-ha, Trinh T. (2022), "Outside In Inside Out (1986/88)," in Balsom and H. Peleg et al. (eds.), *Feminist Worldmaking and the Moving Image*, 67–79. Cambridge: The MIT Press.

Mungai, A., dir. (1992), *Saikati* (film).

Ndisi-Herrmann, P., dir. (2018), *New Moon* (film).

Pete, S. (2018), "Meschachakanis, a Coyote Narrative: Decolonising Higher Education," in G. K. Bambra et al. (eds.), *Decolonising the University*, 173–89. London: Pluto Press.

Smith, A. (2020), *Agnès Varda*, Manchester: Manchester University Press.

Steedman, R. (2023), *Creative Hustling: Women Making and Distributing Films from Nairobi*, Cambridge: The MIT Press.

Vered, A. and G. Gibson (2022), "A Decolonial Dreaming," in A. Nirmal and S. Dey (eds.), *Histories, Myths, and Decolonial Interventions: A Planetary Resistance*, 143–67. New York: Routledge.

Winn, M. (2015), "Imaginal Cells," December 9. https://theviewinside.me/imaginal-cells/

Interviews

Kamau, Toni. Filmed interview. February 2022.
Kibinge, Judy. Filmed interview. February 2022.
Kibinge, Judy. Filmed interview. September 2020.
Kimani, Martin. Filmed conversation with Judy Kibinge. February 2022.
King, Christopher. Filmed interview. February 2022.
Lekow, Maia. Filmed interview. February 2022.
Matata, Lydia. Filmed interview. February 2022.
Murimi, Pete. Filmed interview. June 2022.
Ndisi-Herrmann, Philippa. Filmed interview. June 2022.
Ndisi-Herrmann, Philippa. Audio interview. July 2019.
Nyairo, Joyce. Filmed interview. February 2022.
Wanja, Emily. Filmed interview. February 2022.

Chapter 3

Badran, M. (1995), *Feminists, Islam, and Nation: Gender and the Making of Modern Egypt*, Princeton, NJ: Princeton University Press.

Basu, A. (2000), "Globalization of the Local/Localization of the Global Mapping Transnational Women's Movements," *Meridians,* 1(1): 68–84. http://www.jstor.org/stable/40338428

Benton, S. (2016), "Feminist Views on Solidarity with Palestinians and BDS," *Jews for Justice for Palestinians*, March 20. https://jfjfp.com/feminist-views-on-solidarity-withpalestinians-and-bds/

Caravan (2023), "Women Caravan 2023." https://www.womencaravan.online/2023 (accessed May 20, 2024).

Caravan (2022), "Carte Blanche." https://www.womencaravan.online/october (accessed October 6, 2022).

Desai, M. (2002), "Transnational Solidarity: Women's Agency, Structural Adjustment, and Globalization," in Nancy A. Naples and Manisha Desai (eds.), *Women's Activism and Globalization: Linking Local Struggles and Transnational Politics*, 34–41. New York, NY: Routledge.

Dickinson, K. (2016), *Arab Cinema Travels: Transnational Syria, Palestine, Dubai and Beyond*, London: Palgrave on behalf of the British Film Institute.

Dönmez-Colin, G. (2014), "Women's Film Festivals in the Middle East: Challenges and Rewards," in Dina Iordanova and Stefanie Van de Peer (eds.), *Film Festival Yearbook 6: Film Festivals and the Middle East*, 27–40. St. Andrews: St Andrews Film Studies.

El Khachab, C. (2022), "Cultural Administration in Postcolonial Egypt: The Case of the Mass Culture Institute," University of Wisconsin-Madison, online, October 28.

El Khachab, C. (2021), *Making Film in Egypt: How Labor Technology and Mediation Shape the Industry*, Cairo: The American University in Cairo Press.

El-Sharkawy, Y. (2021), "Women Filmmakers under Spotlight," *The Egyptian Gazette*, November 15. https://egyptian-gazette.com/egypt/women-filmmakers-under-spotlight/.

Espinosa, J. G. (1969), "Por un cine imperfecto," in *Cine cubano*, 66/67 46–53.

Ginsberg, T. (2016), *Visualizing the Palestinian Struggle: Towards a Critical Analytic a Palestine Solidarity Film*, London: Palgrave Macmillan.

Grewal, I. and C. Kaplan (1994), *Scattered Hegemonies: Postmodernity and Transnational Feminist Practices*, Minneapolis: University of Minnesota Press.

Hammami, R. (2023), "Catastrophic Aid: GBV Humanitarianism in Gaza," in Lila Abu-Lughod, Rema Hammami, and Nādirah Shalhūb-Kīfūrkiyān (eds.), *The Cunning of Gender Violence: Geopolitics and Feminism*, 324–60. Durham: Duke University Press.

Hamza, M. (2020), *Women Resisting Sexual Violence and the Egyptian Revolution: Arab Feminist Testimonies*, London: Zed Books.

Iordanova, D. and S. Van de Peer (2014), "Introduction," in *Film Festivals and the Middle East*, St. Andrews: St Andrews Film Studies.

Khader, S. J. (2019), *Decolonizing Universalism: A Transnational Feminist Ethic*, New York: Oxford University Press.

Mendoza, B. (2002), "Transnational Feminisms in Question," *Feminist Theory*, 3(3): 295–314.

Moghadam, V. M. (2005), *Globalizing Women: Transnational Feminist Networks*, Baltimore, MD: The Johns Hopkins University Press.

Mohanty, C. T. (2003), *Feminism without Borders: Decolonizing Theory, Practicing Solidarity*, Durham, NC: Duke University Press.

Naber, N., E. Desouky, and L. Baroudi (2016), "The Forgotten "-ism": An Arab American Women's Perspective on Zionism, Racism, and Sexism," in INCITE! Women of Color Against Violence (ed.), *Color of Violence: The INCITE! Anthology*, 97–112. Durham, NC: Duke University Press.

Palestine Feminist Collective. (2021), "Pledge that Palestine is a Feminist Issue." https://actionnetwork.org/petitions/pledge-declaring-palestine-is-afeminist-issue (accessed September 12, 2023).

Rizov, V. (2023), "At Least 18 Filmmakers Withdraw from IDFA 2023." https://filmmakermagazine.com/123710-at-least-18-filmmakers-withdraw-from-idfa2023/ (accessed December 2).

Saddy, F. (2016), *The Arab World and Latin America: Economic and Political Relations in the Twenty-First Century*, London: I.B. Tauris.

Saglier, V. (2020), "'Not-Yet' an Industry: The Temporalities of Contemporary Palestinian Cinema," in Terri Ginsberg and Chris Lippard (eds.), *Cinema of the Arab World: Contemporary Directions in Theory and Practice*, 125–46. Switzerland: Palgrave Macmillan.

Sharoni, S., R. Abdulhadi, N. Al-Ali, F. Evans, R. Lentin, and D. Siddiqi (2015), "Transnational Feminist Solidarity in Times of Crisis: The Boycott, Divestment and Sanctions (BDS) Movement and Justice in/for Palestine," *International Feminist Journal of Politics*, 17(4): 654–70.

Smaill, B. (2009), "The Documentaries of Kim Longinotto: Women, Change, and Painful Modernity," *Camera Obscura*, 24(71): 43–75.

White, P. (2006), "Cinema Solidarity: The Documentary Practice of Kim Longinotto," *Cinema Journal*, 46(1): 120–8. https://doi.org/10.1353/cj.2007.0008

Chapter 4

Aguilar, C. (2019), "Annecy 2019: First-Ever Inclusion in Animation Study Confirms Obvious Lack of Opportunities For Women In Industry," *Cartoon Brew*, 10 June. Available at: https://www.cartoonbrew.com/artist-rights/annecy-2019-first-ever-inclusion-in-animation-studyconfirms-obvious-lack-of-opportunities-for-women-in-industry-175380.html (accessed November 12, 2023).

Akcay, Z. (2021), "Dance, Long Exposure And Drawing: An Absurd Manifesto about the Female Body," *International Journal of Film and Media Arts*, 6(3): 67–84. Available online: https://revistas.ulusofona.pt/index.php/ijfma/article/view/8102 (accessed November 12, 2023).

Balsom, E. and H. Peleg (2022), *Feminist Worldmaking and the Moving Image*, Cambridge, MA: MIT Press.

Couzin, S. (1997), "An Analysis of Susan Pitt's Asparagus and Joanna Priestley's All My Relations," in J. Pilling (ed.), *A Reader in Animation Studies*, 71–81. Bloomsbury: Indiana University Press.

Cuklanz, L. and H. McIntosh, eds. (2016), *Documenting Gendered Violence: Representations, Collaborations, and Movements*, New York: Bloomsbury Academic.

Ehrlich, N. (2021), *Animating Truth: Documentary and Visual Culture in the 21st Century*, Edinburgh: Edinburgh University Press.

Formenti, C. (2022), *The Classical Animated Documentary and Its Contemporary Evolution*, New York: Bloomsbury Academic.

French, L. (2021), *The Female Gaze in Documentary Film*, Cham, Switzerland: Palgrave Macmillan.

Furniss, M. (2016), *Art in Motion : Animation Aesthetics*, 2nd ed., Eastleigh: John Libbey.

Greenberg, S. (2020), "Drawing the Line," *The Moving Image*, 20(1, 2): 70–84.

Honess Roe, A. (2013), *Animated Documentary*, New York: Palgrave Macmillan.

Kohn, E. (2023), "How to Survive the Documentary Apocalypse by Staying Small and Strange," *Indiewire*. Available online: https://www.indiewire.com/features/general/32-sounds-interviewsam-green-1234833498/ (accessed February 25, 2024).

Law, S. (1997), "Putting Themselves in the Pictures: Images of Women in the Work of Joanna Quinn, Candy Guard and Alison de Vere," in J. Pilling (ed.), *A Reader in Animation Studies*, 48–70. Bloomington: Indiana University Press.

Mukherjee, D. (2020), "Animated Documentary as a Social Tool," *Animation Studies Journal*, 15.

Murray, J. and N. Ehrlich, eds. (2019), *Drawn from Life: Issues and Themes in Animated Documentary Cinema*. Vol. 1, Edinburgh: Edinburgh University Press.

Pilling, J., ed. (2012), *Animating the Unconscious: Desire, Sexuality and Animation*, New York: Columbia University Press.

Ulfsdotter, B. and A. Backman Rogers, eds. (2018), *Female Authorship and the Documentary Image*. Edinburgh: University of Edinburgh Press.

Filmography

Akcay, Zeynep. *KAM*. Zeynep Akcay, 2020. Courtesy of the director.

Avni, Shira and Serne El-haj Daoud, dirs. (2000), *From Far Away* (film), National Film Board of Canada, 7 min. https://www.nfb.ca/film/from_far_away/

Djukić, Urška and Emilie Pigeard, dirs. (2021), *Granny's Sexual Life* (film), Ciclic Animation, Ikki Films, Studio Virc. https://ikkifilms.com/en/films/grannys-sexual-life/

Gunnarsdóttir, Sara, dir. (2022), *My Year of Dicks* (film), Cat's Pajamas, FX Productions, Wonder Killer. 24 minutes. https://myyearofdicks.com/

Kater, Camila, dir. (2019), *Carne* (film), Abano Producions, Doctela. 11 min. https://www.nytimes.com/video/opinion/100000007491017/carne.html

Lingford, Ruth, dir. (2010), *Little Deaths* (film), 12 min. https://vimeo.com/54482361

Lingford, Ruth, dir. (1997), *Death and the Mother* (film), Channel Four Films. 10 min.

Mukherjee, Debjani, dir. (2020), *Awakening the Goddess* (film), Shayok Banerjee Productions. Courtesy of the director.

Rimminen, Marjut, dir. (1987), *Some Protection* (film), Smoothcloud Production. 1h 7 min. https://archive.org/details/SomeProtectionMarjutRimminen

Satrapi, Marjane and Vincent Paronnaud, dirs. *Persepolis* (film), 2.4.7 Films, France 3 Cinéma,

Shi, Domee, dir. (2022), *Turning Red* (film), Disney Pixar. 1h 40 min. Blu-ray disc VD, 4K.

The Kennedy/Marshall Company, 2007. 1h 36 min. https://www.amazon.com/Persepolis-SimonAbkarian/dp/B0083GOVLW

Chapter 5

Arenillas, M. G. and M. J. Lazzara, eds. (2016), *Latin American Documentary Film in the New Millennium*, London: Palgrave Macmillan.

Berrendo Pérez, O., J. A. Serrano Fernández, E. Encinas Puebla, and S. Conejo Ávila (2023), *Panorama Audiovisual Iberoamericano 2023*, Madrid: EGEDA, retrieved from https://www.egeda.com/documentos/PanoramaAudiovisualIberoamericano2023/Panora maIberoamericano2023.pdf

Bourdieu, P. (1990), *Photography, A Middle-brow Art*, Stanford: Stanford University Press.

Bossay, C. and M. P. Peirano (2017), "Parando la olla documental: Women and Contemporary Chilean Documentary Film," in D. Martin and D. Shaw (eds.), *Latin American Women Filmmakers, Production, Politics, Poetics*, 70–95. London: I.B. Tauris.

Burton, J., ed. (1990), *The Social Documentary in Latin America*, Pittsburgh: University of Pittsburgh Press.

Butler, J. ([1990] 2011), *Gender Trouble: Feminism and the Subversion of Identity*, New York and London: Routledge.

Cervera Ferrer, L. (2022), "Reproductive Rights, Othered Women, and the Making of Feminist Documentary in Latin America," *Feminist Media Studies*, retrieved from https://www.tandfonline.com/doi/citedby/10.1080/14680777.2022.2027803?scroll=top&ne edAccess=true

Chanan, M. (2007), *The Politics of Documentary*, London: British Film Institute.

Cumaná González, M. C. and S. Lord (2013), "Deterritorialised Intimacies: The Documentary Legacy of Sara Gómez in Three Contemporary Women Filmmakers," in P. Nair and J. D. Gutierrez-Albilla (eds), *Hispanic and Lusophone Women Filmmakers: Theory, Practice and Difference*, 96–110. Manchester: Manchester University Press.

Cunha da Cruz, A. R. and A. C. Ciotti (2022), "La industria audiovisual Argentina desde una perspectiva de géneros 2021," *Observatorio Audiovisual INCAA*, retrieved from http://www.incaa.gov.ar/wp-content/uploads/2022/06/IIAADUPDG2022.pdf

Foster, D. (2013), *Latin American Documentary Filmmaking. Major Works*, Tucson: The University of Arizona Press.

French, L. (2021), *The Female Gaze in Documentary Film. An International Perspective*, Cham: Palgrave Macmillan.

Haddu, M. and J. Page, eds (2009), *Visual Synergies in Fiction and Documentary Film from Latin America*, New York: Palgrave Macmillan.

Hirsch, M. (1997), *Family Frames: Photography, Narrative, and Postmemory*, Cambridge: Harvard University Press.

Ivanov, D., L. Vieira, A. Selonk, and M. Candido (2021), "Case Study I: Women in the Audiovisual Industry: A Panorama of Latin American Countries and Spain," World Intellectual Property Organization, retrieved from https://www.wipo.int/export/sites/www/ipdevelopment/en/agenda/docs/4_case_study_1_women_av.pdf

Karrer, M. (2022), *No home movies. Usos políticos del archivo familiar en el cine documental de Argentina y Brasil*, PhD thesis, University of Tübingen.

Lazzara, M. J. (2009), "Filming Loss: (Post-) Memory, Subjectivity, and the Performance of Failure in Recent Argentine Documentary Films," *Latin American Perspectives*, 36(5): 147–57.

Lebow, A., ed. (2012), *The Cinema of Me: The Self and Subjectivity in First Person Documentary*, New York and Chichester: Columbia University Press.

Lesage, J. (1990), "Women Make Media: Three Modes of Production," in J. Burton (ed.), *The Social Documentary in Latin America*, 315–47. Pittsburgh: University of Pittsburgh Press.

Llanos, B. (2016), "Caught Off Guard at the Crossroads of Ideology and Affect: Documentary Films by the Daughters of Revolutionaries," in M. G. Arenillas and M. J. Lazzara (eds.), *Latin American Documentary Film in the New Millennium*, 243–58. London: Palgrave Macmillan.

Martin, D. (2012), *Painting, Literature and Film in Colombian Feminine Cultures, 1940-2005,* Woodbridge: Tamesis.

Martin, D. and D. Shaw, eds. (2017), *Latin American Women Filmmakers. Production, Politics, Poetics,* London: I.B. Tauris.

Matusiak, T. (2022), "Family Ties: Mercedes Gaviria's Feminist Critique of Authorship," *Visible Evidence,* paper presentation, Gdańsk.

Navarro, V. and J. C. Rodríguez, eds. (2014), *New Documentaries in Latin America,* New York: Palgrave Macmillan.

Nouzeilles, G. (2005), "Postmemory Cinema and the Future of the Past in Albertina Carri's Los Rubios," *Journal of Latin American Cultural Studies,* 14: 26–78.

Page, J. (2005), "Memory and Mediation in *Los rubios*: A Contemporary Perspective on the Argentine Dictatorship," *New Cinemas: Journal of Contemporary Film,* 3: 29–40.

Polgovsky Ezcurra, M. (2018), *Touched Bodies: The Performative Turn in Latin American Art,* New Brunswick and New Jersey: Rutgers University Press.

Ramírez, E. (2010), "Estrategias para (no) olvidar: notas sobre dos documentales chilenos de las post-dictadura," *Aisthesis,* 47: 45–63.

Rich, B. R. (1997), "An/Other view of the New Latin American Cinema," in M. T. Martin (ed.), *New Latin American Cinema, Vol 1: Theory, Practices, and Transcontinental Articulations,* 273–97,. Detroit: Wayne State University Press.

Sarlo, B. (2005), *Tiempo pasado: cultura de la memoria y giro subjetivo: una discusión,* Buenos Aires: Siglo Veintiuno Editores.

Tadeo Fuica, B. (2015), "Memory or Postmemory? Documentaries Directed by Uruguay's Second Generation," *Memory Studies,* 8(3): 298–312.

Traverso, A. and K. Wilson (2013), "Political Documentary Cinema in Latin America," *Social Identities,* 19(3–4): 275–86.

Zimmermann, P. R. (1995), *Reel Families: A Social History of Amateur Film,* Bloomington: Indiana University Press.

Chapter 6

Asen, R. (2000), "Seeking the 'Counter' in Counterpublics," *Communication Theory,* 10(4): 424446.

Benhabib, S. (1992), *Situating the Self: Gender, Community, and Postmodernism in Contemporary Ethics,* New York: Routledge.

DiNitto, R. (2014), "Narrating the Cultural Trauma of 3/11: The Debris of Post-Fukushima Literature and Film," *Japan Forum,* 26(3): 340-60.

Fraser, N. (1990), "Rethinking the Public Sphere: A Contribution to the Critique of Actually Existing Democracy," *Social Text,* 25/26: 56–80.

Hagino, R. (2013), "Resisting against the Disaster by Images: Documentary Films after the Disaster [Imeji ni yoru hisai ni koshite: shinsai-iko no dokyumentari-eiga]," *Gendaishitecho,* 56: 67–73.

Iwata-Weickgenann, K., ed. (2016), *Fukushima and the Arts: Negotiating Nuclear Disaster,* London and New York: Routledge.

Kahana, J. (2008), *Intelligence Work: The Politics of American Documentary,* New York: Columbia University Press.

Lebow, A., ed. (2012), *The Cinema of Me*: *The Self and Subjectivity in First Person Documentary,* London: Wallflower Press.

Lebow, A. (2008), *First Person Jewish.* Minneapolis: University of Minnesota Press.

Mori, Y. (2013), "3/11 Inspection of the Information Society's Environment Concerning the Fukushima Nuclear Accident: The Characteristics and Challenges of Television, Journalism, and Social Media [3.11 Fukushima daiichi genpatsu hatudensho ziko o meguru shakai joho kankyo no kensho: terebi, janarizumu, sosharu medyia no tokusei to kadai]," Gakujutsu no doko, 18(1): 26–33.

Morioka, R. (2014), "Mother Courage: Women as Activists between a Passive Populace and a Paralyzed Government," in Tom Gill, Brigitte Steger, and David H. Slater (eds.), *Japan Copes with Calamity: Ethnographies of the Earthquake, Tsunami and Nuclear Disasters of March 2011,* 177–200. Oxford: Peter Lang.

Nancy, J. (2014), *After Fukushima: The Equivalence of Catastrophes,* New York: Fordham University Press.

Renov, M. (2004), *The Subject of Documentary,* Minneapolis: University of Minnesota Press.

Tanaka, Y., H. Harutoshi, and M. Toshiyuki (2013), *The Great East Japan Earthquake and Sociology: The Society Emerged after the Disaster [Higashi nihon daishinsai to shakaigaku: daisaigai wo umidashita shakai.],* Tokyo: Mineruva shobo.

Wada Marciano, M. (2012), *No Nukes: The Power of "Post-3/11" Cinema and Art [No Nukes: "posuto 3/11" eiga no chikara, ato no chikara.],* Nagoya: Nagoya University Press.

Yotsumoto, Y. and S. Takekawa (2016), "The Social Structures of Victimization of Fukushima Residents Due to Radioactive Contamination from the 2011 Nuclear Disaster," *Japan after 3,* 11: 251–68.

Yu, K. T. (2018), *My Self on Camera: First Person Documentary Practice in an Individualising China,* Edinburgh: Edinburgh University Press.

Chapter 7

Abe, S. (2012), "Iranian Environmentalism: Nationhood, Alternative Natures, and the Materiality of Objects," *Nature and Culture,* 7(3): 259–84.

Alikarami, L. (2018), "Iranian Lawyers for Human Rights: The Defenders of Human Rights Center," in R. Barlow and S. Akbarzadeh (eds.), *Human Rights and Agents of Change in Iran: Towards a Theory of Change*, 65–80. Singapore: Palgrave Macmillan.

Allen, R. C. and D. Gomery (1985), *Film History: Theory and Practice*, New York: McGraw Hill, Inc.

Atwood, B. (2016), *Reform Cinema in Iran: Film and Political Change in the Islamic Republic*, New York: Columbia University Press.

Balaghati, O. (2016), "Dar Khiaban-haye bi-saranjam: Iran-e napeida dar sinema-ye mostanad-e in sal-ha" ('In Endless Streets: Invisible Iran in These Years' Documentary Cinema'), *Film Monthly*, 516: 66–8.

Barlow, R. and S. Akbarzadeh (2018), "Top-Down or Bottom-Up? Towards a Theory of Change for Human Rights Practice in Iran," in R. Barlow and S. Akbarzadeh (eds.), *Human Rights and Agents of Change in Iran: Towards a Theory of Change*, 3–24. Singapore: Palgrave Macmillan.

Bayat, A. (2013), *Life as Politics: How Ordinary People Change the Middle East*, 2nd ed., Stanford: Stanford University Press.

Documentary and Experimental Film Center. (2019), "Alagheh-ye mostanadsazan-e Irani be sakht e film-e portreh" ('The Interest of Iranian Documentarians in Portrait Filmmaking'), 23 October. Available online: http://www.defc.ir/theme_3/page-defc.php?id_pro=2910 (accessed February 3, 2020).

Fadaee, S. (2012), *Social Movements in Iran: Environmentalism and Civil Society*, London: Routledge.

Fadaee, S. (2018), "Environmentalism and Social Change in Iran," in R. Barlow and S. Akbarzadeh (eds.), *Human Rights and Agents of Change in Iran: Towards a Theory of Change*, 143–55. Singapore: Palgrave Macmillan.

Fadaee, S. (2016), "Rethinking Southern Environmentalism: Iranian Environmental Movement and Its Premises," in S. Fadaee (ed.), *Understanding Southern Social Movements*, 15–26. London: Routledge.

Gaard, G. (2017), *Critical Ecofeminism*, Lanham: Lexington Books.

Hanaway, W. L. (1990), "Half-Voices: Persian Women's Lives and Letters," in A. Najmabadi (ed.), *Women's Autobiographies in Contemporary Iran*, 55–63. Cambridge, MA: Harvard University Press.

Hillmann, M. C. (1990), "An Autobiographical Voice: Forugh Farrokhzad," in A. Najmabadi (ed.), *Women's Autobiographies in Contemporary Iran*, 33–53. Cambridge, MA: Harvard University Press.

Hole, K. L. and D. Jelača (2019), *Film Feminisms: A Global Introduction*, New York: Routledge.

Kara Film Studio. "About." Available online: https://karafilm.ir/en/about (accessed June 15, 2023).

Kara Film Studio. "About Karestan." Available online: https://karafilm.ir/en/karestan/about-karestan (accessed June 15, 2023).

Kara Film Studio. "*All My Trees*." Available online: https://karafilm.ir/en/films/released/24-all-my-trees (accessed June 15, 2023).

Khansalar, F. (2021), "Embracing *All My Trees*: An Ecocritical Reading," in M. Ghorbankarimi (ed.), *ReFocus: The Films of Rakhshan Banietemad*, 206–18. Edinburgh: Edinburgh University Press.

Laylin, D. (2018), "Environmental and Wildlife Degradation in Iran," *Atlantic Council*, 1–14.

Monshipouri, M. (2016), "Introduction: Social Change in Post-Khomeini Iran," in M. Monshipouri (ed.), *Inside the Islamic Republic: Social Change in Post-Khomeini Iran*, 1–20. Oxford: Oxford University Press.

Naficy, H. (2012a), *A Social History of Iranian Cinema, Volume 3: The Islamicate Period, 1978-1984*, Durham: Duke University Press.

Naficy, H. (2012b), *A Social History of Iranian Cinema, Volume 4: The Globalizing Era, 1984-2010*, Durham: Duke University Press.

Naficy, H. (2011), *A Social History of Iranian Cinema, Volume 2: The Industrializing Years, 1941-1978*, Durham: Duke University Press.

Najmabadi, A. (1991), "Hazards of Modernity and Morality: Women, State and Ideology in Contemporary Iran," in D. Kandiyoti (ed.), *Women, Islam and the State*, 48–76. Philadelphia: Temple University Press.

Osanloo, A. (2009), *The Politics of Women's Rights in Iran*, Princeton: Princeton University Press.

Rust, S. and S. Monani (2013), "Introduction: Cuts to Dissolves—Defining and Situating Ecocinema Studies," in S. Rust, S. Monani, and S. Cubitt (eds.), *Ecocinema Theory and Practice*, 1–14. New York: Routledge.

Scollon, M. (2023), "Iran's Environmental Standards, Polluted Reality Mix Like Oil and Water," *RFE/RL*, 1 May. Available online: https://www.rferl.org/a/iran-environmental-standards-pollution-smog/32385813.html (accessed June 15, 2023).

Trofimenkoff, S. M. (1985), "Feminist Biography," *Atlantis*, 10(2): 1–9.

Yarshater Center. (2020), "Eskandar Firouz (1925-2020)," 9 March. Available online: https://cfis.columbia.edu/news/eskandar-firouz-1925-2020 (accessed June 15, 2023).

Chapter 8

Abad, Daniela, dir. (2018), *The Smiling Lombana* (film), Colombia. Producciones La Esperanza.

Adler, K. W. (2023, March 28), "Bianca Graulau Is Sharing the Struggles and Joys of Puerto Rico," *Elle*. Available online: https://www.elle.com/culture/a43251828/bianca-graulauinterview-2023/.

Alexander, M., K. Polimis, and E. Zagheni (2019), "The Impact of Hurricane Maria on Outmigration from Puerto Rico: Evidence from Facebook Data," *Population and Development Review*, 45(3): 617–30.

Aldarondo, Cecilia, dir. (2020), *Landfall* (film), Puerto Rico, Blackscrackle Films.

Aldarondo, Cecilia, dir. (2016), *Memories of a Penitent Heart* (film), Puerto Rico, Blackscrackle Films.

"Bad Bunny & Drake – *Mía* (Video Official)," (2018, October 11), [YouTube]. Available online: https://www.youtube.com/watch?v=OSUxrSe5GbI&ab_channel=BadBunny (accessed February 4, 2024).

"Bad Bunny - *Solo de mí* | X100PRE (Video Official)," (2018, December 15), [YouTube]. Available at: https://www.youtube.com/watch?v=7rbprAR_Reg&ab_channel=BadBunny (accessed February 4, 2024).

"Bad Bunny - *Yo perreo sola* | YHLQMDLG (Video Official)," (2020, March 27), [YouTube]. Available online: https://www.youtube.com/watch?v=GtSRKwDCaZM&ab_channel=BadBunny (accessed February 4, 2024).

"Bad Bunny (ft. Buscabulla) - *Andrea* (360° Visualizer) | Un Verano Sin Ti," (2022, May 6), [YouTube]. Available at: https://www.youtube.com/watch?v=gjvTQTGogUM&ab_channel=BadBunny (accessed February 4, 2024).

Berlant, L. (2011), *Cruel Optimism*, Durham: Duke University Press.

Brown, Mariel, dir. (2017), *Unfinished Sentences* (film), Trinidad & Tobago/Jamaica, SAVANT FILMS.

Bonilla, Y. (2020a), "Postdisaster Futures: Hopeful Pessimism, Imperial Ruination, and La Futura Cuir," *Small Axe: A Caribbean Journal of Criticism*, 24(2): 147–62.

Bonilla, Y. (2020b), "The Coloniality of Disaster: Race, Empire, and the Temporal Logics of Emergency in Puerto Rico, USA," *Political Geography*, 78: 1–12. https://doi.org/10.1016/j.polgeo.2020.102181

Bonilla, Y. (2020c), "The Swarm of Disaster," *Political Geography*, 78. https://doi.org/10.1016/j.polgeo.2020.102182

Bowles, N. (2018), "Making a Crypto Utopia in Puerto Rico," *International New York Times*, 2 February. Available online: https://www.nytimes.com/2018/02/02/technology/cryptocurrency-puerto-rico.html

Cabral, Natalia and Oriol Estrada, dirs (2016), *Site of Sites* (film), Dominican Republic, Faula Films.

Carlos Dávila, Juan, dir. (2021), *Simulacros de liberación* (film), Puerto Rico, Republica 21 Media.

Carney, N. (2016), "All Lives Matter, but so Does Race: Black Lives Matter and the Evolving Role of Social Media," *Humanity & Society*, 40(2): 180–99.

Cheatham, A. and D. Roy. (2022), "Puerto Rico a US Territory in Crisis, Council on Foreign Relations," *Council on Foreign Relations*, 29 September. Available online: https://www.cfr.org/backgrounder/puerto-rico-us-territory-crisis

Clark-Parsons, R. (2021) "'I SEE YOU, I BELIEVE YOU, I STAND WITH YOU': #MeToo and the Performance of Networked Feminist Visibility," *Feminist Media Studies*, 21(3): 362–80.

"Conéctate con AdocPR - Cecilia Aldarondo & Lale Namerrow," (2021), [YouTube] Asociación de Documentalistas de Puerto Rico. 18 March. Available online: https://www.youtube.com/watch?v=vB2ThK7nnlE&ab_channel=Asociaci%C3%B3ndeDoc umentalistasdePuertoRico (accessed December 28, 2023).

Cortés, J. (2018), "Necromedia, Haunting, And Public Mourning in The Puerto Rican Debt State: The Case of 'Los Muertos,'" *Journal of Latin American Cultural Studies*, 27(3): 357–69. https://doi.org/10.1080/13569325.2018.1485562

Crandall, J. (2019), "Blockchains and the "Chains of Empire": Contextualizing Blockchain, Cryptocurrency, and Neoliberalism in Puerto Rico," *Design and Culture*, 11(3): 279–300.

"Detrás de cámaras del video con Bad Bunny: 'Aquí Vive Gente,'" (2022), [YouTube] Bianca Graulau Español. 14 October. Available online: https://www.youtube.com/watch?v=8nxwlVK-zow (accessed September 4, 2024).

Duany, J. (2000), "Nation on the Move: The Construction of Cultural Identities in Puerto Rico and the Diaspora," *American Ethnologist*, 27(1): 5–30. https://doi.org/10.1525/ae.2000.27.1.5

Figueroa Esther, dir. (2018), *Climate Change is a Gender Issue* (film), Jamaica, Panos Caribbean.

Figueroa, Esther, dir. (2017), *Caribbean Climate Change: The Take Away Messages* (film), Jamaica, Vagabond Media.

"Film & Discussion: *Landfall*, Led By: Lale Namerrow Pastor, Associate Producer," (2021), [YouTube] Metropolitan Community College, 6 December. Available online: https://www.youtube.com/watch?v=2ICkXBXc7Jo

Folke, C., S. Carpenter, T. Elmqvist, L. Gunderson, C. S. Holling, and B. Walker (2002), "Resilience and Sustainable Development: Building Adaptive Capacity in a World of Transformations," *Ambio*, 31(5): 437–40. https://doi.org/10.1579/0044-7447-31.5.437

French, L. (2021), *Female Gaze in Documentary Film*, New York: Springer International Publishing.

Fuchs, C. (2014), *OccupyMedia!: The Occupy Movement and Social Media in Crisis Capitalism*, Winchester: John Hunt Publishing.

García-Ortega A. and J. A. García-Avilés (2023), "Innovation in Narrative Formats Redefines the Boundaries of Journalistic Storytelling: Instagram Stories, TikTok and Comic Journalism," in M. C. Negreira-Rey, J. Vázquez-Herrero, J. Sixto-García, and X. López-García (eds), *Blurring Boundaries of Journalism in Digital Media: New Actors, Models and Practices*, 185–97. Berlin: Springer.

Gonzalez, C. G. (2021), "Racial Capitalism, Climate Justice, and Climate Displacement," *Oñati Socio-Legal Series*, 11(1): 108–47.

Gonzalez, D. (2023), "In the Thick of Bad Bunny, there is Reggaeton Feminista," *The Latinx Project*, 12 May. Available online: https://www.latinxproject.nyu.edu/intervenxions/in-thethick-of-bad-bunny-there-is-reggaeton-feminista

Graulau, Bianca, dir. (2022), *Aquí vive gente* (film), Puerto Rico, Independent.

Hermilla, N. D. (1997), "Puerto Rico 1898-1998: The Institutionalization of Second Class Citizenship," *Dick. J. Int'l L*, 16: 275.

Hinojosa, J. (2018), "Two Sides of the Coin of Puerto Rican Migration: Depopulation in Puerto Rico and the Redefinition of the Diaspora," *Centro Journal*, 30(3): 230–52.

"IDA Documentary Screening Series: *Landfall* | Cecilia Aldarondo, Puerto Rico," (2021), [YouTube], International Documentary Association (IDA), 28 January. Available online: https://www.youtube.com/watch?v=yKQjrus3N6Q&ab_channel=InternationalDocumentary Association%28IDA%29 (accessed December 28, 2023)

Juhasz, A. and A. Lebow (2018), "Beyond Story/ An Online, Community-based Manifesto," *World Records Journal*, 2(3): 1–5. Available online: https://worldrecordsjournal.org/beyondstory-an-online-community-based-manifesto

Klein, N. (2018), *The Battle for Paradise: Puerto Rico Takes on the Disaster Capitalists*, Chicago: Haymarket Books.

Klein, N. (2007), *The Shock Doctrine: The Rise of Disaster Capitalism*, New York: Palgrave Macmillan.

La Fountain-Stokes, L. (2023), "Star Studies and Archipelagoes of Pain: Recent Diasporic Puerto Rican Documentary Films," in *Diaspora in Recent Film from the Spanish Caribbean Welcome and Panel 1: Diasporic Representations: Past, Present, Future*. UM Cuban Heritage Collection. Available online: https://www.facebook.com/umchc/videos/934445924262936

"*Landfall*: Conversation with Director Cecilia Aldarondo," (2021), [YouTube] UMassHistory. 21 February. Available online: https://www.youtube.com/watch?v=oz3qbmMdZDk

Lesage, J. (1978), "The Political Aesthetics of the Feminist Documentary Film," *Quarterly Review of Film Studies*, 3(4): 507–23.

Linares Villegas, Victoria, dir. (2022), *It Runs in the Family* (film), Dominican Republic/United States, Viewfinder and Zero Chill.

Maguire, B. and P. Hagan (2007), "Disasters and Communities: Understanding Social Resilience," *The Australian Journal of Emergency Management*, 22(2): 16–20.

Maldonado, A. W. (2020), *Teodoro Moscoso and Puerto Rico's Operation Bootstrap*, Gainesville: University Press of Florida.

María Cabral, José, dir. (2019), *Plastic Island* (film), Dominican Republic, Cacique Films.

Markham, T. (2014), "Social Media, Protest Cultures and Political Subjectivities of the Arab Spring," *Media, Culture & Society*, 36(1): 89–104.

Nagib, L. (2001), *World Cinema and the Ethics of Realism*, New York/London: Continuum.

Nihad, F. N. (2022), "Navigating the Paradox of Resilience: Colonial Legacies, Climate Change, and Hurricanes in Puerto Rico," MA diss. International Studies, University of Oklahoma.

Niney, F. (2009), *Le documentaire et ses faux-semblants*, Paris: Klincksieck.

Phillips, M. and N. Rumens, eds. (2015), *Contemporary Perspectives on Ecofeminism*, London: Routledge.

Polley, Sarah, dir. (2012), *Stories We Tell* (film), Canada, National Film Board of Canada.

Portillo, Lourdes, dir. (2001), *The Devil Never Sleeps* (film), United States/Mexico. Xochitl Films.

Recuber, T. (2013), "Disaster Porn!," *Contexts*, 12(2): 28–33. https://doi.org/10.1177/1536504213487695

Rhiney, K. (2020), "Dispossession, Disaster Capitalism and the Post-Hurricane Context in the Caribbean," *Political Geography*, 78. https://doi.org/10.1016/j.polgeo.2020.102171

Resilience Alliance. (2014), "What is Resilience?," Waterloo Institute. Available online: https://uwaterloo.ca/waterloo-institute-for-social-innovation-and-resilience/about/whatresilience

Rodríguez Coss, N. (2019), "A Feminist Intersectional Analysis of Economic and Resource (in) Equality in Puerto Rico Before and After Hurricane Maria," *Gonz. J. Int'l L.*, 23: 97–113.

Santana, D. B. (1998), "Puerto Rico's Operation Bootstrap: Colonial Roots of a Persistent Model for 'Third World' Development," *Revista Geográfica*, 124: 87–116.

Schuller, M. and J. K. Maldonado (2016), "Disaster Capitalism," *Annals of Anthropological Practice*, 40(1): 61–72. https://doi.org/10.1111/napa.12088

Sheller, M. (2021), "Reconstructing Tourism in the Caribbean: Connecting Pandemic Recovery, Climate Resilience and Sustainable Tourism Through Mobility Justice," *Journal of Sustainable Tourism*, 29(9): 1436–49. https://doi.org/10.1080/09669582.2020.1791141

Smaill, B. (2012), "Cinema Against the Age: Feminism and Contemporary Documentary," *Screening the Past*, 34: 1–12.

Smith, R. M. (2017), "The Unresolved Constitutional Issues of Puerto Rican Citizenship," *Centro Journal*, 29(1): 56–75.

Puerto Rico | Sotheby's International Realty. (2018), "Act 22 Individual Investors Act: Puerto Rico Tax Incentives," http://puertoricotaxincentives.com/act-22-individual-investors-act

Torre, C. A. and W. Burgos, eds. (1994), *The Commuter Nation: Perspectives on Puerto Rican Migration*, San Juan: La Editorial UPR.

Ulfsdotter, B. and A. Backman Rogers (2018a), *Female Agency and Documentary Strategies: Subjectivities, Identity and Activism*, Edinburgh: Edinburgh University Press.

Ulfsdotter, B. and A. Backman Rogers (2018b), *Female Authorship and the Documentary Image: Theory, Practice and Aesthetics*, Edinburgh: Edinburgh University Press.

Waldman, D. and J. Walker, eds. (1999), *Feminism and Documentary*, Minneapolis: University of Minnesota Press.

White, P. (2015), *Women's Cinema, World Cinema: Projecting Contemporary Feminisms*, Durham: Duke University Press.

Chapter 9

Baron, J. (2014), *The Archive Effect: Found Footage and the Audiovisual Experience of History*, London: Routledge.

Baron, J. (2014), *The Archive Effect: Found Footage and the Audiovisual Experience of History*, London: Routledge.

Balsom, E. and H. Peleg, eds. (2022), *Feminist Worldmaking and the Moving Image*, Cambridge, MA: The MIT Press.

Balsom, E. and H. Peleg, eds. (2016), *Documentary Across Disciplines*, Cambridge, MA: The MIT Press.

Bammer, A. (2015), *Partial Visions*, Bern: Peter Lang.

Blonski, A., B. Creed, and F. Freiberg (1987), *Don't Shoot Darling!: Women's Independent Filmmaking in Australia*, Richmond, Vic: Greenhouse.

Boal, A. (2008), *Theatre of the Oppressed*, trans. M.O. Leal McBride, C. A. Leal McBride and E. Fryer, London: Pluto Press.

Bruzzi, S. (2020), *Approximation: Documentary, History and Staging Reality*, Abingdon; New York: Routledge.

Candy, L. and E. Edmonds (2018), "Practice-Based Research in the Creative Arts: Foundations and Futures from the Front Line," *Leonardo*, 51(1): 63–9.

Chambers-Letson, J., T. Nyong'o, and A. Pellegrini (2019), "Foreword" in *Cruising Utopia, 10th Anniversary Edition: The Then and There of Queer Futurity* by José Esteban Muñoz, ix–xvi. New York: New York University Press.

Cvetkovich, A. (2003), *An Archive of Feelings: Trauma, Sexuality, and Lesbian Public Cultures,* Durham: Duke University Press.

Daniels, J. (2022), "The Way of the Bricoleuse: Experiments in Documentary Filmmaking," *Studies in Documentary Film*, 16(2): 127–39.

Dolan, J. (2005), *Utopia in Performance: Finding Hope in the Theatre,* Ann Arbor: University of Michigan Press.

Fischer, J. (2014), *To Create Live Treatments of Actuality: An Investigation of the Emerging Field of Live Documentary Practice.* Unpublished MSc Thesis, Department of Comparative Media Studies, Massachusetts Institute of Technology.

French, L., ed. (2003), *Womenvision: Women and the Moving Image in Australia,* Melbourne: Damned Publishing.

Gibson, R. (2018), "Foreword: Cognitive Two-Steps," in C. Batty and S. Kerrigan (eds.), *Screen Production Research: Creative Practice as a Mode of Enquiry,* v–xiii. Cham: Palgrave Macmillan.

Harper, D. (2002), "Talking about Pictures: A Case for Photo Elicitation," *Visual Studies*, 17(1): 13–26.

Hjorth, L., A. Harris, K. Jungnickel, and G. Coombs (2019), *Creative Practice Ethnographies*, London: Lexington Books.

Juhasz, A. and A. Lebow (2018), "Beyond Story: An Online, Community-Based Manifesto," *World Records*, 2(3). https://vols.worldrecordsjournal.org/02/03

Kerrigan, S. (2018), "A 'Logical' Explanation of Screen Production as Method-Led Research," in C. Batty and S. Kerrigan (eds.), *Screen Production Research: Creative Practice as a Mode of Enquiry,* 11–27. Cham: Palgrave Macmillan.

Lesage, J. (1978), "The Political Aesthetics of the Feminist Documentary Film," *Quarterly Review of Film Studies,* 3(4): 507–23.

Lesage, J. and S. Warren (2022), "'It was there all along': An Intergenerational Dialogue about Feminism, Realism, and Documentary," in E. Balsom and H. Peleg (eds.), *Feminist Worldmaking and the Moving Image,* 141–57. Cambridge, MA: The MIT Press.

Loveless, N. (2019), *How to Make Art at the End of the World: A Manifesto for Research-Creation,* Durham: Duke University Press.

Martinis Roe, A. (2018), *To Become Two: Propositions for Feminist Collective Practice*, Berlin: Archive Books.

Muñoz, J. E., J. Chambers-Letson, T. Nyong'o, and A. Pellegrini (2019), *Cruising Utopia, 10th Anniversary Edition: The Then and There of Queer Futurity*, New York: New York University Press.

Munro, K. (2023), "Live Documentary Performance in the Time of COVID-19," in D. Sills-Jones and P. Kääpä (eds.), *Documentary in the Age of Covid,* 85–107. Oxford: Peter Lang.

Odell, J. (2023). *Saving Time: Discovering a Life Beyond the Clock,* New York: Random House.

Radhakrishnan, S. (2022), "Trinh T. Minh-ha by Shivani Radhakrishnan," https://bombmagazine.org/articles/trinh-t-minh-ha/ (accessed October 20, 2023).

Steedman, C. (2001), *Dust,* Manchester: Manchester University Press.

Sundar, S. (2023), "Foreword: Performance, Memory and Absence," in A. Potter and S. Saha (eds.), *Performance Making and the Archive,* xxii–xxix. Abingdon; New York: Routledge.

Trinh, Minh-ha T. (2013), *D-Passage,* ed. Minh-ha T. Trinh, Durham: Duke University Press

Trinh, T. Minh-Ha. (2012), *Cinema Interval,* New York: Routledge.

Zimmermann, P. (1999), "Flaherty's Midwives," in D. Waldman and J. Walker (eds.), *Feminism and Documentary,* 64–83. Minneapolis: University of Minnesota Press.

Chapter 10

Anderson, K. (2016), *A Recognition of Being: Reconstructing Native Womanhood,* 2nd ed, Toronto: Women's Press.

Anderson, K. (2010), "Affirmations of an Indigenous Feminist", in Cheryl Suzack, Shari M. Huhndorf, Jeanne Perreault, and Jean Barman (eds.), *Indigenous Women and Feminism,* 81–91. Vancouver: University of British Columbia Press.

Archibald, J. (2008), *Indigenous Storywork: Educating the Heart, Mind, Body, and Spirit,* Vancouver: UBC Press.

Archibald Q'um Q'um Xiiem, J., J. B. J. Lee-Morgan, and J. De Santolo, eds. (2019), *Decolonizing Research: Indigenous Storywork as Methodology,* London: Zed Books.

Baker, E. (2005), "Loving Indianess: Native Women's Storytelling as Survivance," *Atlantis,* 29(2): 111–21.

Bancroft, C. (2018), "The Braided Narrative," *Narrative,* 26(3): 262–81.

Barclay, B. (2003), "Celebrating Fourth Cinema," *Illusions Magazine,* 1: 2–11.

Boutsalis, K. (2021), "Elle-Máijá Tailfeathers' *Kímmapiiyipitssini* Brings Empathy to an Opioid Crisis," *POV Magazine,* 114: 30–3.

Christian, D. (2019), "Indigenous Visual Storywork for Indigenous Film Aesthetics," in J. Archibald Q'um Q'um Xiiem, J. B. J. Lee-Morgan, and J. De Santolo (eds.), *Decolonizing Research: Indigenous Storywork as Methodology,* 40–55. London: ZED Books.

Crenshaw, K. (1989), "Demarginalizing the Intersection of Race and Sex: A Black Feminist Critique of Antidiscrimination Doctrine, Feminist Theory and Antiracist Politics," *University of Chicago Legal Forum,* 1: 139–67.

Green, J., ed. (2017), *Making Space for Indigenous Feminism*, 2nd ed. Toronto, Fernwood Publishing. Kindle version.

Hubbard, Tasha, dir. (2019), *nîpawistamâsowin: We Will Stand Up* (film), Canada: Downstream Documentary Productions Inc. and the National Film Board of Canada.

Kaiser, B. M. and K. Thiele (2017), "What is Species Memory? Or, Humanism, and the Afterlives of '1492,'" *Parallax*, 23(4): 403–15.

King, T. (2014), *The Inconvenient Indian: A Curious Account of Native People in North America*, Doubleday Canada.

Manuel, A. with Grand Chief Ronald Derrickson (2017), *The Reconciliation Manifesto: Recovering the Land Rebuilding the Economy*, Toronto: James Lorimer & Company Ltd, Publishers.

Manuel, G. and M. Posluns (1974, 2019), *The Fourth World*, Minneapolis: University of Minnesota Press.

Maracle, L. (1990), *Sojourner's Truth and Other Stories*, Vancouver: Press Gang Publishers.

McLeod, N., ed. (2014), *Indigenous Poetics in Canada*, Waterloo: Wilfrid Laurier University Press.

Murray, Stuart (2008), *Images of dignity: Barry Barclay and Fourth Cinema*. Wellington, NZ: Huia Publishers.

Posca, E. (2023), "Indigenizing the Academy," *Canadian Woman Studies/les cahiers de la femme*, 36(1,2): 68–76.

Razack, S., ed., (2015), *Dying from Improvement: Inquests and Inquiries into Indigenous Deaths in Custody*, Toronto: University of Toronto Press.

Sharma, Nandita (2015), "Strategic Anti-Essentialism: Decolonizing Decolonization," in K. McKittrick (ed.), *Sylvia Wynter: On Being Human as Praxis*, 164–82. Durham and London: Duke University Press.

Simpson, L. B. (2021), *A Short History of the Blockade: Giant Beavers, Diplomacy, and Regeneration in Nishnaabewin*, Edmonton: University of Alberta Press.

Simpson, L. B. (2017), *As We Have Always Done: Indigenous Freedom Through Radical Resistance*, Minneapolis: University of Minnesota Press.

Tailfeathers, Elle-Máijá, dir. (2021), *Kímmapiiyipitssini: The Meaning of Empathy* (film), Canada: Seen Through Women Productions and the National Film Board of Canada.

Vanstone, G. and B. Winston (2019), "'This Would be Scary to Any Other Culture … But to Us It's So Cute!' The Radicalism of Fourth Cinema from *Tangata Whenua* to *Angry Inuk*," *Studies in Documentary Film*, 13(3): 233–49.

Wynter, S. and K. McKittrick (2015), "Unparalleled Catastrophe for Our Species? Or, to Give Humanness a Different Future: Conversations," In (ed.), *Sylvia Wynter: On Being Human as Praxis*, 9–80. Durham and London: Duke University Press.

Chapter 11

MacDougall, D. (1998), *Transcultural Cinema*, Princeton, NJ: Princeton University Press.
Shahani, Kumar, dir. (1991), *Bhavantarana* (film), India: Ministry of External Affairs.
Vertov, Dziga, dir. (1929), *The Man With The Movie Camera* (film), USSR.
Williams, R. (1989), *Resources of Hope*, ed. Robin Gable, London & New York: Verso.

Chapter 12

Frampton, Hollis, dir. (1970), *Zorn's Lemma* (film), USA: The Filmmakers Cooperative.
Godmilow, J. (2022), "Kill the Documentary: A Letter to Filmmakers, Students, and Scholars," *Journal of Film and Video*, 54(2/3): 3–10.
Guzmán, Patricio dir. (2010), *Nostalgia for the Light* (film), France: Pyramide Distribution.
Jayanti, Hannah, dir. (2021), *Truth or Consequences* (film), USA: Sentient. Art.Film.
Jayanti, Hannah and Alexander Porter, dirs (forthcoming), *Topography* (film, Performance, Installation), USA.
Lorde, A. (1984), *Sister Outsider: Essays and Speeches*, Trumansburg NY: Crossing Press.
Lusztig, Irene, dir. (2023), *Richland* (film), USA: Komsomol Films.
Lusztig, Irene, dir. (2001), *Reconstruction* (film), Lusztig, USA: Women Make Movies.
Mirza, Noorafshan and Brad Butler, dirs (2018), *The Scar* (film) [Multi-screen immersive video installation], UK: HOME and Delfina Foundation.
Mirza, Noorafshan and Brad Butler, dirs (2013), *Hold Your Ground* (film), [Multi-screen public art installation], Butler, UK: Canary Wharf Tube Station.
Tarkovsky, Andrei, dir. (1979), *Stalker* (film), Soviet Union: Mosfilm.
Uddoh, Irene and Louis Brown, dirs (2021), *Practice Makes Perfect* (Single-channel video), UK: Focal Point Gallery and Bluecoat.
Varda, Agnès, dir. (1975), *Daguerréotypes* (film), France: L'Epée de Bois.
Waldman, D. and J. Walker, eds. (1999), *Feminism and Documentary*. Minneapolis: University of Minnesota Press.
Zimmerman, Andrea Luka, dir. (2015), *Estate: A Reverie* (film), UK: Grasshopper Films.

Index

3CM Less (2003) 63
9/11 attacks 154
311 (documentary film, 2011) 118
1975 New York Conference of
 Feminist Film and Video
 Organizations 13
1999 series Girls Around the World 19
2009 FESPACO film festival 27
2018 Durban International Film
 Festival 43

Abad, Daniela 157
Abbass, Hiam 24–5

El Abnoudy, Ateyyat 16
accented cinema 18, 25
affected party-ism 113, 116
affective relations 98–101, 109, see
 also Como el cielo después de
 llover (2021)
Afghanistan Unveiled 20
After the Earthquake/Despues del
 Terremoto (1979) 17
Afzali, Mahnaz 140
Agencia Española de Cooperación
 Internacional (AECID) 57
Agnès Varda 242–3
Aguilar, Carlos 78
Al-e Ahmad, Jalal 136
Ahmadinejad, Mahmoud 140
Aina Women Filming Group 20
Akbarzadeh, Shahram 140
Akerman, Chantal 174
Aldarondo, Cecilia 153, 156–60, 164
Algerian anti-colonial struggle 67–8
Al-Ali, Nadje 62
Alliance Française 42
All My Trees (2015)
 Banietemad, Rakhshan 141–5
 Damavand collage 144
 intimate scenes shot in
  Mallah's home 143
 Iran's lack of proper management 143

Mallah, Mahlagha
 contributions of 141–2
 vigor as a woman 145
 national Clean Air Day, event to
  commemorate 144
All the Beauty and the
 Bloodshed (2022) 1
Almada, Natalia 18
Alvarez, María José 16
Álvarez-Mesa, Pablo 160
Anatomy of a Fall 1
Anderson, Kim 190
Andrea (2022) 163
Anglophone hegemony 16
Another Gaze (journal) 22
antiracism 16
apartheid 23
APHIDS 175
Apolonia, Apolonia (2022) 1
Aquí vive gente (People Live
 Here, 2022) 152
 archival footage 162
 Graulau, Bianca 153, 156, 161
 imagery and representations of the
  island 163
 international affairs 164
 mechanism of control and mass state
  surveillance 164
 rhythmic editing 163–4
 social media feminism 165
Arab and Latin American countries
 cultural bonds 69 n.1
Arab Film Festival in Berlin
 (ALFILM) 65
Arab Fund for Arts and Culture (AFAC)
 58
Arabyya epistemologies
 and Chicana feminist, similarities
  between 66
 and Egyptian feminism 65–8
 Shahadat 66
 transnational Haki 66
 the Archive Fever 181

art movements 73
The Art of Work Is a Work of Art (2023) 7, *see also* theater and live documentary
　archive as space for possibility 180
　consciousness-raising meetings 177
　formally experimental 177
　hybrid documentary-theater project 176
　by Kim Munro 169, 173, 182
Asen, Robert 124
Association of Independent Video and Filmmakers 16
Aston, Judith 180
As Women See It (1983) 14–16, 19
Atwood, Blake 139
authorship 3–4, 153, 176
　and agency, concepts of 20
avant-garde film movements 13, 21, 218
Awakening the Goddess (2020) 74, 84–7
　animated documentaries 84
　audio track 85–6
　creative social protest 84
　description 84–5
　feminism 87
　Kali's emergence 86
　Mukherjee, Debjani 84
　woman's body, objectification and commodification of 86

Babri Masjid, destruction of 218
Bad Bunny 154, 162–3, 168 n.11
Balaghati, Omid 139
Balsom, Erika 3, 76
Balvin, J. 163
Bammer, Angelika 174
Barclay, Barry 187
Barea, Maria 16, 19
Barlow, Rebecca 140
Barnaby, Jeff 199
Basu, Amrita 52
Battaglia, Letizia 53
Battle of the Sacred Tree (1994) 28
Bazargan, Mehdi 136
Because Roots Don't Die (1977) 64
Becoming a Woman (documentary) 16
Benamou, Catherine 17
Benhabib, Seyla 115
Berlant, Lauren 156

Bhavantarana (Shahani) 227
big-budget documentaries 20
biographical documentaries in Iran 149 n.1, *see also All My Trees* (2015); *Poets of Life* (2017)
biography and environmentalism 134–5
　environmentally conscious practices 141
　establishment of city councils 138
　feminist biographical approach 133
　"personal is political," notion of 134
　popularity of Khatami 137
　resistance, creative and flexible forms 140
　significance of feminist biography 133–4
　societal issues, connecting private to the public 139
　technological advancements 139
　tenets of Khatami's presidential campaign 137
　traditions and environmental conditions of Iran 135–7
　women
　　empowerment in a society 149
　　and environmentalism 137–41
　　sociopolitical participation 137
bisexuality 101
#BlackLivesMatter 168 n.13
Blackwood, Maureen 18
Blanche, Carte 64
The Blonds (2003) 18
Blonski, Annette 177
Blood Quantum (2019) 199
Boal, Augusto 175
The Body Remembers When the World Broke Open (2019) 199
Bongela, Milisuthando 23–4
Bonilla, Yarimar 155–6, 160
Borden, Lizzie 13
Boycott, Divestment, Sanctions (BDS) movement 61
Brown, Mariel 82, 157
Burton, Julianne 97
Busan International Film Festival in 2014 117
Butler, Brad 237, 252
Butler, Judith 99
Bye Bye Tiberias (2023) 24–5

Cabral, José María 160
Cairo International Women's Film Festival (CIWFF) 55
California Newsreel 14
Calling the Ghosts (1996) 20
Cameraperson (2016) 12
Campbell, Maria 202
Campion, Jane 1
Candy, L. 170
Cannes Film Festival 1–2
   Golden Eye Award 2
Cannes' Palme d'Or 1
capitalism 3, 7, 65–6, 68, 81, 153–6, 160, 164–5, 234, 247
Caravan 70 n.12
   culture Caravan 51
   development of women's cinema in Egypt 55
   Egyptian fanbase 59
   Facebook account 65
   funding 60
   gender-specific struggles 58
   history of 55–9
   inspiration and funding 56–9
   intergenerational dialogue and knowledge, promotion of 64
   limitations of transnational collaboration 60
   model of transnational feminist film culture 68
   operations in the MENA 68
   organization 'Between Women Filmmakers Caravan' 7, 51, 62
   Palestinian Cinema Guide 65
   politics 59–65
   restrictions on the participation 64
   workshops and mentorship 58
Cardi B. 163
Carne (2019) 74, 80–4
   change and physical signs of aging 81, 83
   forms of discursive and epistemic violence 84
   Kater, Camila 80
Carri, Albertina 18
Carthage Film Festival (JCC) or Damascus Film Festival 59
Cervera, Lorena 7
Cheatam, Amelia 152
Chenzira, Ayoka 16

Children of Shatila (1988) 63
Chipko forest preservation activism, India 16
Christian, Dorothy 201
chrononormativity 179
cinema solidarity 53
Cine Mujer in Mexico, women's film groups 17
Cine Pobre Film Festival, Cuba 56
Circles and COW, UK 14
Citizen 4 23
Coded Bias (2020) 12
Colombian conflict 111 n.10
colonialism 3, 65, 68, 151, 157, 159, 165, 197, 223
colonization, Canadian context, *see also Kímmapiiyipitssini: The Meaning of Empathy* (2021); *nîpawistamâsowin: We Will Stand Up* (2019)
   attempted cultural genocide 191–2
   Indian Act 191
   Residential School system 191
   troubled relationship 190–1
   Truth and Reconciliation Commission (TRC) 191
Comedi, Agustina 99–103
Coming of Age (2008) 28, 37–8
commercial films 60
community group 12, 14
Como el cielo después de llover (2021)
   description 107–9
   family's home movies 107
   Gaviria, Mercedes 106–9
   woman's aspirations 106
Comprehensive Employment and Training Act (CETA) 13
Conference of Feminist Film and Video Organizations 26, 26 n.2
Connell, Raewyn 5
consciousness raising 68, 143–4, 172, 177, 244
   (C-R) groups 245, 252 n.11
conversational approach 48 n.5
counterpublic(s) 21, 121–6, *see also A Lullaby under the Nuclear Sky* (2016); *The Road Home* (2017)
   cinematically mediated 126–7
Covid-19 49 n.24, 55, 73, 154, 156, 214

CPH:DOX in Copenhagen   23
Creed, Barbara   177
cross-generational and affective
    discourse   7
Culture, Communication, and
    Development Fund (KCD)   60
*Curating Africa in the Age of Film
    Festivals* (2015)   41

Daguerréotypes (1975)
Dangerous Affair (2002)   27, 36
Dash, Julie   16
The Days of Cinema, Palestinian film
    festival   59
debut films, description   110 n.6
deep image   8
    cinematic mode of inquiry   7
    description   213, 221–2, 227, 229–30
    practice of   212–13
Department of Environment
    (DOE)   136–40
de Peer, Stefanie Van   58
Desai, Manisha   52, 61
The Devil Never Sleeps (2001)   157
Dhanraj, Deepa   16
Dhofar rebellion in the Arabian Gulf   66
Dickinson, Kay   58–9
digital culture   12
digital expansion   3
digital technologies, power of   2
Dirty War (1976–83)   111 n.8
"disaster porn" narratives   158
discourses of sobriety   21
distribution
    acquisitions on global issues in the
        1990s   19–20
    alternative distribution method   162
    description   14
    educational   14, 21
    experience   139
    inadequate public funding   19
    nontheatrical distribution
        catalog   12–13
    partnerships with filmmakers   19
    WMM, distribution service   14, 16,
        20, 21, 24, 26
Divorce Iranian Style (1998)   19
"doc apocalypse"   13
Docubox   7, 34–48, 49 n.15, 50
    n.29, 50 n.31

Documentary and Experimental Film
    Center (DEFC)   141
documentary filmmaking   1–2, 4–5, 15,
    30, 39, 44, 46, 50 n.31, 51, 55, 70
    n.12, 79, 84, 137–41, 166, 175,
    178, 235, 241
Domee Shi   74
Dönmez-Colin, Gönül   58
Don't Shoot Darling (1987)   176
Dosa, Sara   1
Dougherty, Ariel   13
Dovey, Lindiwe   6, 33, 40
    and Judy Kibinge in conversation   33
DoxBox   58
Dream Girls (1993)   19
Dubai International Film Festival
    (DIFF)   58–9
Ducournau, Julia   1
Dunye, Cheryl   181
Eaker, Quinn   160
earthquake, Tohoku region of Japan
    in 2011   112
East Africa, documentary film cultures
    collaboration and intimacy   32
    collaborative curating   30–1
    criteria for the films   42
    Docubox's films   42–4
    female friendship and feminist
        curation in film   27–34
    female-led film industry   43
    identity-related quotas   43
    Kibinge, Judy   34–41
    power of female friendships   27
    self-reflexive tone   30
    Starry Nights, open-air screenings   42
    transformation of documentary
        culture   41–5
    transparency   34–41
Ebtekar, Masumeh   137
ecofeminism   165
    critical   134
Edmonds, E.   170
Egyptian Feminist Union (EFU)   61
El Futuro Es Nuestro (2014)   66
El General (2009)   18
Ellerson, Betti   29
El silencio es un cuerpo que cae (2017)
    Comedi, Agustina   99–103
    first-person enunciation   101–2
    new trends in political art   102

     portrait of an Argentinian family   100
     reframing of home movies   103
     school shows   100
Enemies of Happiness (2006)   2
Entrepreneurship Development
          Foundation for Women and
          Youth (NGO)   145
environmental issues   141
environmental non-government
          organisations (NGOs)   137
ERC-funded "African Screen Worlds:
          Decolonising Film and Screen
          Studies" project   28
Al-Erhayem, Anja   2
Erickson, McCann   35
Escher, Celina   18
Eskandar Firouz   136
Espinosa, Julio Garcia   56
essentialism   4
Estate, a Reverie (2015)   249
Eurocentric practices of
          development aid   36
European Research Council (ERC)   47
Experimental Film Fund   177

Faasla (2021)   214
Fadaee, Simin   138
Father, Son and Holy War (1994)   218
Faye, Safi   29
*Female Agency and Documentary
          Strategies: Subjectivities, Identity
          and Activism* (Ulfsdotter and
          Rogers)   3, 20
*Female Authorship and the Documentary
          Image: Theory, Practice and
          Aesthetics* (Ulfsdotter and
          Rogers)   3, 20
female gaze   4, 153
*The Female Gaze in Documentary
          Film: An International
          Perspective* (2021)   3
"Female Only Filmmakers" program   28
Feminism and Documentary (Walker and
          Waldman)   3, 233
feminism as documentary method
     art is healing   247–8
     Black self-formation   235
     consciousness-raising groups   245
     cracks   244
     creative practices   233–4
     embedded conditioning   238
     female verité cinematographers   242
     feminist practice and
          sustainability   246
     forced assimilation   245
     generosity and reciprocity   239–40
     good practices of documentaries   239
     history of feminism   244
     importance of representation   235
     inequality and structural
          violence   236
     intergenerational dialogue and
          learning   241
     limits of representational politics   241
     listening-centered and relational   240
     making mistakes   250
     narrative structures   247
     notions of inclusivity   246
     patriarchy   250
     place-based films   235–6
     popular culture   241
     practice legislates   248
     Practice Makes Perfect (2021)   235
     practice of self-re-imagining   236
     process-based emergent form   238
     radical self-love, idea of   234
     Reconstruction (2001)   234
     Reflecting on the Museum of Non-
          Participation (project)   236
     representation of Black people   237
     self-education.   245
     Third Cinema   243
     time-traveling   242
     traumatic experience   244
     Truth or Consequences (2021)   235
     violence   243
     Vision Machine   236
feminist activism   165
feminist animated documentary
     feminism and animation and
          documentary   75–7
feminist archival film curators (2024)   30
feminist distribution and exhibition
          networks   2
Feminist Elsewheres program, 2023   22
feminist film workers   176
Feminist Media Histories (Hennefeld
          and Horak)   32
*Feminist Worldmaking and the Moving
          Image* (Balsom and Peleg)   3

Ferdowsi, Abolqasem   135
festival presentations   1
Figueroa, Esther   160
Film Forum Nairobi   21
filmmaking practices of Black
    African women   47
Filmmor in Turkey   22
Firdausi (1934)   135
Fire of Love (2022)   1
first-person aesthetics of feminist
    cinematic practices   129 n.9
first-person documentary
  dialectical representations of public
    and private life   115
  plurality of   120
first-person enunciation   101, *see also*
    El silencio es un cuerpo que
    cae (2017)
Fischer, Julie   180
Flanders, Elle   64
Florencia Marchetti   29
Fly So Far (2021)   18
Ford Foundation's JustFilms and Chicken
    and Egg   12
Fountain-Stokes, Larry La   158
Four Daughters (2023)   2
Fourth Cinema, concept of   188–90
Freeman, Elizabeth   179
Freiberg, Freda   177
French, Lisa   3, 98
Friedrich, Su   13
From One Woman to Another: The
    Screen Worlds of Bongiwe
    Selane (2023)   28
Frontiers of Dreams and Fears (2001)   63
Fukushima
  nuclear catastrophe   114
  scholarship on cinematic
    (and other artistic)
    representation   128 n.6
Fukushima Daiichi nuclear power plant
  accident   112
Full Frame Film Festival
  Center for Documentary Studies
    Filmmaker Award   2

Gaza
  brutal attack on   63
  catastrophization of   68–9
  gender-based violence (GBV)   68

Gerima, Haile   29
Ghaemmaghami, Rokhsareh   2, 12
Ghods, Saideh   145
Gibson, Linda   16
Gibson, Ross   171
Girish, Devika   32
Glob, Lea   1
globalization   3
global women's documentary practices   5
Goat   35
Godmilow, Jill   247
Goulet, Danis   199
Gramann, Karola   22
Grandi, Nicolas   214
Granny's Sexual Life (2021)   87–91
  animation   90
  César Award-the National Film Award
    in France   74
  description   89–90
  Djukiæ, Urška   87
  fact and fiction   90
  hand-drawn animation   88
  images   90
  minimalist environment   88–9
  Pigeard, Émilie   87
  scribbled, smeared cartoon
    technique   88
  sound as powerful strategy   88–9
  women's sexual violence   89
  youth and intimacy of women   88
Graulau, Bianca   153–4
The Greatest Silence: Rape in the
    Congo (2007)   20
Green, Joyce   193
Grigor, Mish   174
Grizim, Shelly   61
Grupo Chaski in Peru   17
Guatemalan Civil War (1960–
    96)   103, 111 n.9
Gunnarsdóttir, Sara   73

Hagino, Ryo   117
Haiti's earthquake in 2010   154
Hammami, Rema   68
Hammer, Barbara   13, 174
Hamza, Manal   65
Hanaway, William L.   135
Hania, Kaouther Ben   2
el-Hassan, Azza   63
  Q&A with   63

Hatoum, Mona 18
Healthcaring: From Our End of the Speculum (1976) 13
hemispheric gathering *Cocina de imágenes* in 1987 21–2
Hennefeld, M. 30
heteronormativity 65
Hillmann, Michael Craig 135
Hiroshima and Nagasaki, destruction by atomic bombs 128 n.5
Hirsch, Marianne 98, 99
History and Memory: For Akiko and Takashige (1991) 26
Hjort, Mette 37, 41
Hoffmann, Pierre 15
Hold Your Ground (2013) 237–8
Hole, Kristin Lené 134
"Homage to Lebanon", category films 54
Hooligan Sparrow (documentary) 23
Horak, L. 30–2, 47
Hot Docs Canadian International Film Festival (2021) 199
Hot Docs in Toronto 23
The Hour of Liberation Has Arrived (1974) 66
Houston, Whitney 177, 178
Hubbard, Tasha 188
Human Rights Watch Film Festival 2
Hurricane Fiona, 2022 152
Hurricane Katrina, 2005 154
Hurricane Maria, 2017 152
Hussein, Imam 135

Ibermedia Program 110 n.1
imaginal cells, concept of 46
an imperfect cinema 56
Imre, Anikó 53
inclusivity 16, 246
Independent Television Service 16
India
    Chipko forest preservation activism 16
    Indianess 189–90
    as a media-infested landscape 211
    parallel cinema 227
    social realities in contemporary 8
Indigenous cinema 188–9
Indigenous storytelling 188
informal networks of collaboration 5
International Documentary Film Festival Amsterdam (IDFA) 1–2, 23, 44, 62
Internationales Frauenfilm Festival in Dortmund/Köln 22
International Faire of Rashid Karameh 56
international markets for documentary 23
International Women Suffrage Alliance in Copenhagen 61
In The Claws of a Century Wanting (2017) 66
intimacy 4, 31–2, 47, 85, 88, 144, 167 n.4, 181
Iran, *see also* biographical documentaries in Iran
    films by women in 22
Iranian Documentary Filmmakers Association (IRDFA) 137–9
Iris and Serious Business in California (1979) 13
Islamic Revolution, 1979 135–6
Islamism 65
Islamophobia 20
Israel-Hamas War 26
Israel/Palestine, political conflict in 62–3
It Runs in the Family (2022) 157
I've Heard The Mermaids Singing and *When Night Is Falling* (1984) 218

Jackson, Lisa F. 20
Japan
    aesthetic strategies by women filmmakers 7
    emphasis on social harmony and conformity 121
    historical legacies of postwar 114
    nuclear power policy 113
Jayanti, Hannah 8, 233–50
Jelaèa, Dijana 134
journalistic narrative 168 n.10

K-12 education 14
Kahana, Jonathan 115
KAM (2020) 74, 91–4
    Akcay, Zeynep 91
    celebratory power dance 91

collective feelings and grievances
  of women 92
dance, expressing through 93–4
feminist and feminine energy 93
fictitious ritual 91
liminal transformation concept 93
long-exposure pixilation and 2D
  animation 92–3
punk culture 94
Kamakha: Through Prayerful Eyes
  (2012) 224, 226
Kantayya, Shalini 12
Kapadia, Payal 2
Keller, Marjorie 13
Kenyan Human Rights Commission 39
Kenyatta, Uhuru 36, 39
El Khachab, Chihab 60
Khaled, Laila 67
Khansalar, Fatemeh-Mehr 142
Khosrovani, Firouzeh 1
Kibera, Leonard 35
Kibinge, Judy 7, 27
  awards 36
  Coming of Age (2008) 37–8
  commentary on the violence 49 n.16
  Dangerous Affair (2002) 36
  as filmmaker 34–41
  first-person" filmmaking 37
  Headlines in History (2010) 37
  key documentary films 36
  knowledge of Africa 36
  magical realism 35
  motivation for making her
    fiction films 36
  Project Daddy (2004) 36
  Scarred: Anatomy of a Massacre
    (2015) 37–8
  Something Necessary (2013) 34
Killer Necklace (2009) 28, 35, 48 n.3
Kill the Documentary as We Know It
  (2022) 247, 252
Kimiavi, Parviz 135
*Kímmapiiyipitssini: The Meaning of
  Empathy* (2021) 188–
  90, 198–207
  awards 198–9
  braided narrative
    structure 202–3, 205
  collective struggle with opioid
    crisis 199

Community Managed Alcohol
  Program Coop 203
description 200–5
Fourth World perspective 190, 206
Naloxone kits 203
strategy of braiding individual stories
  together 204
Supportive Recovery Program 203
Tailfeather, Elle-Máijá 188–9,
  198, 201, 203
King, Christopher 31, 38, 43–4
King, Thomas 189
Kingdom of Women (2010) 64
Kinyanjui, Wanjiru 28
Klein, Naomi 154

La asfixia (2018)
  Bustamante, Ana 103–6
  current state of Guatemala 104
  inherited trauma 105–6
  postmemory 103
  scarcity of family images 105
Lady of the Roses (2008) 140
Landfall (2020) 152–3
  Aldarondo, Cecilia 152
  anti-colonial stance 159
  collective conversations on
    politics 161
  exploitative practices to plantation
    economy 159–60
  #Rickyrenuncia campaign 161
  role of diasporic Puerto Ricans 159
  self-governed socialism 160
  vulnerability and colonial
    legacies 158–61
Larijani, Ali 139
*Las Madres: The Mothers of Plaza del
  Mayo* (1985) 18
Latin American documentary,
  reformulation of, *see also
  Como el cielo después de
  llover* (2021); *El silencio es
  un cuerpo que cae* (2017);
  La asfixia (2018)
  concept of *postmemory* 98–9
  documentary practices and
    discourses 109
  shift from exteriority to interiority
    98
Latin American filmmakers 52

Lebow, Alisa   37, 99, 103, 120, 153, 170
Lekow, Maia   31, 43
   change of course   44
   The Letter (dir. Lekow and King, 2019)   43–4
   musician and composer   45
   unique creative vision   45
Lesage, Julia   35
The Letter (2019)   43
LGBTQA+ community   163
Llanos, Bernardina   99
Longinotto, Kim   19, 53–4, 69
López, Jennifer   163
Love, Women and Flowers (1988)   18
A Lullaby under the Nuclear Sky (2016)
   counterpublics   121
   demonstration   119–20
   experience of pregnancy   116
   journalistic report about Fukushima   118
   maternal connectivity of bodies   127
   private/public dynamics   120
   sense of responsibility and guilt   119
   "the narrative of arrival"   117–18
   threat of radiation   117
   Tomoko Kana   116
Lusztig, Irene   8
Lutfi, Nabiha   64

MacDougall, David   227–9
macho-masculinity   101
Madi, Sandra   64
Mahak: A World She Founded (2017)   145
Maldonado, J.K.   151, 155
Maldoror, Sarah   22, 29
Mallah, Mahlagha (mother of Iran's environment)   141–5
Mallet, Marilu   18
Mani, Sahra   2
Manna, Jumana   62
Manuel, George   190, 195
The Man with the Movie Camera (1929)   226
Maracle, Lee   206
Maranan, Jewel   66
Marciniak, Katarzyna   53
marginalization of scholarship   15
Marin, Luis Muñoz   151

Marina (2018)   66
Marson, Una   241
Masri, Mai   63–4
Mass Culture Institute   51
Matías, Bienvenida   17
Matsubayashi, Yoji   118
Matusiak, Thomas   108
media art centers   14
media privatization   20
Melbourne Women's Film Group   176
Memories of a Penitent Heart (2016)   157–8
memory of the disaster   128 n.7
Merrison, Lindsey   84
#MeToo movement   11, 21, 65, 73, 168 n.13
Middle East and North Africa (MENA) region   52
Mihin Sutta, Mihin Jibon (2019)   224
Miklavèiè, Milena   87
Milisuthando (2023)   23–6
militarism   65, 234
military coup, 2013   60
Mills, Jen   172, 181
Minh-ha, Trinh T.   12, 15, 18, 20, 169, 174
Mirtahmasb, Mojtaba   140
Mirza, Noorafshan   8, 240
mission-driven peer organizations   14
M-Net New Directions filmmaking initiative   28
Moffatt, Tracey   18
Mohammad Khatami   137–40
Mohanty, Chandra   16, 53
Moi, Daniel Arap   37
Monani, Salma   149
Moradiyan-Rizi, Najmeh   7
Mori, Tatsuya   118
Morita, Mika   120
Mother of the Earth (2017)   140, 145
A Mulher de Todos (1969)   83
Mulvad, Eva   2
Mungai, Anne   27
Muñoz, Jose Esteban   17, 169, 178
Muñoz, Susana Blaustein   17
Munro, Kim   7, 173, 182
Murimi, Pete   38
Mwenza, Mekatilili Wa   44
Myhr, Ken   45
My Year of Dicks (2022)   73

Naficy, Hamid   18, 25, 135–6, 138
Nagib, Lúcia   4–5
Nancy, Jean-Luc   113
Nanfu Wang   23
narrative filmmaking   1
the narrative of arrival   117–18
National Association of Women Entrepreneurs (Tehran-based NGO)   147
National Black Women's Health Collective   16
National Film Board of Canada   16
National Women's Studies Association (NWSA)   61
Nation Media Group   37, 39
Ndisi-Herrmann, Philippa   37, 42–5
   "cinécriture"   45
   creative vision to their work   45
   New Moon (2018)   43
   photographer and poet   45
Negotiating Dissidence: The Pioneering Women of Arab Documentary (2017)   3–4
neoliberalism   3, 65
Nestor Almendros Prize   2
Netflix   20, 23
New Historicism   181
New Latin American Cinema   97
New Moon (2018)   43–5
News Time (2001)   63
New York, film festivals in   21
Nichols, Bill   21
A Night of Knowing Nothing (2021)   2
Night Raiders (2019)   199
Nihad, Fathimath Nayifa   155
nîpawistamâsowin: We Will Stand Up (2019)   188–9, 192–200, 202, 205–6
   anti-Indigenous racism   192
   awards   192
   description   193–8
   Fourth World perspective   190
   graphic film   197
   Hubbard, Tasha   188–9
   maternal authority   193, 196
   settler narrative   196–7
Nomadland (2020)   1
non-fictional work   8
Nostalgia for the Light (2010)   249

No Stranger At All (2022)   214
Novaro, María   17
nuclear disaster   116, 118–19, 124, 126, 127 n.1, 128 n.5
nuclear power village   128 n.4
Nyairo, Joyce   37, 39
   and Judy Kibinge in conversation   40

Ocasio, Benito Antonio Martínez, *see* Bad Bunny
Octavia Butler Collection   249
Odell, Jenny   179
O'Healy, Áine   53
O'Malley, Hayley   29
Only Dreams (2005)   56
Onwurah, Ngozi   18
opioid crisis   189–200, 209 n.21
Out of the Box: The Screen Worlds of Judy Kibinge (2023)   28, 43

Palestinian-Israeli conflict   62, 65
Pan y Dignidad (1982)   16
Parkerson, Michelle   16
Parmar, Pratibha   18–19
Parsi, Shirin   145–6
patriarchy   3, 250
Patwardhan, Anand   218
PAWA254   42
Peleg, Hila   3, 76–7
performance art collectives   175
Permissible Dreams (1983)   16
Pink Saris (2010)   19
Piper, Adrian   242
pixilation   74, 79, 93
P like Pelican (1972)   135–6
Poets of Life (2017)   135, 140, 145–9
   Barghnavard, Shirin   140
   description   146–7
   environmental and social activism   147
   life and achievements of Shirin Parsi   145–6
   obstacles to sustainable farming   147–8
   support for women farmers   148
Poitras, Laura   1, 23
Polley, Sarah   157
pop culture   73
Porter, Dawn   23
Portillo, Lourdes   17, 157

post-Fukushima documentaries   7, 115,
    see also *A Lullaby under the
    Nuclear Sky* (2016); *The Road
    Home* (2017)
  as the creation of
      counterpublics   121–2
  feminist aesthetics   116
  post-Fukushima social
      movements   126
postmemory
  concept of   98
  corpus of films   99
  documentaries   99, 103, 109, 110 n.5
post-vérité documentaries   115
Potter, Sally   15, 249
The Power of the Dog (2022)   1
Practice Makes Perfect (2021)   235
Precarious Workers Brigade   248, 252
private and the public spheres
  aesthetics of the personal and radical
      rethinking   116
  dialectical relations   115
Production Assistance Program   11–
    13, 17, 23
programming   1, 6, 16, 22
progressive social changes and
    movements   5
Project Daddy (2004)   27
Pro Quote in Germany   22
pro-Zionist feminists   62
Public Broadcasting Service (PBS)   153
Puerto Rico, social justice documentary
  anti-colonial struggle   157
  colonialism   151
  Covid-19 crisis   156
  cultural politics of   163
  digital activism   166
  ecological disasters   152
  feminist and ecocritical
      narratives   166
  feminist documentary studies   153
  massive emigration   152
  notions of female authorship and
      agency   153
  Operation Bootstrap   151
  post-Hurricane Maria Era
    critical approaches   152, 154–8
    disaster capitalism   154–5
    resilience as survival   155
    racio-colonial capitalism   155–6

self-referential documentaries   157
socioeconomic policies favoring
    foreign investment   152
Puerto Rico Oversight, Management
    and Economic Stability Act
    (PROMESA)   166 n.1
Punto de Vista: Latina   14, 17–18

racio-colonial capitalism   155
racism   61, 189, 192, 195
  anti-Indigenous   192
  antiracism   16
  cyber racism   196
  structured   192
  systemic   198
radiation   113–14, 116–21, 124, 128 n.5
Radiograph of a Family (2020)   1
Raheb, Eliane   64
Rahme, Dahna Abou   64
Ram Ke Naam (1992)   218
Ramsis, Amal   55–7, 59–60, 63
*Realist Cinema as World
    Cinema* (2020)   5
Reassemblage (1982)   15
Reconstruction (2001)   234
Red Pheasant Reserve   197
Reel Women (1979–83)   176
Reverie (2023)   32
Revolution in Egypt, 2011   66, 67
Ribon, Pamela   73
Rich, B. Ruby   11, 98
#Rickyrenuncia campaign   153, 161
The Road Home (2017)   115–16, 121–5
  activating the communicative
      action   127
  coming-of-age story   123
  counterpublic, process of
      communication   124–5
  creation of a counterpublic   121–3
  disillusionment with promotion of
      nuclear power   123
  Oura, Miran   122
  shift in the familial relationship   122
  social change as anti-nuclear
      movement   126
  trial of utilizing conversation   122
Roe, Alex Martinis   176, 179, 182
Roesler, Julia   66
Roe v. Wade   20
Rogers, Anna Backman   3, 6, 20, 75

Roselló, Ricardo   153, 157–9, 162
Roy, Diana   152
Royal Canadian Mounted Police (RCMP)   196, 208 n.16
Royal Commission on Aboriginal Peoples   191
Rozema, Patricia   218
Ruby, Rich, B.   11, 98
Rust, Stephen   149

Saglier, Viviane   59
Saikati (1992)   28
Saken (2014)   64
Sandler, Kathe   16
Sarlo, Beatriz   98
Sarmiento, Valeria   17
Sarukkai, Sundar   180
Saving Face (2012)   12
Saving Time (Odell)   179
The Scar (2018)   240
Schlüpmann, Heidi   22
Schuller, M.   155
Search, Jess   46
Selane, Bongiwe   28
Selbe: One among Many/Selbe et tantes d'autres (1983)   15–16
self-reflexivity, practice of   20, 63
Sembene, Ousmane   29
Sen, Mrinal   226
Sen, Priya   7, 212, see also *Faasla* (2021); *No Stranger At All* (2022)
  black and white reversal film   219
  deep image   222
  experimental documentary   220
  as a filmmaker   222
  filmmaker and people, relationship   216
  moving image practices   216
  observational and interactive style of filming   216–17
  political work   221
  relationship to practice   215
  self and other   221
  thesis film and love for poetry through Qawwali   219
  urgencies   217–18
Sepanta, Abdolhosain   135
settler-colonialism   65
Shafek, Amal   7
Shahani, Kumar   227

Sharawi, Huda   61
Shariati, Ali   136
alSharif, Basma   62
Sharma, Aparna   8, 212–13, 222, 224, 228, 231, see also *Kamakha: Through Prayerful Eyes* (2012); *Mihin Sutta, Mihin Jibon* (2019)
  concept of deep reflexivity   228–9
  deep image and time   229–30
  as a filmmaker   230–1
  films on artisans and craftspersons   222–3
  guest-lecture and workshops   223
  people and environments, relationship   225–6
  relationship with poetic registers   226–7
  sustained and long-term collaboration with people   230
  voice in a documentary   225
  working in Assam   222
Shirkers (documentary)   23
Shirzadi, Hayedeh   145
The Shock Doctrine (Klein)   154
Shohat, Ella   18, 25, 53
Shooting the Mafia (2019)   53–4
Shreir, Daniella   22
Shu Lea Cheang   16
Silent Waters/Khamosh Pani (2003)   20
Silva, Jorge   18
el-Sisi, Abdel Fattah   55
Sisters in Law (2005)   19
Sisters of the Screen: African Women in the Cinema (2002)   29
Sixties Scoop   195, 208 n.15
Smaill, Belinda   53, 69
The Smiling Lombana (2018)   157
Smith, John   249
social justice documentary, see Puerto Rico, social justice documentary
social movements
  after the Tohoku earthquake   120
  post-Fukushima   126 (*see also* post-Fukushima documentaries)
  role of women   120
  for women's rights and awareness about violence   73
Society of Women and Youth Protectors of the Environment (NGO)   148

Sojourner Truth Festival of the
    Arts, 1976   22
Sojourner Truth Symposium, 1976   29
Solo de mí (2018)   163
Sonita (2015)   2, 12
South African National Film and Video
    Foundation   28
Speed Sisters (2015)   57, 64
Steedman, Carolyn   180
stop-motion puppet animation   79
Stories We Tell (2012)   157
"Strategic Anti-Essentialism/Decolonizing
    Decolonization" (Nandita
    Sharma)   187
Stuart, Moira   241
Studio D   16, 19
*Subject to Reality: Women and
    Documentary* (2019)   3
Sudesha (1983)   16
Sumar, Sabiha   19
Supreme Council for Media
    Regulation   55
Surname Viet Given Name Nam
    (1988)   18, 26
Susana (1980)   17
Svilova, Elizaveta   226
Sydney Film Festival, 2024   29
Sydney Women's Film Group   176

Tabari, Ula   64, 67
Tafakory, Maryam   62
Tailfeathers, Esther   202
Tailfeathers, Elle-Máijá   188,
    198, 201, 203
Tajiri, Rea   16, 26
Taleqani, Ayatollah   136
*Talking Visions: Multicultural
    Feminism in a Transnational
    Age* (1998)   53
Tan, Sandi   23
Tanaka, Janice   16
Tell Your Tale, Little Bird (2007)   67–8
Tel Zaatar Massacre of Palestinians   64
theater and live documentary
    background and the event   172–4
    creative practice
        methodologies   170–2
    feminist filmmaking and
        utopias   174–8
    feminist queer archives   180–4

live theater and documentary,
    intersection   181–2
non-traditional forms of
    historiography   170
plays about issues
    affecting women   172
"polydisciplinary" approach to
    research creation   170–1
queer temporalities   178–9
Vitalstatistix archives   183
women role in network of
    production   175–6
Third World Newsreel   13
A Thousand Girls Like Me (2018)   2
The Times of Harvey Milk (1984)   218
Titane (2021)   1
To Kill a Tiger (2022)   12
Tokyo Electric Power Company
    (TEPCO)   116, 123, 128 n.1
Tootoosis, Jade   198–9
Topography, multi-media documentary
    project   235, 250 n.1
Touran Khanom (2018)   145
transnational feminism   8, 19, 52–4, 61,
    68, *see also* Caravan
    collaboration   52
    in Egypt   61–2
    practice of reflexive thinking   54
    scholarship on transnational feminist
        filmmaking   54
    as theory and praxis   53
    transnational feminist
        collaboration   62
    solidarity   52
*Transnational Feminism in Film
    and Media: Visibility,
    Representation, and Sexual
    Differences* (2007)   53
"Transnational Solidarity: Women's
    Agency, Structural
    Adjustment, and Globalization"
    (Desai)   52
Triet, Justine   1
Trofimenkoff, Susan Mann   133
Truth or Consequences (2021)   235, 248
tsunami   113–14, 118, 154
Turning Red (2022)   74

Uddoh, Rosa-Johan   8
UK Black British workshops   19

Ukraine war   154
Ulfsdotter, Boel   3–4, 6, 7, 20, 75, 153
UN Convention on the Elimination of All Forms of Discrimination Against Women (CEDAW)   140
UN End of Decade for Women in 1985   16
Unfinished Diary (1989)   18
Unfinished Sentences (2017)   157
Un hombre, cuando hombre es (1982)   17
United Nations Permanent Forum on Indigenous Issues (UNPFII)   198, 209 n.19
UN's World Conferences on Women in Mexico City (1975) and Copenhagen (1980)   61
UN World Conferences on Women   52
US-based Palestinian Feminist Collective (PFC)   61
USC Annenberg Inclusion Initiative   78
US university library market   14
utopianism   184

Van de Peer, Stefanie   3, 58
Vásquez, Teodora   18
Venice International Film Festival, 79th   1
Veras, Christine   7, 79
Vertov, Dziga   226–7
Villegas, Victoria Linares   157
violence
   of atomic bomb explosions   128 n.5
   awareness about   73
   definition   80
   domestic   92, 107, 245, 252 n.12
   epistemic   83
   extreme and sustained forms   223
   gender-based violence (GBV)   66, 68, 77–8, 87, 163
   inequality and structural   236
   oppression and structural   152, 155, 236–7
   police   217
   and poverty   42
   radioactive   114
   sexual   20, 66, 74, 76, 89–90, 108
   supported by data   80
virtual screening program   56

Vision Machine Film Project (1999–2010)   250 n.3
Vitalstatistix, South Australian queer feminist theater company   169–70, 172, 175–7, 182–3
Voices of Afghan Women   2

Wainaina, Binyavanga   31
Wakae Nakane   7
Waldman, Diane   3, 75, 233
Walker, Janet   3, 75, 233
Warren, Shilyh   3, 7, 35
Watai, Takeharu   118
The Watermelon Woman (1996)   181
What About China? (2021)   20
When I Saw You (2012)   64
White, Patricia   4, 6, 53
Williams, Raymond   228
Winn, Marc   46
women in animation, *see also Awakening the Goddess* (2020); *Carne* (2019); *Granny's Sexual Life* (2021); *KAM* (2020)
   body politics   80–1
   challenges faced by women of color   78–9
   democratization of the internet   77
   feminist animations   78
   in-person screening event   79
   interviews, role of   79–80
   social-issue documentaries: 81
   technology-facilitated violence   80
   violence   80
   women face in private and public spaces   80
   Women in Animation student club at the University of Texas   79
Women Make Movies (WMM)   2, 6, 11–24, 51
   distribution collection   26
   as a distributor within the feminist media   12
   feminist commitments   12–13
   films by and about Muslim women   20
   functions   11–12
   Global South   15–16
   non-fiction feminist films   11

Production Assistance Program 23
transnational feminist politics 11
Women of El Planeta (1983) 16
Women Resisting Sexual Violence and the Egyptian Revolution: Arab Feminist Testimonies (Hamza) 65–6
Women's Cinema, World Cinema (2015) 4
Women's Film Unit 176
Women's Society for Fighting Environmental Pollution (NGO) 142
Woods, Fronza 16
Wynter, Sylvia 187, 207

Yamagata International Documentary Film Festival, 2017 122, 126, 128
Yangon Film School (YFS) 84
Yeh Freedom Life (2019) 216, 221
Yo perreo sola (2020) 163
Yugantar Collective 16

Zarza, Zaira 7
Zero Degrees of Separation (2005) 64
Zhao, Chloé 1
Zimmerman, Andrea Luka 8
Zimmerman, Debra 2, 11
Zimmermann, Patricia 107
Zionism 61
Zorn's Lemma (1970) 237